HUMAN RESOURCE INFORMATION SYSTEMS

For
MPM Semester-IV and MBA Semester-III (HRM Specialization)

As per New Revised Syllabus of Pune University

NITIN C. KAMAT
B.E. (Elect.)

CHINMAY N. KAMAT
D.C.E., P.G.D.B.M.

Dr. POOJA UPADHYAY
M.Com., M.B.A.

HUMAN RESOURCE INFORMATION SYSTEMS　　　　　　　ISBN 978-93-5164-268-8
First Edition　:　February 2015
©　:　Authors

The text of this publication, or any part thereof, should not be reproduced or transmitted in any form or stored in any computer storage system or device for distribution including photocopy, recording, taping or information retrieval system or reproduced on any disc, tape, perforated media or other information storage device etc., without the written permission of Authors with whom the rights are reserved. Breach of this condition is liable for legal action.

Every effort has been made to avoid errors or omissions in this publication. In spite of this, errors may have crept in. Any mistake, error or discrepancy so noted and shall be brought to our notice shall be taken care of in the next edition. It is notified that neither the publisher nor the authors or seller shall be responsible for any damage or loss of action to any one, of any kind, in any manner, therefrom.

Published By :	Printed at
NIRALI PRAKASHAN Abhyudaya Pragati, 1312, Shivaji Nagar, Off J.M. Road, PUNE – 411005 Tel - (020) 25512336/37/39, Fax - (020) 25511379 Email : niralipune@pragationline.com	**Repro Knowledgecast Limited** **India**

DISTRIBUTION CENTRES
PUNE

Nirali Prakashan	*Nirali Prakashan*
119, Budhwar Peth, Jogeshwari Mandir Lane Pune 411002, Maharashtra Tel : (020) 2445 2044, 66022708, Fax : (020) 2445 1538 Email : bookorder@pragationline.com	S. No. 28/27, Dhyari, Near Pari Company, Pune 411041 Tel : (022) 24690371 Email : dhyari@pragationline.com bookorder@pragationline.com

MUMBAI
Nirali Prakashan
385, S.V.P. Road, Rasdhara Co-op. Hsg. Society Ltd.,
Girgaum, Mumbai 400004, Maharashtra
Tel : (022) 2385 6339 / 2386 9976, Fax : (022) 2386 9976
Email : niralimumbai@pragationline.com

DISTRIBUTION BRANCHES

NAGPUR	**JALGAON**
Pratibha Book Distributors Above Maratha Mandir, Shop No. 3, First Floor, Rani Jhanshi Square, Sitabuldi, Nagpur 440012, Maharashtra, Tel : (0712) 254 7129	*Nirali Prakashan* 34, V. V. Golani Market, Navi Peth, Jalgaon 425001, Maharashtra, Tel : (0257) 222 0395 Mob : 94234 91860
BENGALURU	**KOLHAPUR**
Pragati Book House House No. 1, Sanjeevappa Lane, Avenue Road Cross, Opp. Rice Church, Bengaluru – 560002. Tel : (080) 64513344, 64513355, Mob : 9880582331, 9845021552 Email:bharatsavla@yahoo.com	*Nirali Prakashan* New Mahadvar Road, Kedar Plaza, 1st Floor Opp. IDBI Bank Kolhapur 416 012, Maharashtra. Mob : 9855046155

CHENNAI
Pragati Books
9/1, Montieth Road, Behind Taas Mahal, Egmore,
Chennai 600008 Tamil Nadu, Tel : (044) 6518 3535,
Mob : 94440 01782 / 98450 21552 / 98805 82331, Email : bharatsavla@yahoo.com

RETAIL OUTLETS
PUNE

Pragati Book Centre	*Pragati Book Centre*
157, Budhwar Peth, Opp. Ratan Talkies, Pune 411002, Maharashtra Tel : (020) 2445 8887 / 6602 2707, Fax : (020) 2445 8887	676/B, Budhwar Peth, Opp. Jogeshwari Mandir, Pune 411002, Maharashtra Tel : (020) 6601 7784 / 6602 0855
Pragati Book Centre Amber Chamber, 28/A, Budhwar Peth, Appa Balwant Chowk, Pune : 411002, Maharashtra, Tel : (020) 20240335 / 66281669 Email : pbcpune@pragationline.com	*PBC Book Sellers & Stationers* 152, Budhwar Peth, Pune 411002, Maharashtra Tel : (020) 2445 2254 / 6609 2463

MUMBAI
Pragati Book Corner
Indira Niwas, 111 - A, Bhavani Shankar Road, Dadar (W), Mumbai 400028, Maharashtra
Tel : (022) 2422 3526 / 6662 5254, Email : pbcmumbai@pragationline.com

www.pragationline.com　　　　　　　　　　　　　　　　　　info@pragationline.com

Preface ...

We are happy to launch this book on **Human Resource Information Systems**. Contents of this book are completely aligned with Pune University as per new Syllabus 2013-14 for MBA, Semester III (HRM Specialization) (course code 310 HR), MPM, Semester IV, (course code 403) and many Indian Universities with comprehensive coverage of various topics have been included.

This book is organized in six chapters dealing with major aspects of Human Recourse Information System. Many snapshots of HRIS applications are added to understand practical in depth of understanding the subject.

Data bank for Questions and MCQ for Guidelines for students appearing for Pune University MBA and MPM is illustrated in Appendix, which will be useful for preparing examination.

This book will be an important resource for students, faculties as well as practicing mangers as text as well as reference book.

We being visiting faculty in many leading Business Institutes in Pune and also instrumental in developing educational contents for Welingkar Distance Education Institute, have paid to the practical use of HRIS techniques and included various Snapshots for various modules.

We are thankful to our Guru Padmashri Dr. S. B. Muzumdar, President and founder director of Symbiosis International University and also giving blessings for this book.

Our heartfelt thanks to **Mr. Dineshbhari Furia** and **Mr. Jignesh Furia** of **Nirali Prakashan** Mr. Girish Redkar (Head Sales and Marketing), Mr. Amar Salunkhe (Technical Editing), Mrs. Prachi Sawant (Typing and Drawing Designing), instrumental in front and back end in marketing and publishing this book in various Management Institute all over India and also for giving useful feedback for modifying contents of this book.

Reader's feedback is highly appreciated. Feel free to contact us or mail to communicate your views for improvement of the book.

nitin.kamat2012@gmail.com,
nitin.kamat2008@yahoo.com
Authors

Dedicated to...

*We are grateful for blessing from our **Guru Padmashri Dr. S. B. Mujumdar** Founder of Symbiosis Group of Institutes*

Syllabus ...

FOR MPM : IV

1. **Different Types of Computer Based Information Systems** (7+2)

    Computers and Computer Based Information Systems/Introduction to Computer Based Information Systems : TPS/MIS/EIS/ES/DSS/OA

    HRMS Planning : HRIS Introduction

    Human Resource and HRMS

    Planning an HRMS

    Designing an HRMS

    Software for HRMS

    Hardware for HRMS

2. **Management Information Systems** (7+2)

    Functional Applications/ Exercise

    HRIS Life Cycle/HR Responsibility in each Phase of HRIS Development

    Pre Implementation Stage of HRIS :

    HRIS Planning

    HRIS Expectation

    HRIS Cost-benefit Value Analysis

    Getting Management Support for HRIS

    Limitations of Computerization of HRIS

3. **Implementation of HRIS** (7+2)

    Tools in HRIS Development

4. **HRIS Applications** (8+2)

    Applicant and Employment Management

    EEO and Affirmative Action

    Compensation

    Benefits

    Employee and Industrial Relations

    Training and Development

    Human Resource Planning

    OSHA

    Payroll

    Other HRIS Applications

5. **Emerging Trends in HRIS, Networking, Internet, Intranet, Technology Implications, etc.** (6+2)

FOR MBA : III
(HRM Specialization)

1. **Introduction to Human Resource Management and Human Resource Information Systems** (5+1)

   Evolution of Human Resource Management and Human Resource Information Systems: The Role of Information Technology, Database Concepts and Applications in Human Resource Information Systems, Systems Considerations in the Design of an HRIS: Planning for Implementation

2. **Determining Human Resource Information System's Needs** (5+1)

   Human Resource Information Systems Needs Analysis, System Design and Acquisition, HR Metrics and Workforce Analytics, Cost Justifying Human Resource Information Systems Investment

3. **Resource Information Systems Implementation and Acceptance** (3+1)

   Human Resource Information Systems Project Management, Change Management: Implementation, Integration and Maintenance of the Human Resource Information Systems

4. **Human Resource Information Systems Applications** (7+1)

   Human Resource Administration and Human Resource Information Systems, Talent Management 1: Job Analysis and Human Resource Planning, Recruitment and Selection in an Internet Context, Training and Development: Issues and Human Resource Information Systems Applications, Performance Management, Compensation, Benefits, Payroll and the Human Resource Information Systems, International Human Resource Management

5. **Special Topics in Human Resource Information Systems** (5+1)

   Information Security and Privacy in Human Resource Information Systems, The Future of Human Resource Information Systems: Emerging Trends in Human Resource Management and Information Technology

Contents ...

1. **Different Types of Computer Based Information Systems**   1.1 – 1.30

2. **Management Information Systems**   2.1 – 2.30

3. **Implementation of HRIS**   3.1 – 3.18

4. **HRIS Applications**   4.1 – 4.68

5. **Other HRIS Applications**
   (Ancillary Modules in the HRIS System)   5.1 – 5.10

6. **Emerging Trends in HRIS**   6.1 – 6.34

*   **Appendices**   A.1 – A.19

Chapter 1...

Different Types of Computer Based Information Systems

Objectives ...
After discussing this chapter, you will be able to:
- Explain the concept of HRIS and describe its Importance in HRM.
- Discuss the Significance of Computerization in the HR Field.
- Enlist and describe the Significant aspects of the Contemporary HRIS Systems.
- Describe in detail the Benefits of an HRIS System.

Structure ...
1.1 Introduction
1.2 Computers and Computer Based Information Systems
    1.2.1 Introduction to Computers
    1.2.2 Overview of Computer Based Information System
    1.2.3 Evolution of Human Resource Management and Information System
1.3 Computer Based Information System
    1.3.1 Transaction Processing Systems (TPS)
    1.3.2 Mananagement Information Systems (MIS)
    1.3.3 Executive Information Systems (EIS)
    1.3.4 Expert System (ES)
    1.3.5 Decision Support Systems (DSS)
    1.3.6 Office Automation (OA) System
1.4 HRMS Planning
    1.4.1 HRIS Introduction
        1.4.1.1 Definitions
    1.4.2 Human Resources and HRMS
    1.4.3 Planning on HRMS
    1.4.4 Designing a HRMS
    1.4.5 Software for HRMS
    1.4.6 Hardware for HRMS
1.5 Benefits of Human Resource Information System
- Activities
- Summary
- Self-assessment Questions

1.1 INTRODUCTION

Human Resource Information System – normally called as HRIS is the general term indicating to any data framework utilized for getting pertinent and prompt data on which to base human asset choices. A HR Information Systems is a software application planned explicitly for the accumulation and blend of employee data. These HR frameworks can furnish functions differing from payroll and compensation breakdown to the pertinent association of accessible positions with qualified provisions already existing inside the framework.

The mechanization of the information altogether diminishes the probability of mistakes in entries disparities between records. With the information of the employees perfectly woven into a proper web of HRIS databases, HR executives come to be allowed to seek after additional discriminating and inventive thinking ventures. The HRIS system facilitates the development of an integrated and vast repository of employee data taking into account more mind boggling and mixed investigation by organization executives, expediting better choice making and enhanced business productivity. With everything taken into account, this system can't neglect to enhance the execution of business operations, merging diverse HR forms and altering the routes in which an organization administers its representatives.

1.2 COMPUTER AND COMPUTER BASED INFORMATION SYSTEMS

Information Systems (IS) is a set of interrelated elements or components that collect (input), manipulate (process), and disseminate (output) data and information and provide a feedback mechanism to meet an objective.

Definition: IS Pronounced as separate letters, and short for Information Systems or Information Services. For many companies, IS is the name of the department responsible for computers, networking and data management. Other companies refer to the department as IT (Information Technology) and MIS (Management Information Services).

What is an Information System?

Schematic model of an information system

Schematic model of an information system consists of :

1. **Input:**
   - The activity of gathering and capturing data.
   - Whatever goes into the computer.

2. **Processing:**
   - Converting or transforming data into useful outputs.
3. **Output:**
   - Useful information, usually in the form of documents and/or reports.
   - Anything that comes out of a computer.

   Whatever goes into the computer. Input can take a variety of forms, from commands you enter on a keyboard to data from another computer or device. A device that feeds data into a computer, such as a keyboard or mouse, is called an input device.

4. **The act of entering data into a computer:**
   (i) **Feedback:** Output that is used to make changes to input or processing activities
   (ii) **Forecasting:**
   - A proactive approach to feedback.
   - Use for estimating future sales or inventory needs.

Information as a Strategic Resource:

Business environment is prone to changes and this factor makes business planning very complex. Some factors such as the market forces, technological changes, complex diversity of business and competition have a significant impact on any business prospects. MIS is designed to assess and monitor these factors. The MIS design is supposed to provide some insight into these factors enabling the management to evolve some strategy to deal with them.

Since, these factors are a part of the environment, MIS design is required to keep a watch on environment factors and provide information to the management for a strategy formulation. Strategy formulation is a complex task based on the strength and the weakness of the organization and the mission and goals it wishes to achieve. Strategy formulation is the responsibility of the top management and the top management relies on the MIS for information.

There are various business strategies such as overall company growth, product, market, financing and so on. MIS should provide the relevant information that would help the management in deciding the type of strategies the business needs. Every business may not require all the strategies all the time.

The type of strategy is directly related to the current status of business and the goals it wishes to achieve. The MIS is supposed to provide current information on the status of the business visa-a-visa the goals. MIS is supposed to give a status with regard to whether the business is on a growth path or is stagnant or is likely to decline, and the reasons thereof. If the status of the business shows a declining trend, the strategy should be of growth. If business is losing in a particular market segment, then the strategy should be a market or a product strategy.

The continuous assessment of business progress in terms of sales, market, quality, profit and its direction becomes the major role of MIS. It should further aid the top management in strategy formulation at each stage of business.

The business does not survive on a single strategy but it requires a mix of strategy operating at different levels of the management. For example, when a business is on the growth path, it would require a mix of price, product and market strategies. If a business is showing a decline, it would need a mix of price-discount, sales promotion and advertising strategies.

The MIS is supposed to evaluate the strategies in terms of the impact they have on business and provide an optimum mix. The MIS is supposed to provide a strategy-pay off matrix for such an evaluation.

In business planning, MIS should provide support to top management for focusing its attention on decision making and action. In business management, the focus shifts from one aspect to another. In the introductory phase, the focus would be on a product design and manufacturing. When the business matures and requires and requires to sustain or to consolidate, the focus would be on the post sales services and support. The MIS should provide early warning to change the focus of the management from one aspect to the other.

Evolving the strategies is not the only task the top management has to perform. It also has to provide the necessary resources to implement the strategies. The assessment of resource need, and its selection becomes a major decision for the top management. The MIS should provide information on resources, costs, quality and availability, for deciding the cost effective resource mix.

When the strategies are being implemented, it is necessary that the management gets a continuous feedback on its effectiveness in relation to the objective which they are supposed to achieve. MIS is supposed to give a critical feedback on the strategy performance. According to the nature of the feedback, the management may or may not make a change in the strategy mix, the focus and the resource allocation.

Characteristics of Strategic Information:

Integrated	Must have a single, enterprise-wise view.
Data Integrity	Information must be accurate and must confirm to business rules.
Accessible	Easily accessible with intuitive access paths, and responsive for analysis.
Credible	Every business factor must have one and only one value.
Timely	Information must be available within the stipulated time frame.

The Data:

The word data is the plural of Latin datum. In English, the word datum is still used in the general sense of "something given".

Raw data are numbers, characters, images or other outputs from devices to convert physical quantities into symbols, in a very broad sense. Such data are typically further processed by a human or input into a computer, stored and processed there, or transmitted (output) to another human or computer.

The Data Entry:

Data entry is the process of converting raw data to the Digital form by physically entering or Scanning.

The Data Storage:

The process of data storage enables the reduction in cost and improvement in the data management.

Data is stored in secondary devices such as hard disk, CDs, floppies, Pen drive.

The difference between Data and Information?

It is important that you understand the difference between "data" and "information".

Think of data as a "raw material" - it needs to be processed before it can be turned into something useful. Hence the need for "data processing". Data comes in many forms - numbers, words, symbols. Data relates to transactions, events and facts. On its own - it is not very useful.

1.2.1 Overview of Computers

The computer comprises of technologically advanced hardware put together to work at great speed. To accomplish its various tasks, the computer is made of different parts, each serving a particular purpose in conjunction with other parts. In other words, a 'computer' is an ensemble of different machines that you will be using to accomplish your job.

Computer is primarily made of the Central Processing Unit (usually referred to as the Computer), the monitor, the keyboard and the mouse. Other pieces of hardware, commonly referred to as peripherals, can enhance or improve your experience with the computer.

Advantages of Computers :

Compared to traditional systems, computers offer many noteworthy advantages. This is one reason that traditional systems are being replaced rapidly by computer-based systems.

The main advantages offered by computers are as follows :
1. High Accuracy.
2. Superior Speed of Operation.
3. Large Storage Capacity.
4. User-friendly Features.
5. Portability.
6. Platform independence.
7. Economical in the long term.

Computers that process digital signals are known as Digital Computers. The Digital signal is a discrete signal with two states 0 and 1. In practice, the digital computers are used and not analog. Examples of digital computers are personal computers, supercomputers, mainframe computers etc.

Supercomputers are the most powerful computers in terms of speed of execution and large storage capacity. NASA uses supercomputers to track and control space explorations.

Mainframe computers are next to supercomputers in terms of capacity. The mainframe computers are multi terminal computers, which can be shared simultaneously by multiple users. Unlike personal computers, mainframe computers offer time-sharing. For example, insurance companies use mainframe computers to process information about millions of its policyholders.

Minicomputers these computers are also known as midrange computers. These are desk-sized machines and are used in medium scale applications. For example, production departments use minicomputers to monitor various manufacturing processes and assembly-line operations.

Microcomputers as compared to supercomputers, mainframes and minicomputers, microcomputers are the least powerful, but these are very widely used and rapidly gaining in popularity.

Personal Computer (PC) is the term referred to the computer that is designed for use by a single person. PCs are also called microcontrollers because these are smaller when compared to mainframes and minicomputers. The term 'PC' is frequently used to refer to Desktop computers. Although PCs are used by individuals, they can also be used in computer networks.

Desktop Computer this is the most commonly used personal computer. It comprises of a keyboard, mouse, monitor and system unit. The system unit is also known as cabinet or chassis. It is the container that houses most of the components such as motherboard, disk drives, ports, switch mode power supply and add-on cards etc. The desktop computers are available in two models-horizontal model and tower model.

Laptops are also called notebook computers. These are the portable computers. They have a size of 8.5 × 11 inch and weigh about three-to-four kilos.

Palmtops are also called handheld computers. These are computing devices, which are small enough to fit into your palm. The size of a palmtop is like an appointment book. The palmtops are generally kept for personal use such as taking notes, developing a list of friends, keeping track of dates, agendas etc.

The Palmtop can also be connected to a PC for downloading data. It also provides value-added features such as voice input, Internet, cell phone, camera, movie player and GPS.

Basic Elements of Computer System :

Basic elements of a computer system are mouse, keyboard, monitor, memory, CPU motherboard, hard disk, speakers, modem, power supply and processor.

1. **Mouse :** Mouse is used for operating the system. Nowadays, optical mouse is more popular as compared to simple mouse.
2. **Keyboard :** Keyboard is used to input data in to the system so that the system gives output to the user. Therefore, the keyboard is an integral part of the input system. A computer is essentially Incomplete without a keyboard.
3. **Monitor :** Monitor, which again is a very essential part of the computer system, displays the actions that the computer performs on our command.
4. **Motherboard :** Motherboard again a necessary element of the computer system contains different elements as memory, processor, and modem, slots for graphic card and LAN card.
5. **Hard Disk :** Hard disk is used to store data permanently on computer.
6. **Modem :** Modem is used to connecting to the Internet. Two types of modems are widely used. One is known as software modems and the other is known as hardware modems.
7. **Speakers :** Speakers are also included in basic elements of a computer. It's not indispensable, because a computer can perform its function without speakers. However, we use them to for multiple purposes.

Basic Computer Functioning :

A computer can be defined as "an electronic device that accepts data from an input device, processes it, stores it in a disk and finally displays it on an output device such as a Monitor".

This flow of information holds true for all types of computers such as Personal Computers, Laptops, and Palmtops etc. In other words, the fundamental principle of working is the same.

Components of Computer System :

1. Motherboard :

The motherboard is the main component inside the case. It is a large rectangular board with integrated circuitry that connects the various parts of the computer as the CPU, RAM, Disk drives (CD, DVD, Hard disk or any others) as well as any other peripherals connected via the ports or the expansion slots.

Components directly attached to the motherboard include :

(a) The Central Processing Unit (CPU) performs most of the calculations that enable computer to function and is sometimes referred to as the "brain" of the computer. It is usually cooled by a heat sink and fan.

(b) The chip set aids communication between the CPU and the other components of the system, including main memory.

(c) RAM (Random Access Memory) stores all run processes (applications) and the current running OS.

(d) The BIOS includes boot firmware and power management. The Basic Input Output System (BIOS) tasks are handled by operating system drivers.

(e) Internal Buses connect the CPU to various internal components and to expansion cards for graphics and sound.

2. Removable Media Devices :

(a) **CD (Compact Disc) :** The most common type of removable media, suitable for music and data.

(b) **CD-ROM Drive :** A device used for reading data from a CD.

(c) **CD Writer :** A device used for both reading and writing data to and from a CD.

(d) **DVD (Digital Versatile Disc) :** A popular type of removable media that is the same size as a CD but stores up to 12 times as much information - the most common way of transferring digital video and is popular for data storage.

1.2.2 Overview of Computer Based Information System

We are living in a time of great change and working in an Information Age. Managers have to assimilate masses of data, convert that data into information, form conclusions about that information and make decisions leading to the achievement of business objectives. For an organization, information is as important resource as money, machinery and manpower. It is essential for the survival of the enterprise.

Before the widespread use of computers, many organizations found difficulties in gathering, storing, organizing and distributing large amounts of data and information. Developments in computer technology made possible for managers to select the information they require, in the form best suited for their needs and in time they want. This information must be current and in many cases is needed by many people at the same time. So it has to be accurate, concise, timely, complete, well presented and storable.

Most firms now-a-days depend on Information Technology (IT).

A computer based information system is a subset of the overall internal controls of a business covering the application of people, documents, technologies, and procedures by management accountants to solve business problems such as costing a product, service or a business-wide strategy. Management Information Systems are distinct from regular information systems in that they are used to analyze other information systems applied in operational activities in the organization. Academically, the term is commonly used to refer to the group of information management methods tied to the automation or support of human decision making, e.g. Decision Support Systems (DSS), Expert Systems (ES), and Executive Information Systems (ESS).

In any organization, small or big, a major portion of the time goes in data collection, processing, documenting it to the people. Hence, a major portion of the overheads goes into this kind of unproductive work in the organization. Every individual in an organization is continuously looking for some information which is needed to perform his/her task. Hence, the information is people-oriented and it varies with the nature of the people in the organization.

The difficulty in handling this multiple requirement of the people is due to a couple of reasons. The information is a processed product to fulfill an imprecise need of the people. It takes time to search the data and may require a difficult processing path.

Since the people are instrumental in any business transaction, a human error is possible in conducting the same. Since a human error is difficult to control, the difficulty arises in ensuring a hundred per cent quality assurance of information in terms of completeness, accuracy, validity, timeliness and meeting the decision making needs.

In order to get a better grip on the activity of information processing, it is necessary to have a formal system which should take care of the following points :

1. Handling of a voluminous data.
2. Confirmation of the validity of data and transaction.
3. Complex processing of data and multidimensional analysis.
4. Quick search and retrieval.

5. Mass storage.
6. Communication of the information system to the user on time.
7. Fulfilling the changing needs of the information.

The computer based information system uses computers and communication technology to deal with these points of supreme importance.

1.2.3 Evolution of Human Resource Management and Information System

Historical Evolution of HRM and HRIS :

One can analyze the historical trends of the HR function from different viewpoints: the evolution of HRM as a professional and scientific discipline, as an aid to management, as a political and economic conflict between management and employees, and as a growing movement of employee involvement influenced by developments in industrial/organizational and social psychology. This historical analysis will demonstrate the growing importance of employees from being just one of the means of production in the 20th -century industrial economy to being a key source of sustainable competitive advantage in the 21st-century knowledge economy.

Since, this is a book on HRIS, we will examine the development of the fields of both HR and IT in terms of their evolution since the early 20th century. This means examining the evolution of HRM intertwined with developments in IT and describing how IT has played an increasing role in the HRM function. In addition, this historical analysis will show how the role of HRM in the firm has changed over time from primarily being concerned with routine transactional HR activities to dealing with complex transformational ones. Transactional activities are the routine bookkeeping tasks – for example, changing an employee's home address or health care provider – whereas transformational activities are those actions of an organization that "add value" to the consumption of the firm's product or service.

Pre–World War II :

In the early 20th century and prior to World War II, the personnel function (the precursor of the term human resource management) was primarily involved in record keeping of employee information; in other words, it fulfilled a "caretaker" function. During this period of time, the prevailing management philosophy was called "scientific management."

At this point in history, there were very few government influences in employment relations, and thus, employment terms, practices, and conditions were left to the owners of the firm.

Post–World War II (1945–1960):

The mobilization and utilization of labor during the War had a great impact on the development of the personnel function. Managers realized that employee productivity and motivation had a significant impact on the profitability of the firm. The human relations movement after the War emphasized that employees were motivated not just by money but also by social and psychological factors, such as recognition of work achievements and work norms.

Due to the need for classification of large numbers of individuals in military service during the war, systematic efforts began to classify workers around occupational categories in order to improve recruitment and selection procedures. The central aspect of these classification systems was the job description, which listed the tasks, duties, and responsibilities of any individual who held the job in question. These job description classification systems could also be used to design appropriate compensation programs, evaluate individual employee performance, and provide a basis for termination.

Social Issues Era (1963–1980):

As a result, the personnel department was burdened with the additional responsibility of legislative compliance that required collection, analysis, and reporting of voluminous data to statutory authorities. For example, to demonstrate that there was no unfair discrimination in employment practices, data pertaining to all employment functions, such as recruitment, training, compensation, and benefits, had to be diligently collected, analyzed, and stored.

Emergence of Strategic HRM (1990 to Present):

The economic landscape underwent radical changes throughout the 1990s with increasing globalization, technological breakthroughs (particularly Internet-enabled Web services), and hyper competition. Business process reengineering exercises became more common and frequent, with several initiatives, such as right sizing of employee numbers, reducing the layers of management, reducing the bureaucracy of organizational structures, autonomous work teams, and outsourcing.

Firms today realize that innovative and creative employees who hold the key to organizational knowledge provide a sustainable competitive advantage because unlike other resources, intellectual capital is difficult to imitate by competitors. A good example is when accompany is considering a strategic decision to expand by establishing a production facility in a new location.

Therefore, in determining the strategic fit between technology and HR, it is not the strategy per se that leads to competitive advantage but rather how well it is "implemented, "taking into account the environmental realities that can be unique to each organization and, indeed, between units and functions of the organization.

1.3 COMPUTER BASED INFORMATION SYSTEM

Fig. 1.1 shows various kinds of systems applied at different levels in Management.

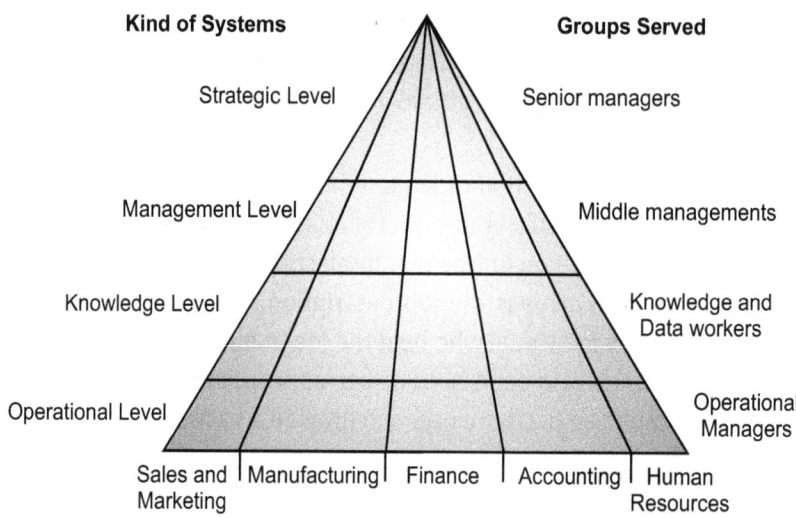

Fig. 1.1

1.3.1 Transaction Processing Systems (TPS)

As the name implies, Transaction Processing Systems (TPS) are designed to process routine transactions efficiently and accurately.

Order tracking	Machine control	Securities trading	Payroll	Compensation
Order processing	Plant scheduling	Cash Management	Accounts payable	Training and development
	Material movement and control		Accounts receivable	Employee records
Sales/ Mktg.	Mfg	Finance	Account	HR

A business will have several (sometimes many) TPS; for example: Billing systems to send invoices to customers- Systems to calculate the weekly and monthly payroll and tax payments - Production and purchasing systems to calculate raw material requirements - Stock control systems to process all movements into, within and out of the business.

1.3.2 Management Information System (MIS)

A Management Information System (MIS) is mainly concerned with internal sources of information. MIS usually take data from the transaction processing systems (see below) and summaries it into a series of management reports.

MIS reports tend to be used by middle management and operational supervisors.

Systems that serve planning, control and decision-making through routine summary and reports.

Management-level Systems				
Sales management	Inventory control	Annual budgeting	Capital investment	Relocation analysis
Sales and Mktg.	Mfg	Finance	Account	HR

1.3.3 Executive Information Systems (EIS)

An Executive Support System (ESS) is designed to help senior management make strategic decisions. It gathers analyses and summarizes the key internal and external information used in the business.

Strategic-level Systems				
5-year sales trend forecasting	5-year operating plan	5-yearbudget forecasting	Profit planning	Personnel planning
Sales/Mktg.	Mfg	Finance	Account	HR

A good way to think about an ESS is to imagine the senior management team in an aircraft cockpit - with the instrument panel showing them the status of all the key business activities. ESS typically involve lots of data analysis and modeling tools such as "what-if" analysis to help strategic decision-making.

1.3.4 Expert System (ES)

An expert system is a software system that attempts to reproduce the performance of one or more human experts, most commonly in a specific problem domain, and is a traditional application and/or subfield of artificial intelligence. A wide variety of methods can be used to simulate the performance of the expert however common to most or all are : (1) the creation of a so-called "knowledgebase" which uses some knowledge representation formalism to capture the Subject Matter Experts (SME) knowledge and (2) a process of gathering that knowledge from the SME and codifying it according to the formalism, which is called knowledge engineering. Expert systems may or may not have learning components but a third common element is that once the system is developed it is proven by being placed in the same real world problem solving situation as the human SME, typically as an aid to human workers or a supplement to some information system.

Computer programs that are derived from a branch of computer science research called Artificial Intelligence (AI). AI's scientific goal is to understand intelligence by building computer programs that exhibit intelligent behavior. It is concerned with the concepts and methods of symbolic inference, or reasoning, by a computer, and how the knowledge used to make those inferences will be represented inside the machine.

Of course, the term intelligence covers many cognitive skills, including the ability to solve problems, learn, and understand language; AI addresses all of those. But most progress to date in AI has been made in the area of problem solving -- concepts and methods for building programs that reason about problems rather than calculate a solution.

Building an expert system is known as knowledge engineering and its practitioners are called knowledge engineers. The knowledge engineer must make sure that the computer has all the knowledge needed to solve a problem. The knowledge engineer must choose one or more forms in which to represent the required knowledge as symbol patterns in the memory of the computer -- that is, he (or she) must choose a knowledge representation. He must also ensure that the computer can use the knowledge efficiently by selecting from a handful of reasoning methods.

Expert Systems				
Sales trend forecasting	Operating plan	Budget forecasting	Profit planning	Personnel planning
Sales/Mktg	Mfg	Finance	Account	HR

1.3.5 Decision Support Systems (DSS)

Decision Support Systems (DSS) are specifically designed to help management make decisions in situations where there is uncertainty about the possible outcomes of those decisions. DSS comprise tools and techniques to help gather relevant information and analyses the options and alternatives. DSS often involves use of complex spreadsheet and databases to create "what-if" models

Systems that combine data, models and analysis tools for non-routine decision-making.

Management-level Systems				
Sales region analysis	Production scheduling	Cost analysis	Pricing/ profitability analysis	Contract cost analysis
Sales/Mktg	Mfg	Finance	Account	HR

1.3.6 Office Automation (OA) System

Office Automation Systems are systems that try to improve the productivity of employees who need to process data and information. Perhaps the best example is the wide range of software systems that exist to improve the productivity of employees working in an office (e.g. Microsoft Office XP) or systems that allow employees to work from home or whilst on the move.

Systems that are designed to increase the productivity of data workers.

Knowledge-level Systems		
Word processing	Document imaging	E-mail/electronic calendars

1.4 HRMS PLANNING

1.4.1 HRIS Introduction

In a growing number of organizations human resources are now viewed as a source of competitive advantage. There is greater recognition that distinctive competencies are obtained through highly developed employee skills, distinctive organizational cultures, management processes, and systems. This is in contrast to the traditional emphasis on transferable resources such as equipment. Increasingly, it is being recognized that competitive advantage can be obtained with a high quality work force that enables organizations to compete on the basis of market responsiveness, product and service quality, differentiated products, and technological innovation.

The economic landscape underwent radical changes throughout the 1990s with increasing globalization, technological breakthroughs (particularly Internet enabled Web services), and hyper competition. Business process reengineering exercises became more common and frequent, resulting in several initiatives, such as the rightsizing of employee numbers, reducing the layers of management, reducing the bureaucracy of organizational structures, creating autonomous work teams, and outsourcing.

Accordingly, the people management function has become strategic in its importance and outlook and is geared to attract, retain, and engage talent. These developments have led to the creation of the HR balanced scorecard as well as to added emphasis on the Return on Investment (ROI) of the HR function and its programs.

The effective management of human resources in a firm to gain a competitive advantage in the marketplace requires timely and accurate information on current employees and potential employees in the labor market. With the evolution of computer technology, meeting this information requirement has been greatly enhanced through the creation of HRIS. A basic assumption here is that the effective management of employee information for decision makers will be the critical process that helps a firm maximize the use of its human resources and maintain competitiveness in its market.

Even small and medium firms could afford computer-based HR systems that were run by increasing user-friendly microcomputers and could be shown to be cost-effective. The prevailing management thinking regarding the use of computers in HR was not that their use would result in a reduction in the number of employees needed in HR departments but that employee activities and time could be shifted from transactional record keeping to more transformational activities that would add value to the organization. This change in the function of HRM could then be clearly measured in terms of cost-benefit ratios to the "bottom line" of the company.

1.4.1.1 HRIS Definitions

HRIS can be briefly defined "as integrated systems used to gather, store and analyze information regarding an organization's human resources" (Hedrickson).

HRIS "which is used to acquire, store, manipulate, analyze, retrieve and distribute information about an organization's human resources" (Tannenbaum).

"HRIS is not limited to the computer hardware and software applications that comprise the technical part of the system; it also includes the people, policies, procedures and data required to manage the HR function." (Hedrickson).

A Human Resource Information System (HRIS) is "software containing a database that allows the entering, storage and manipulation of data regarding employees of a company. It allows for global visualization and access of important employee information". (Marcia Moore)

Human assets are critical for any company and explicitly the IT industry where representatives perform the functions of the talent stores. Because of the vitality of human assets, human asset data frameworks have come into the spotlight. To use the representative's productivity it is basic to have full depiction about the worker and in addition the employment for which he/she is accessible. At times the representative could be the legacy for the association yet the person might not be successful in his present position or part in the organization. In many instances, surplus and lack of workers influences the organizations. HRIS supports the companies to overcome such challenges by planning the amount of employees, and also their set of responsibilities. Fig 1.2 shows how HRIS works.

Fig. 1.2

1.4.2 Human Resources and HRMS

In today's information economy, organizational triumph depends immensely on the execution of HRM (Human Resource Management) and HRIS (Human Resource Information Systems). Besides, HRIS has as of late turned its focus on sharing of learning and study of employee in a strategic manner and has been progressively developing into a critical donator for the organizational vital administration. HRIS comprises of efficient systems and capacities to gain, store, recover, study, control, and disseminate pertinent data concerning strategic practices from the organizational context. To expand the viability of HRM, companies are relying immensely on HRIS systems. HRIS can stay informed concerning representatives', candidates', and unexpected specialists' capabilities, demographics, execution assessment, expert advancement, payroll, recruitment, and maintenance on the functional level. With HRIS, the regulatory proficiency keeps up quicker data preparing, enhanced worker correspondences, and more stupendous data precision, lower HR costs and generally speaking HR capability upgrades. Strategic value could be inferred utilizing HRIS devices that support making of decisions concerning indispensable HR functions.

For instance, a system for HRIS might be acknowledged as an apparatus that furnishes strategic decision-makers with the required data empowering them to estimate future workforce request and supply prerequisites. In addition, it might be recognized as an instrument that helps managements in holding the right workers. This could be carried out by paying them focused compensations contrasted with the business, and preparing them to advance their abilities and capabilities to do their existing and future occupations. It goes without saying that no two HRIS programming results are precisely much the same. Hence there is a standardized set of common characteristics that each HR framework is basically anticipated to deliver.

The following are the most generic attributes :

1. **Payroll** : This module gathers attendance information and time related data from the databases, computes taxes and other deductions, and automatically creates paychecks as per the management's directive.

2. **Time and Labor Management** : This module pools and studies data on employee work/time so that the management can precisely supervise work assets. This regularly prompts lessened work costs and enhanced comprehension of work capacities.

3. **Profits Administration** : This module empowers the management to watch and supervise employee co-operation in the different benefits programs provided by the organization in a convenient manner. Certain modules even feature a self-service capacity which allows employees to audit their program choices, access their benefits any time of the day, and effortlessly select the plans for which they qualify.

4. **HR Management** : The HR Management module aggregates the sum of an organization's workforce information, permitting executives to stay informed concerning employees, for example contact data, status on any training programs, development of expertise, and compensation and benefits programs.

5. **Worker Self-Service** : As you have undoubtedly acknowledged at this point, a HRIS can work marvels regarding lightening the managerial load for a business' HR division. Be that as it may HRIS was not made singularly for the managerial advantage. This framework also opens the route to an entirely new level of self-service for the employees, permitting them to remotely access functional devices and crucial information through the utilization of the framework's networked databases.

6. **Cost** : Obviously, one of the primary concerns when it comes to investing in an HRIS is cost. The truth of the matter is that the "average cost" of an HRIS system can be difficult to narrow down; these applications can range from many thousands to even millions of dollars. Then factor in the costs of hardware, installation, integration, customization, and technical support, and the price of your comprehensive software solution will probably total several times the cost of the HRIS package on its own.

Last, but certainly not least, it is vital that you remember the cost of training your employees to use the new HRIS. Getting workers to learn the ropes of a new system can be expensive, but failing to push their adoption of the software can be downright disastrous.

Another key thing to keep in mind – when calculating the HRIS package's projected return on investment, don't forget the intangible efficiency benefits that can't always be assigned a simple dollar value.

1.4.3 Planning on HRMS

Project plans are established to meet strategic, tactical, and operational goals.

Plans can be too broad, or too detailed. Over-planning, or taking too much time to plan, can doom a project as can jumping into developing a system without a plan. Planning is a pragmatic process, with the aim of developing plans that are effective and efficient, not that are all inclusive or perfect. Plans, like their financial counterparts, budgets, represent the planner's best estimate at a specific point in time.

Plans should be flexible. It is the realization of the plan, through sound management of it, including adjusting for intangibles, and reacting to resource changes, which yields success.

Major Steps in Planning :

Step 1 : Recognition of need for new HRMS.

Step 2 : If there is an existing system, determine if it can be modified at a reasonable cost.

Step 3 : If there is no system, or if the cost of modifying it is not reasonable, conduct an analysis of whether buying a system or building a system is preferred.

Step 4 : Prepare detailed needs analysis.

Step 5 : Prepare a Request For Information (RFI) or Request For Proposal (RFP) and send it to selected vendors.

Step 6 : Analyse the results, reducing the short-list until only one or two options remain, and select finalist product and vendor.

Step 7 : Negotiate price and conditions, while conducting final vendor references, and financial review.

Step 8 : Select implementation project team.

Step 9 : Project management combines planning with a controlled use of resources to develop and implement specific end results, or projects, such as designing and implementing a new HRMS.

Project planning must clearly specify the following resources :

1. Time (start/end dates).
2. People (identification; specific skills they bring to project; availability; cost).
3. Tools (equipment, software).
4. Money (budget).

1.4.4 Designing a HRMS

An HRIS can be defined as "a composite of database, computer applications, hardware and software necessary to collect/record, store, manage, deliver, present, and manipulate data for human resource".

Functions and Attributes of Modern Human Resource Information System :

HRIS differs in its functionality and application from administrative applications, talent management applications, workforce management applications, service delivery applications and workforce analysis and/or decision support applications. This means a shift has been made from labor-intensive HRM to technology-intensive HRM. The transformation has not been trivial, considering "getting the staff to adapt and adapt to a new system, which is actually a new business process for them" to be the most important difficulty.

Fig. 1.3 : HRIS Model

Many studies came out with many functions that represent an HRIS. For example, HRIS functions include corporate communication, recruitment, selection, training, employee opinion survey, compensation, payroll services and employee verification as well as general staff related information and demographics. Recent studies added that the functions of HRIS comply with organizational interests in maintaining and managing the human capital based on the organizational vision and the strategy of achieving that vision. It supports and integrates various aspects in relation to organizational sustainability. In their study, Mayfield and his colleagues identified seven main component of an HRIS model. They commented that those components are considered to be the primary components of this model which form a comprehensive framework of an HRIS. They stated that "more specifically, our model addresses all major HRIS components and offers information on how these facets interact to support each other and larger organizational outcome". These components (functions) are portrayed in figure provided below:

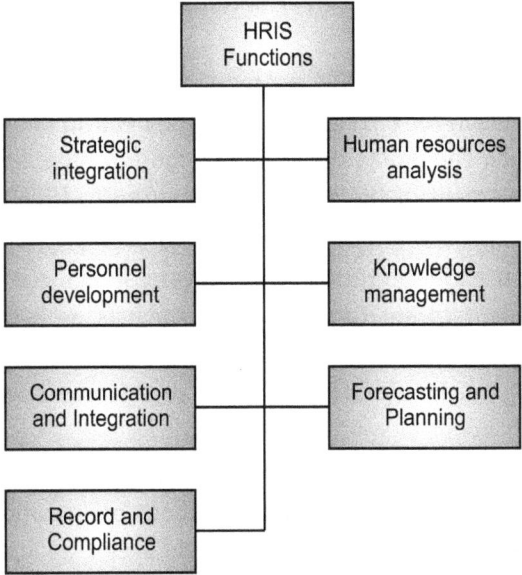

Fig. 1.4 : HRIS Functions

The above framework is divides the seven functions into two dimensions. The four functionalities for HRIS are related to HR practices concerned directly with the organizational employees. These functions are personnel development, communication and integration, records and compliance and HR Analysis. The additional three functionalities (strategic integration, forecasting and planning and knowledge management) represent HR department role in the organizational practices in general and the strategic management in specific.

1. **Strategic Integration :** HRIS leads to an improvement in organizational performance and changes the method in which organizations are managed. HRIS facilitates strategic value generation by helping design and implement internally consistent policies and practices which ensure the human resources contribute to accomplishing business objectives. Strategic value can be derived by HRIS tools that assist with decision-making regarding essential HR functions.

2. **Human Resources Analysis :** Most of the HR decisions are based on this function. Using this function, an organization makes a decision of whether their personnel capabilities are congruent or not. Human resource analysis is considered to be an ongoing mean of collecting and identifying human resource needs.

3. **Personnel Development :** In this function, an organization can decide on any deficiency an employee has, accordingly, make a decision of the most appropriate training and/or development method to use to overcome that deficiency. Such a deficiency can be determined using an individual employee performance, appraisal, and career development which all can be accomplished through an HRIS.

4. **Knowledge Management :** HRIS are mostly created for knowledge management of HRM. The reason for having an HRIS is the need to control the basic data on personnel, which constructs organizations more profitable and effective. These concerns are element of the big challenge linked to HRIS development, one of which is also the abilities to design and implement HRIS.

5. **Communication and Integration :** Inter-organizational communication supports and coordinates different organizational activities as well as changes. In this function, an appropriate HRIS involves a communication mechanism suitable for communicating necessary information to all customers within and outside an organization.

6. **Forecasting and Planning :** This function is used to transform the input of an HRIS analysis into its predictive feedback about organizational future personnel and skill needs. Data maintained in an HRIS can be used as a competitive information resource.

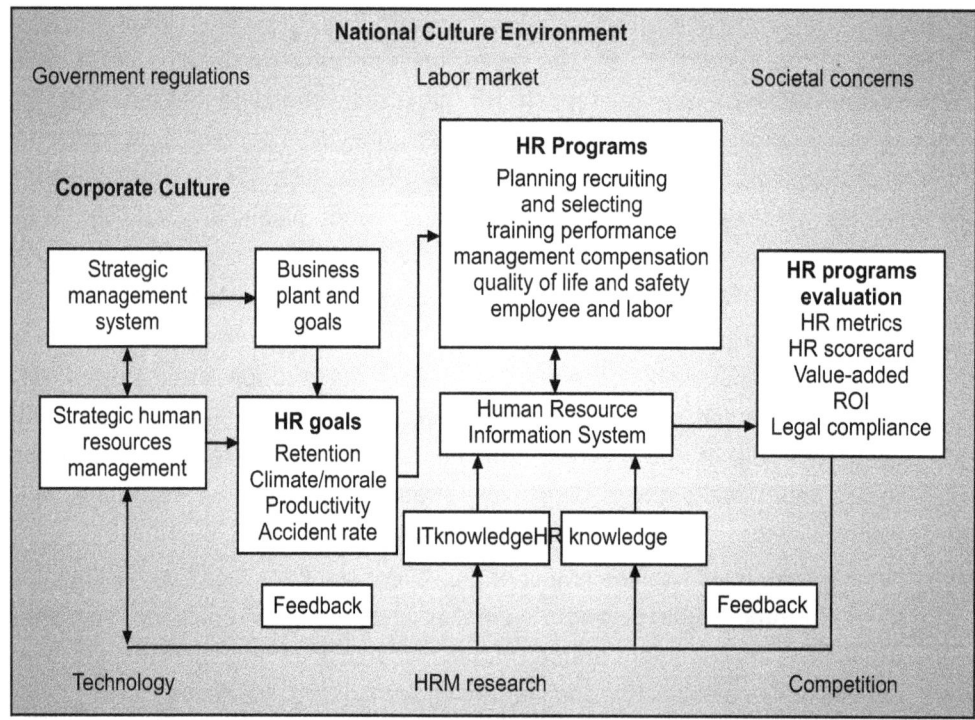

Fig. 1.5 : Model of an Organizational System Centered on HRIS

1.4.5 Software for HRMS

The developments in the Indian industry has also seen the implementation of Enterprise Resource Planning (ERP) configuration in HRM with extensive use of manager and employee self-portals. Most critically, these changes ensure that firms can significantly advance in the use of people knowledge in managerial decision. They can access people's knowledge more rapidly with a higher degree of accuracy. The system of applications of Information Technology (IT) in HRM is referred to as Human Resource Module. HRIS merges some of HRM functions with the IT field, wherein the planning and programming of data processing systems have evolved into standardized routines and packages of Enterprise Resource Planning (ERP) software.

ERP integrates the human resource module with finance, production, sales and administration modules. Technology-driven automation (IT) processes certainly help reduce costs and cycle times as well as improve quality. Information System (IS) can further help decision makers to make and implement strategic decisions. HR data, if collected effectively and contained within computerized and accessible systems, can compare organizational HR 'bottom line' outcomes of HRM function i.e. between functions and with national or international performance benchmark.

Ten step Plan for HRM Software Selection :
1. Improve your HRMS software knowledge.
2. Determine your needs.
3. Create a detailed HRMS software needs and requirements spreadsheet.
4. How much can you spend ?
5. Pick a handful of HRMS software systems to evaluate.
6. Demo advice.
7. Research the short list.
8. Determine the implementation scope.
9. Make the decision.
10. Getting approval.

1. Improve your HRMS Software Knowledge :

Before you can determine your needs, budget, or anything, you have to understand what the overall capabilities, features, and options are of the various HRIS software applications. There are a number of ways you can educate yourself on these capabilities. One is to look up articles, such as this one. There are tremendous online resources and articles created on this exact subject. There are also a number of sites that show a number of HRIS software applications and provide helpful information for your education, as well.

2. Determine your needs :

Everything you read about buying HRIS software is going to say exactly the same thing. Telling you to determine your needs is nothing new.

The concept is used so often it is almost considered a click. The point of this section is to tell you what this statement means and why this step is extremely important when starting your search for HRIS software.

Exactly what reports do you need, what data do you need to track, how would you populate the database fields, and would you need to interface with any of your other software applications ?

In this process of determining your needs and requirements, make sure to also confer with other departments who might end up utilizing portions of your HRIS product, as well.

3. **Create a detailed HRM software needs and requirements spreadsheet:**

You will likely look at a number of systems and, like looking for a house, eventually you are going to forget which system did what and offered what advantages.

I recommend creating a detailed spreadsheet to assist with this process. Down the left side, list your needs and across the top, list each vendor. If you want to offer more detail, you might end up reviewing several HR information systems to score each product.

4. **How much can you spend ?**

Now that you have improved your HRIS knowledge and you have a detailed list of your needs, you need to determine how much you can spend before deciding which applications you want to evaluate.

How much you can spend can be a little tricky because of the various pricing options vendors offer.

5. **Pick a handful of systems to evaluate :**

The first thing to do is find the short list that seems to meet your needs. Perform a few searches and you will find a hand full of sites that list a number of HRIS systems on their sites. Some even offer the capability of filtering the products by options or features.

The sales people for those companies, while they might not offer the prices up front if you call and tell them what your max budget is, will at least tell you if that is possible or not. At the end of this process, you should have your list scaled down to four or five systems of which you will want to see a demo.

6. **Demo advice :**

With each demo, have your spreadsheet in hand and make sure that each need or requirement you have identified is shown during the demo. With your score spreadsheet in hand, provide a score for each need. This step is actually pretty easy because you did your homework up front.

7. **Research the short list :**

After reviewing the four or five products, you will likely cut this list in half. From here, do a little research on each company. Ask for references, see how long the company has been in business, and how many installs they have.

8. **Determine the implementation scope :**

You will know exactly what you are paying for the software, service and/support. Some companies may fix cost the implementation costs. Others will provide an estimate of time to complete the work and training. In either case, if the scope of the project is not determined in detail before the project begins, this is where you are going to go over budget.

Make sure you receive an implementation quote that shows hours for each phase of the project. Look it over and make sure that each of your needs is met with the process.

9. **Make the decision :**

Looking over your spreadsheet is the easiest step in the entire process. By now, you have likely narrowed your list to two or three systems and there is no confusion because the best solution is scored the highest.

10. **Getting approval :**

Sadly, many companies view HR as a cost center. As a cost center, it can be difficult to get approval for a system that may benefit a single department.

This is part of the reason, under determining your needs, I recommended involving other departments. Determine what the company objectives are and try to tie your case for HRIS software to these objectives. A system that benefits the entire organization makes a stronger case for need.

Primary Modules for HRM Software :
1. Human Resource Tracking and Reporting system.
2. Applicant and Employment Management.
3. Recruitment Core System to Manage Complete Hiring Life-Cycle.
4. Payroll Module.
5. Performance Management Module.
6. Training and Development.
7. Employee Self-Service Model.

Major HRIS Solution Providers :

1. **SAP HR - SAP Human Resources :**

The Human Resources module (SAP HR) consists of all master data, system configuration, and transactions to complete the Hire to Retire (or, as some say, Fire) process. It includes the following information and processes.

2. **JD Edwards Enterprise One :**

Oracle's JD Edwards is one of today's leading Enterprise Resource Planning (ERP) software and supply chain management software solutions. An integrated applications suite, JDE E1 combines business value, standards-based technology, and deep industry experience into a business solution with a low total cost of ownership.

3. **Simple HR :**

Track It, Retrieve It, Document It! with Simple HR. Human Resources Information Systems should make your HR tasks easier. And SimpleHR will do that. This employee management system can simplify your workflow, increase your efficiency and quickly become an essential tool in your HR workday.

4. Apex Software :

Powerful and cost-effective HR software FMLA software time and attendance software and absence management software. Multi-user with e-mailed alerts leaves calendaring and Web access. Integrates with ADP, Quick books and biometric terminals.

1.4.6 Hardware for HRMS

The computer comprises of technologically advanced hardware put together to work at great speed. To accomplish its various tasks, the computer is made of different parts, each serving a particular purpose in conjunction with other parts. In other words, a 'computer' is an ensemble of different machines that you will be using to accomplish your job.

Computer is primarily made of the Central Processing Unit (usually referred to as the Computer), the monitor, the keyboard and the mouse. Other pieces of hardware, commonly referred to as peripherals, can enhance or improve your experience with the computer.

Basic elements of a computer system are Mouse, Keyboard, monitor, memory, CPU Motherboard, Hard Disk, Speakers, Modem, power supply and processor.

HRMS Hardware Requirement :

1. **Development Environment :**
   (i) Microsoft Windows XP Professional 2002 SP3 (Development, Browser Client).
   (ii) Microsoft Windows 2000 Server (Web Server).
   (iii) Microsoft .Net 2008.
   (iv) Microsoft SQL Server 2005.
   (v) Microsoft Internet Explorer 7.0.
   (vi) Microsoft Internet Information Service 5.1.
2. **Recommended Client-side Environment (Intranet or Internet) :**

(i) **Database Server :**
   - Database Software.
   - Microsoft SQL Server Professional 2005.
   - Operating System.
   - Microsoft Windows 2003 Server.

(ii) **Hardware Configuration is the recommended environment for the organization whose employee number exceeds 5000) :**
   - CPU: Intel Xeon 5320(Dual-Core), [Intel Xeon 5500(4-Core)] Memory: 4G, [16G - 32G].

- Hard Disk: 250G+, [5*160G, SCSI, 15000rps, RAID5].

(iii) **Web Server :**
- Web Server Software.
- Microsoft Internet Information Service 5.1.NET Framework 3.5.

Operating System :
- Microsoft Windows 2003 Server.
- Hardware Configuration ([] is the recommended environment for the organization whose employee number exceeds 5000).
- CPU : Intel Xeon 5320(Dual-Core), [Intel Xeon 5500 (4-Core)].
- Memory: 4G, [16G - 32G].
- Hard Disk : 160G, [5*160G, SCSI, 15000rps, RAID5].

(iv) **Browser Client :**
- Browser Software.
- Microsoft Internet Explorer 6.0.
- Microsoft Internet Explorer 7.0.
- Microsoft Internet Explorer 8.0.
- Mozilla Firefox 3.62011-07-01.

(v) **Operating System :**
- Microsoft Windows XP Professional 2002 SP3.
- Microsoft Windows Vista.

(vi) **Hardware Configuration :**
- CPU: Intel Pentium E2160 (1.8GHz).
- Memory: 1G+.
- Hard Disk: 80G+.

1.5 BENEFITS OF HUMAN RESOURCE INFORMATION SYSTEM

The Human Resource Information System is by no means a new phenomenon – on the contrary, HRIS technology has been around for years. Only recently, however, have people begun to realize the serious benefits such systems have to offer. Nearly every business can stand to gain something in the realm of efficiency and operational cohesion, and HR information software is designed to provide exactly those improvements. It helps, too, that HR software vendors have been coming out with increasingly bigger and better offerings. Evolving technology is allowing HRIS to perform tasks that no one could have even dreamed of back when the systems were first introduced. Consider talent management: an HRIS helps companies to streamline the hiring process, formulating better recruitment strategies and decreasing time-to-hire, which results in an improvement in the quality of the workers hired and, consequently, an improvement in the quality of the business as a whole.

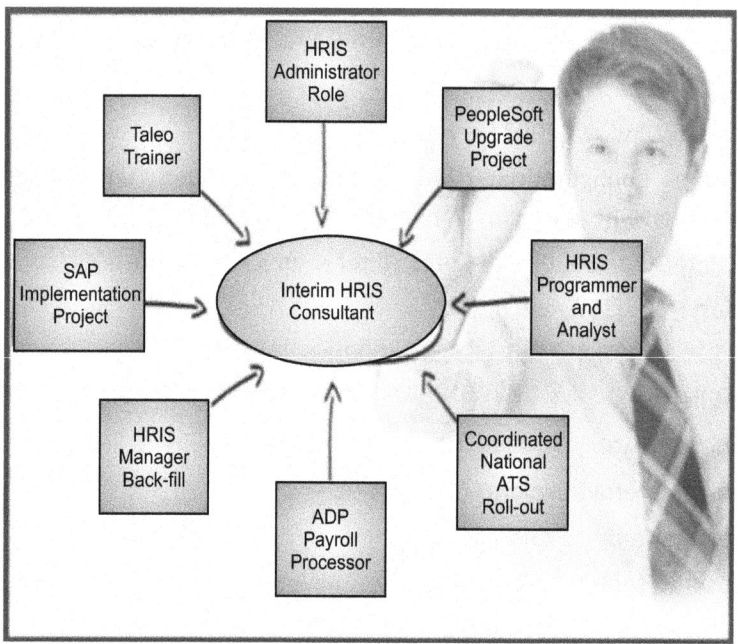

Fig. 1.6

An HRIS benefits management module, meanwhile, is a legitimate revolution for those still stuck doing the work manually. With HRIS, executives can track a variety of different benefits plans, electronically set certain eligibility requirements, and instantaneously calculate costs and details. The list goes on – compliance management protects confidential employee information, recruitment tracks applicants and analyzes available positions, payroll crunches those numbers so you don't have to. Put simply, HRIS exists to make your job easier – it takes care of the routine administrative tasks so that you can focus on more important issues.

1. **Reporting :** Perhaps the biggest benefit that the use of an HRIS system adds to a business is its ability to create reports and presentations. An HRIS system typically holds all information surrounding the firm's human resources initiatives, including details regarding the group's hiring practices, such as a comprehensive listing of all job applicants, an up-to-date index of job openings and electronic copies of each employee's on boarding paperwork, such as I-9 and W2 forms. For example, when looking to hire additional staff, he/she can run a report of past candidates who possess a specific skill set. Alternatively, he can run a compensation report to obtain needed information when preparing the annual budget.

2. **Recruitment :** In support of a firm's staffing efforts, many HRIS systems provide a sophisticated interface allowing its use by both internal employees, as well as external job applicants. An HRIS system allows candidates for open positions to submit their resumes and contact information to a potential employer from a remote computer. The system then collects the information and archives it so it is easily accessible by the hiring manager. When seeking candidates, the manager is able to perform detailed searches of collected resumes, using a variety of queries, including location, level of education, years of professional experience and technical skill set. In addition, the software also allows current employees to electronically apply for new positions.
3. **Benefits Administration :** An HRIS system allows a business to streamline the administration of employee benefits. In many cases, employees and new hires may electronically enroll in benefit plans. They may also have the capability of logging onto the system to monitor and update their current coverage throughout the year, changing status, dependent information and contact data as required. A self-service system allows for benefits to be efficiently administered with as little manpower as possible, saving an organizations time and money.

HRIS gives firms several other benefits and advantages. They include the following :

1. Increasing competitiveness by improving HR operations and management processes.
2. Providing a comprehensive information picture as a single, integrated database; this enables organizations to provide structural connectivity across units and activities and to increase the speed of information transactions.
3. Collecting appropriate data and converting them to information and knowledge for improved timeliness and quality of decision making.
4. Producing a greater number and variety of accurate and real-time HR-related reports.
5. Streamlining and enhancing the efficiency and effectiveness of HR administrative functions.
6. Shifting the focus of HR from the processing of transactions to strategic HRM.
7. Reengineering HR processes and functions.
8. Improving employee satisfaction by delivering HR services more quickly and accurately.

Activities

1. Visit the websites of PeopleSoft.com and enlist the benefits that their HRIS products offer to their clients.
2. Browse the internet and obtain more insight on snapshots provided for Recruitment.

Summary

In this chapter we have discussed about, Human Resource Information System which is commonly known as HRIS is the generic term referring to any information system used for obtaining relevant and timely information on which to base human resource decisions. Human resources are asset for any organization and specifically the IT organizations where employees act as the talent warehouse. Due to the importance of human resources, human resource information systems have come into focus. To utilize the employee's efficiency it is imperative to have full description about the employee as well as the job for which he is available.

In a growing number of organizations human resources are now viewed as a source of competitive advantage. There is greater recognition that distinctive competencies are obtained through highly developed employee skills, distinctive organizational cultures, management processes, and systems.

The effective management of human resources in a firm to gain a competitive advantage in the marketplace requires timely and accurate information on current employees and potential employees in the labor market.

The Human Resource Information System is by no means a new phenomenon – on the contrary, HRIS technology has been around for years. Only recently, however, have people begun to realize the serious benefits such systems have to offer. Nearly every business can stand to gain something in the realm of efficiency and operational cohesion, and HR information software is designed to provide exactly those improvements. HRIS gives firms several other benefits and advantages. They include the following:

1. Increasing competitiveness by improving HR operations and management processes.
2. Producing a greater number and variety of accurate and real-time HR-related reports.
3. Shifting the focus of HR from the processing of transactions to strategic HRM.
4. Improving employee satisfaction by delivering HR services more quickly and accurately.

Self-assessment Questions

1. Discuss in detail the importance of Human Resource Information Systems from the context of human resources.
2. Enlist and discuss the factors that Human Resource Information System (HRIS) has recently turned its concentration on?
3. Enlist and discuss in detail the attributes that an HRIS system can keep track of at the functional level?
4. Explain in brief the functions of the Payroll module of an HRIS system.
5. Explain in brief the functions of the Benefits Administration module of an HRIS system.

❖❖❖

Chapter 2...

Management Information Systems

Objectives ...

After discussing this chapter, you will be able to :

- Enlist and describe different Departments that HRIS caters to and their Functionality.
- Discuss the Role and Skills of the Personnel in charge of HRIS Systems.
- Enlist and describe the Design Considerations for HRIS Systems.
- Understand HRIS Life Cycle.

Structure ...

2.1 Introduction
    2.1.1 Need of MIS
    2.1.2 Purpose and Objectives of MIS
    2.1.3 MIS Definitions
2.2 Functional Applications/Exercise of HRIS
    2.2.1 Database Concept and Applications in HRIS
    2.2.2 HRIS Needs Analysis
    2.2.3 The Main Objectives of HR Metrics and Workforce Analytics
2.3 HRIS Life Cycle
2.4 Responsibility in Each Phase of Development
2.5 Pre-implementation Stage of HRIS
    2.5.1 HRIS Planning
    2.5.2 HRIS Designing Issues
2.6 HRIS Expectation
2.7 HRIS Cost Benefit Value Analysis
2.8 Getting Management Support for HRIS
2.9 Limitations of Computerization of HRIS
2.10 Human Resources (HR) Metrics and Work Force Analytic
- Activities
- Summary
- Self-assessment Questions

2.1 INTRODUCTION

A Management Information System (MIS) is a broadly used and applied term for a three-resource system required for effective organization management. The resources are people, information and technology, from inside and outside an organization, with top priority given to people. The system is a collection of information management methods involving computer automation (software and hardware) or otherwise supporting and improving the quality and efficiency of business operations and human decision making.

As an area of study, MIS is sometimes referred to as IT Management (Information Technology Management) or Information Services (IS). Neither should be confused with computer science.

It is important to note that a management information system should not only indicate the status of a business's conditions, but also indicate why the conditions are improving or deteriorating. For example, an MIS should report performance relative to cost and profitable or unprofitable projects, while identifying individual accountability — both current and past. This can be done only if such reports are based on constantly updated information accessible to those in authority who are responsible for assessing and assuring it is used for timely decision-making.

Examples of the broad scope and varied contexts of MISs are :
1. Decision Support Systems (DSS).
2. Enterprise Resource Planning (ERP).
3. Supply Chain Management (SCM).
4. Customer Relationship Management (CRM).
5. Project Management (PM).
6. Executive Information Systems (EIS).

The term MIS and "information system" are often confused. Information systems, by themselves, are differentiated from the decision-making process. Of course, the data within them may facilitate the decision-making process.

2.1.1 Need of MIS

1. Information is necessary input for achieving our objectives to learn.
2. Information can be considered as the essence of all human intellectual activities.
3. It is well fact that information is fundamental input for activities.
4. Information would acquire importance like raw material natural resources, and energy as commodities.

5. Chief Information Officer is common designation in any enterprise today.
6. It is not only business executives and managers who need information support.
7. Without MIS, it would be impossible for information to be made available.
8. Organizations involve several people with different background, culture, aspirations.
9. A single organization consists of multiple business units located indifferent cities.
10. Materials a manager need information about inventory and capital blocked in inventory.
11. HR managers need information about attendance for preparing payroll.
12. Plant manager for resource allocation.
13. Need in manufacturing and service sector.

2.1.2 Purpose and Objectives of MIS

The fundamental purpose is to provide information support to management functions within an organization MIS is designed to and implemented with view to provide the required information support to undertake managerial activities such as planning, organizing, staffing, co-ordination, control and decision making.

Its purpose is to help managers to solve structured problems. But it should also fulfill a number of other purposes :

1. It should provide a basis to analyze warning signals that can originate both externally and internally; this is the main function of data base;
2. It should automate routine operations thus avoiding human work in the processing tasks;
3. It should assist management in making routine decisions;
4. It should provide the information necessary to make non-routine decisions;
5. It should serve as a strategic weapon to gain competitive advantage.

MIS in a business organization has several objectives. They are dependent on different factors specific to particular business.

Some of common objectives are :

1. To provide right type of information at lowest cost and right time.
2. To ensure managerial activities are provided adequate and appropriate information support.
3. To ensure information overloads well as generation of redundant information is avoided.

2.1.3 MIS Definitions

An organized approach to the study of the information needs of an organization's management at every level in making operational, tactical, and strategic decisions. Its objective is to design and implement procedures, processes, and routines that provide suitably detailed reports in an accurate, consistent, and timely manner.

In a management information system, modern, computerized systems continuously gather relevant data, both from inside and outside an organization. This data is then processed, integrated, and stored in a centralized database (or data warehouse) where it is constantly updated and made available to all who have the authority to access it, in a form that suits their purpose.

1. **Kelly** defines Management information System as "a combination of human and computer based resources that result in collection, storage, communication and use of data for the purpose of efficient management of operations and for business planning".

2. **T. Lucey** defines MIS as "a system to convert data from external and internal sources into information and to communicate that information in an appropriate form to managers at all levels in all functions to enable them to make timely and effective decisions for planning, directing and controlling the activities of organization".

3. According to **Davis Gordon** "integrated user machine system for providing information to support operations, management decision making functions in an organization. The system uses computer hardware and software, manual procedures, models for analysis, planning control and decision making, and a database".

4. According to **Barry Cushing** "MIS is a set of human and capital resources within an organization which is responsible for the collection and processing of data to produce information which is useful to all levels of management in planning and controlling activities in organization".

Now if we put discussion together, we can say :
- MIS is defined as computer based information system.
- MIS is system based on the database of the organization evolved.

2.2 Functional Applications/Exercise of HRIS

A HRIS generally should provide the capability to more effectively plan, control and manage HR costs; achieve improved efficiency and quality in HR decision making; and improve employee and managerial productivity and effectiveness. A HRIS offers HR, payroll, benefits, training, recruiting and compliance solutions. Most are adaptable outlined with mixed databases, an extensive exhibit of characteristics, and capable reporting capacities and examination abilities that you have to supervise your workforce. This can give back hours of the HR manager's day previously used going through routine worker demands.

Some of the most popular modules are :

1. Organization charts (Create professional looking, dynamic organization charts).
2. Employee self-service (Employees can update personal information and view benefits elections, absence transactions, time-off balances and payroll information).
3. Benefits Administration (Save paper and postage, take weeks off the benefits open enrollment period, reduce administration time, and improve data accuracy).
4. Track training for employees.

Skills required for HRIS Practitioners :

The essential authority of the HRIS Practitioner is benefits and compensation, staffing, recruitment and employee relations capacities. The HRIS Practitioner gives authoritative support to the association's HR programs by utilizing and keeping up the human assets data frameworks (HRIS). Selecting the right HRIS is essential. Associations will determine that they can alter the framework to help and that it is a framework that will develop with your organization.

A typical set of responsibilities for the HRIS Practitioner part might incorporate :

1. Performing routine managerial errands in support of the HRIS (Human Resources Information Systems) group.
2. Inputting information into a computer processing framework and audits yield for correctness.
3. Generating standard reports for Human Resources or supervising staff.
4. Requiring a secondary school certificate or its comparable and 0-3 years of experience in the field or in an identified territory.

Organizational Role :

The HRIS Practitioner ordinarily serves as part of specialist, trainee and Manager. As being what is indicated, this Practitioner furnishes routine specialized or authoritative undertakings. The association will hinge on upon this individual's following of policies and procedures.

HRIS Practitioner Job Responsibilities :

The HRIS Practitioner for the most part has the accompanying obligations :

1. Performs an assortment of administrative undertakings as per HRIS guidelines and approaches.

2. Enters information into the HRIS, audits information precision, and stays informed regarding information overhauls.
3. Generates standard HRIS reports for human asset administration.
4. Assists in HRIS training and helps end users with HRIS problem reporting.

HRIS Practitioner Competencies :

Eleven critical proficiencies are expected of HRIS Practitioners as per the comprehensive HRIS Practitioner Manager's Guide. Each capability is defined in detail in the report in the above context. The report also explains what level of proficiency the Practitioner should have in that competency, as well as how important that competency is to performing the role well.

Some of the major competencies for HRIS Practitioners are as follows :

1. The HRIS Practitioner is required to exhibit Working knowledge in the Data Entry Management competency. To show Working background in the Data Entry Management competency, one may as well exhibit information of procedures, instruments and administrations for supervising information section and reporting comes about.
2. Reviews contractual, legitimate, and moral access contemplations and commitments.
3. Experience in a data entry operations center or role.
4. Maintains the lists of inward and outer sources, administrations and outlets, services and vendors.
5. Plays a part in major data entry operations department or roles.
6. Documents operation reports or problems in the data entry process.

2.2.1 Database Concept and Applications in HRIS

The HRIS achieved new dimension with development of computer networks. By then, only trained employees, mainly from the HR department could perform operations in separated computers or in mainframes, through a local network of terminals. However, the sudden expansion of networks and falling prices of computers enabled everyone to become part of the system, no matter where they are. Under the new conditions each employee can use the HRIS. The level of use is determined by the need and permissions. Structure of the HRIS becomes significantly more complex, and the new problems appear, primarily related to security and privacy of information about employees.

Important Data :

As is evident in the above sections, each customer/user of the HRIS has slightly different needs with regard to what information he or she will be using. Some users simply input data and information; a few simply look at data and information provided in the form of reports, while a few others analyze the data and information to make decisions.

What these users all have in common is that all the information is about potential and current employees with a focus on managing the organization's human capital to achieve strategic organizational goals. Specific data from the HRIS database fit into three categories :

1. Information about people, such as biographical information and competencies (knowledge, skills, abilities, and other factors).
2. Information about the organization, such as jobs, positions, job specifications, organizational structure, compensation, employee/labor relations, and legally required data.
3. Data that are created as a result of the interaction of the first two categories, for example, individual job history, performance appraisals, and compensation information.

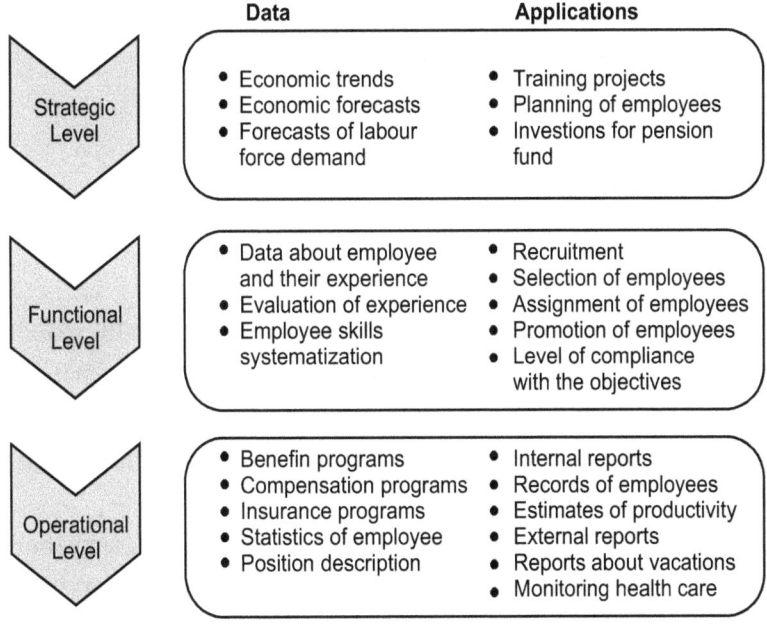

Fig. 2.1

The managers referred to within this section may have a variety of titles such as manager, director, vice president, and even CEO. What they all have in common is that their primary HRIS need is to have real-time access to accurate data that facilitate decision making with regard to their people. The HRIS provides the manager with data for performance management, recruiting and retention, team management, project management, and employee development. The HRIS must also provide the information necessary to help the functional manager make decisions that will contribute to the achievement of the unit's strategic goals and objectives. Easy access to accurate employee data enables the manager for each employee to view and engage in employee life cycle changes such as salary decisions, job requisitions, hiring, disciplinary action, promotions, and training program enrollment.

The HRIS provides the manager with data for performance management, recruiting and retention, team management, project management, and employee development. The HRIS must also provide the information necessary to help the functional manager make decisions that will contribute to the achievement of the unit's strategic goals and objectives. Easy access to accurate employee data enables the manager for each employee to view and engage in employee life cycle changes such as salary decisions, job requisitions, hiring, disciplinary action, promotions, and training program enrollment.

What is a Database ?

A **structured** collection of information captures the **semantics** of an application :
1. Logically coherent - so it makes sense.
2. Inherent meaning - information vs. data.
3. Specific purpose - intended user group.
4. Representation of the real world - changes in the real world reflected in the database.

Database Users :

Users are differentiated by the way they expect to interact with the system.
1. Application programmers – interact with system through DML calls.
2. Sophisticated users – form requests in a database query language.
3. Specialized users – write specialized database applications that do not fit into the traditional data processing framework.
4. Naïve users – invoke one of the permanent application programs that have been written previously, e.g. people accessing database over the web, bank tellers, clerical staff.

Database Administrator :

Coordinates all the activities of the database system; the database administrator has a good understanding of the enterprise's information resources and needs.

Database administrator's duties include :
1. Schema definition.
2. Storage structure and access method definition.

3. Schema and physical organization modification.
4. Granting user authority to access the database.
5. Specifying integrity constraints.
6. Acting as liaison with users.
7. Monitoring performance and responding to changes in requirements.

Transaction Management :
1. A transaction is a collection of operations that performs a single logical function in a database application.
2. Transaction-management component ensures that the database remains in a consistent (correct) state despite system failures (e.g., power failures and operating system crashes) and transaction failures.
3. Concurrency-control manager controls the interaction among the concurrent transactions, to ensure the consistency of the database.

2.2.2 HRIS Needs Analysis

Need Analysis : Enlisted below are the set of activities and tasks which are critical in this particular phase:
1. Evaluate HR department and business models.
2. Form project team.
3. Determine automation needs.
4. Develop system specifications.
5. Analyze current and future reporting needs.
6. Develop REP.
7. Identify and evaluate vendor packages.
8. Select vendor.
9. Develop proposal for management decision makers.
10. Establish formal guidelines and procedures to resolve inefficiencies

These are actual Measures in the Human Resources Effectiveness Report required in any Industry; the need of each business depends upon type of business :
1. Revenue per Employee.
2. Expense per Employee.
3. Compensation as a Percentage of Revenue.
4. Compensation as a Percentage of Expense.
5. Benefit Cost as a Percentage of Revenue.

6. Benefit Cost as a Percentage of Expense.
7. Benefit Cost as a Percentage of Compensation.
8. Retiree Benefit Cost per Retiree.
9. Retiree Benefit Cost as a Percentage of Expense.
10. Hires as a Percentage of Total Employees.
11. Cost of Hire.
12. Time to Fill Jobs.
13. Time to Start Jobs.
14. HR Department Expense as a Percentage of Company Expense.
15. HR Headcount Ratio - HR Employees: Company Employees.
16. HR Department Expense per Company Employee.
17. Supervisory Compensation Percentage.
18. Workers' Compensation Cost as a Percentage of Expense.
19. Workers' Compensation Cost per Employee.
20. Workers' Compensation Cost per Claim.
21. Absence Rate.
22. Involuntary Separation.
23. Voluntary Separation.
24. Voluntary Separation by Length of Service.
25. Ratio of Offers Made to Acceptances.

2.2.3 The Main Objectives of HR Metrics and Workforce Analytics

Despite reporting more metrics with greater frequency to a wider group of managers, many HR professionals tasked with this reporting question whether these efforts have had a significant impact on organization effectiveness.

Often, these individuals report frustration with their inability to get managers to :
1. Tell them what information they need,
2. Use the HR metrics information included in existing reports, or
3. Even acknowledge receipt of the reports. These perceptions represent a fundamental problem in the approach organizations take toward the utilization of metrics and analytics.

Many managers perceive the increased interest in metrics and analytics as simply a mandate to compute and report more metrics. The assumption behind assessing and reporting HR metrics is that it results in better organizational performance. But it is not clear that generating and reporting more HR metrics will necessarily result in better individual, unit, or organizational performance.

HR metrics and analytics comprise an information system, and information systems can only have an impact on organizations if, as a result of the information they receive, managers make different and better decisions than they would have without that information. No information system, including HR metrics and analytics, generates any return on the investment unless managers change their decision behavior for the better. If managers do not make different and better decisions as a result of the information reported to them, the time and effort expended in conducting and reporting HR metrics and analytics is wasted.

The emphasis on improving managerial decisions changes the dynamics driving metrics and analytics assessment efforts; that is, it raises the bar. It is not simply good enough to "do" metrics and analytics. These activities need to be approached in a way that increases the possibility that access to the information from these efforts will change managerial decisions, making them more effective. A fundamental problem is that many of the currently popular HR metrics do not provide a clear impact on important managerial decisions. The challenge, therefore, is to identify metrics and analytics that provide managers with the information they need to make better decisions regarding the acquisition and deployment of an organization's human capital.

Using HR Metrics and Workforce Analytics :

Human capital metrics has become an umbrella term that encompasses a wide range of activities and processes. There is a fundamental distinction between HR metrics and workforce analytics. Metrics are data (numbers) that reflect some descriptive detail about given processes or outcomes, for example, success in recruiting new employees. In the domain of human capital, these reflect characteristics of the organization's HR programs and activities. The importance of this view is that the analytics an organization needs depend on the problems and opportunities that currently face its managers. This path leads to the metrics that the organization needs in order to compute these analyses. A number of important HR activities fall within HR metrics and workforce analytics.

1. **Reporting :**

    A substantial amount of effort in the study and practice of metrics and analytics has focused on reporting. Reporting incorporates decisions about,

    (a) What metrics will be reported ?
    (b) How these metrics will be packaged; and
    (c) When, and to whom they should be reported.

Effort has focused on attempting to identify what metrics an organization should use. This approach can be done by posting the metrics on company Web sites.

2. **Dashboards :**

   Dashboards are an enriched component of reporting. Dashboards reflect efforts to align real-time analysis of organizational and HR processes as well as an increased capacity to aggregate organizational data. The dashboard allows users to maintain a current snapshot of key HR metrics.

3. **Benchmarking :**

   The Saratoga Institute's benchmarking efforts were the first to develop information on standard HR metrics regarding the use and management of human capital. Benchmarking data is useful in that it provides insights into what is possible.

4. **Data Mining :**

   Interest in data mining human capital information has been on the rise since the implementation of integrated HRIS and digitized HRM processes. Data mining refers to efforts to identify patterns that exist within data and that may identify unrecognized causal mechanisms that can be used to enhance decision making. Data mining has a number of important applications, but the caveat with its use is that it can also uncover spurious and nonsensical relationships (e.g., taller employees make better leaders; older employees have longer tenures).

5. **Predictive Analyses :**

   Predictive analysis is the goal of many metrics and analytics efforts. Predictive analysis involves attempts to develop models of organizational systems that can be used to predict future outcomes and understand the consequences of hypothetical changes in organizations, for example, a change in existing organizational systems. Engaging in efforts to test the assumptions in these models over time can lead to enhancements in the quality of the models' underlying predictive analyses, either by identifying additional leading indicators or better specifying the nature of the relationships between predictors and outcomes.

6. **Operational Experiments :**

   The evidence-based management movement argues that managers should base their decisions on data drawn from the organization and evidence about the actual functioning of its systems rather than using personal philosophies or untested personal models or assumptions about "how things work." One of the most effective methods for developing the evidence on which to base decisions is through operational experiments conducted within the organization.

7. Workforce Modeling :

Workforce modeling attempts to understand how an organization's human capital needs would change as a function of some expected change in the organization's environment. This change may be a shift in the demand for the organization's product, entry into a new market, divestiture of one of the organization's businesses, or a pending acquisition of or merger with another organization.

8. Putting HR Metrics and Analytics Data in Context :

Reporting HR metrics data alone is ineffective in leading to improvement in managerial decision making. Reporting trend information for metrics is one way to provide the context that gives meaning to the data, thus creating useful information.

9. **Benchmarking** is a second method for adding context to an organization's metrics.

Data on metrics from other organizations in the same industry can provide information that offers insight into an organization's performance relative to its peers.

2.3 HRIS LIFE CYCLE

Fig. 2.2 shows acquisition phases of HRIS.

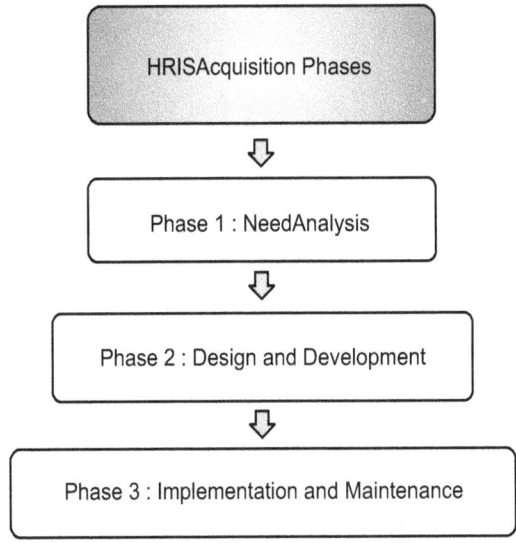

Fig. 2.2 : HRIS Acquisition Phases

Phase 1 : Need Analysis : Enlisted below are the set of activities and tasks which are critical in this particular phase:

1. Evaluate HR department and business models.
2. Form project team.
3. Determine automation needs.

4. Develop system specifications.
5. Analyze current and future reporting needs.
6. Develop.
7. Identify and evaluate vendor packages.
8. Select vendor.
9. Develop proposal for management decision makers.
10. Establish formal guidelines and procedures to resolve inefficiencies.

Phase 2 : Design and Development : Enlisted below are the set of activities and tasks which are critical in this particular phase :

1. Develop detailed project plan.
2. Develop user groups.
3. Purchase hardware.
4. Develop independent, focused computer applications.
5. Implement independent applications as ready.
6. Modify in-house forms.
7. Customize initial system.
8. Establish procedures and guidelines to support system.
9. Test system and user acceptance.
10. Convert data.
11. Train HRIS Staff and/or project team.

Phase 3 : Implementation and Maintenance : Enlisted below are the set of activities and tasks which are critical in this particular phase:

1. Implement HR Core.
2. Train other HR user.
3. Make system available to HR.
4. Refine HR core.
5. Establish mainframe-micro link.
6. Develop/Refine user documentation.
7. Conduct field analysis.
8. Development procedures for distributed processing.
9. Prepare technical documentation.
10. Develop other modules.
11. Test system and user acceptance.
12. Maintain/enhance modules.

13. Distribute to the field.
14. Evaluate effectiveness.

Systems Development Life Cycle :

The system life cycle is the evolutionary process that is followed in implementing a computer-based information system. It consists of a series of tasks that follows a systematic approach for solving or developing solution to problems. In this life cycle, the tasks follow an orderly pattern and are performed in a top-down fashion.

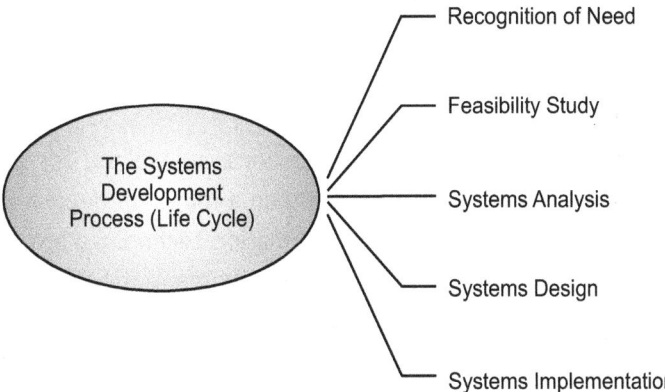

Fig. 2.3 : The Systems Development Process

Numerous HRIS applications give continuous reporting and even screen-based chronicled data about the workers or the useful unit that can furnish the director with the data they require. There are additionally numerous third party programming items accessible that furnish supervisors with very nearly constant information about the status of their unit and the association much as a dashboard on an auto gives prompt data.

Samples of this data incorporate worker execution records, work petitioner following information and payroll organization frameworks. An HRIS director gets, actualizes and works these frameworks. Unlike a standard data engineering work, nonetheless, this part requires the single person in it to have an exhaustive comprehension of the information and how it identifies to the organization.

Some of the important sub-roles of a Manager in this context are :

1. **Acquisition :** Quite regularly, a manager related to the HRIS application is engaged in by an association much sooner than an HRIS framework is set up. The point when a business discovers that it should obtain a framework, the administrator will support in confirming the innovative needs of the aggregation. He will then research the different HRIS frameworks accessible, giving the administration group a short rundown of fitting databases.

2. **Execution :** Once a HRIS framework has been obtained, an HRIS supervisor is answerable for its usage. The manager guarantees that all needed systems are fixed to representative machines. Before enacting the framework or "going live," tests are conducted for each of its characteristics to guarantee that they capacity legitimately.

3. **Operation :** An HRIS administrator operates the framework, performing different errands as asked. Case in point, he/she might run reports that highlight particular data captured by the framework, for example recruitment measurements. He/she might additionally enter new information into the framework, for example representative profits decisions throughout the yearly open enlistment handle.

4. **Instructive Requirements :** In most occasions, an aspirant for the part of HRIS supervisor is instructed to have no less than a four-year degree so as to acquire job. Application of Computers and Information technology are proper fields of study, as are human assets administration and organizational improvement.

Some other sub-parts of HRIS administrators could be :

1. Participating in gatherings with administration and authoritative staff to examine existing frameworks and strategies.
2. Evaluation, with the end goal of redesigning frameworks in a savvy way.
3. Preparing workflow investigations of manual courses of action for transformation to automated frameworks.
4. Assessing computer hardware and software configuration alternatives to present management with viable options.
5. Participating in short and long-range departmental information technology planning.

2.4 RESPONSIBILITY IN EACH PHASE OF DEVELOPMENT OF HRIS

The managers referred to within this section may have a variety of titles: manager, director, vice president, and even CEO. What they all have in common is that their primary HRIS need is to have real-time access to accurate data that facilitate decision making with regard to their people.

Some other sub-parts of HRIS administrators could be :

1. Reviewing and evaluating potential information systems.
2. Diagnosing and troubleshooting computer problems.
3. Monitoring the operations of the machine testing rooms.

4. Assisting in the determination and utilization of any new provisions.
5. Participating in meetings.
6. Monitoring the operations of the machine testing rooms.
7. Assisting in the determination and utilization of any new provisions.

2.5 PRE-IMPLEMENTATION STAGES OF HRIS

2.5.1 HRIS Planning

Human Resource Planning (HRP) process reviews human resources requirements to ensure that the organization has the required number of employees, with the necessary skills, to meet its goals, also known as employment planning. HRP is a proactive process, which both anticipates and influences an organization's future by systematically forecasting the demand for and supply of employees under changing conditions, and developing plans and activities to satisfy these needs. Key steps include forecasting demand for labor considering organizational strategic and tactical plans, economic conditions, market and competitive trends, social concerns, demographic trends, and technological changes.

1. **Recognition of Need :**

   Once the task manager realizes that a problem exists, a clear understanding of the problem is required before moving on to the solution. He has to identity, where the problem exists and the cause of the problem. The major information needs required for developing human resource information systems as defined by its sub-systems are illustratively listed below:

   (i) Payroll processing.
   (ii) Organization/Position management.
   (iii) HR process automation.
   (iv) Recruitment and Selection.
   (v) Central employee database.
   (vi) HR planning.
   (vii) Compensation planning.
   (viii) Employee training and Development.

2. **Feasibility Study :**

   A feasibility study is a brief look at major factors that will influence the ability of the system to achieve the objectives. This study for any system seeks to determine whether it is desirable to implement it or not or whether it fulfills the user requirements. Feasibility study involves the studying of the following aspects :

(i) **Technical :** Availability and technicality of the infrastructure required, (including software and hardware).

(ii) **Economic :** Justification in terms of measurable cost and benefits.

(iii) **Behavioral :** Active involvement of the persons, all involved in the implementation/use and the associated psychological issues.

3. **Systems Analysis :**

This phase includes a review of the existing procedures and information flow. It focuses on isolation of deficiencies from the existing system. Various operations performed by system and their relationship, within and outside of the system fall within this phase. The solution to the critical question of - what must be done to solve the problem is provided in this phase. The information technology or information systems department is responsible for developing the information systems solutions of HR functions.

The fundamental activities involved in the system analysis are :

(i) Definition of the overall system.

(ii) Separation of the system into smaller and manageable parts.

(iii) Understanding the nature, function and interrelationships of various subsystems.

The analysis of the information systems could be done with the help of various tools. Some of the tools, which are frequently used, are described below :

(i) **Review of Documentation :** Documentation on the existing system could be reviewed and analyzed to study the objectives, reports, procedures being followed and equipment being used.

(ii) **Observation of the Situation :** The System Analyst works in the actual system or can be a mere observer. The systems under study can always be observed by getting involved in the system.

(iii) **Conducting Interviews :** Interviews are conducted with the user managers by the System Analysts. The managers are asked questions related to problem domain. These interviews could be formal or informal ones and may span over a period of time.

(iv) **Questionnaire Administration :** The questionnaire survey helps in saving time as compared to interviews as well as getting more committed data. A printed structured or unstructured questionnaire may be administered to find out the information needs of the individual managers.

4. Systems Design :

The stage of system design begins after the functional specification and requirement specification documents are ready and accepted by the users. The conceptual design of the model, which has been developed in the problem definition phase, is enlarged to understand the actual flow of data and the logical model. The logical model is developed to work out to finally develop and test the system in the design phase. This phase defines the way things are, and also defines the way things should be for the same problem. This phase includes mapping of business requirements of the managers on to the proposed system.

The three important objectives the designer has to bear in mind are: performance, control and ability to change.

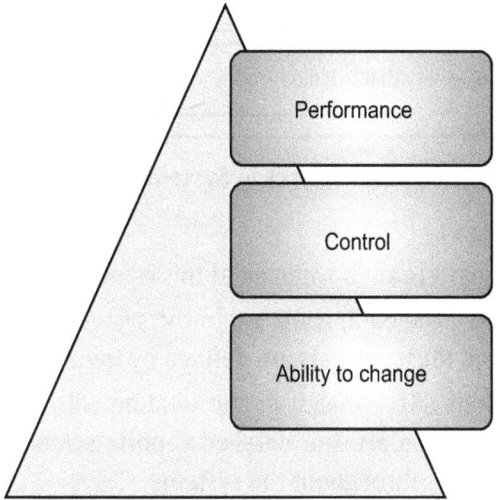

Fig. 2.4 : Systems Designer's Objectives

The system design should be as hardware and software environment independent as possible. The system development team should always keep in mind the cost effectiveness. The below provided are some of the important factors as to understand the reasons behind the need to design a system :

(i) Structure problem solving.
(ii) Explore multiple solutions.
(iii) Decrease cost.
(iv) Decrease time.
(v) Manage mistakes.

The critical design tools used in System analysis are as follows: DFD, ERO, OOD, STD, and UML.

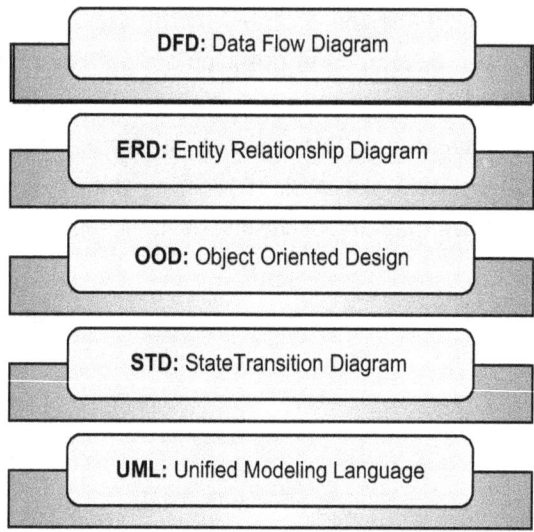

Fig. 2.4 : Phases in Systems Design

Phases in Systems Design :

A multitude of parameters are developed at this stage which is as follows:

(i) **Input Definitions :** The data, coming into the system, has to come through some input formats and these formats are defined by the design of input documents.

(ii) **Output Definitions :** The Analyst in consultation with the end-user finalizes the system outputs. These are the detailed reports screen and file layouts which outline the programs throughout the system.

(iii) **Programme Design :** The actual logic built up for individual programmes is defined in the programme specifications by way of data flow diagrams decision tables, decision trees and structured English.

(iv) **System Specifications :** The system specifications include, description the relationships of various modules of the system among each other's relationships between different programmes with a subsystem. Though the specifications do not give details of logic being followed, it gives the flow of processing among the programs, files and reports, apart from using descriptive English, the system developers also use System Flow Charts for depicting system specifications.

(v) **Testing :** Testing involves code testing (the logic of the programme) and specification testing (what should the program do under various conditions). System testing is a costly but important exercise that it is a requisite phase at this stage. Systems analysis describes a system in terms of its inputs, outputs, data, and processes. The Analysts while testing use various modeling tools and techniques related to data and process. This process is conducted to show how system process transforms data into useful information. A Logical model is thus created that supports business operations and meets the needs of managers and users.

5. **Systems Implementation :**

The Implementation phase involves integration, implementation, user training and documentation. It includes implementation of hardware and software, training of the users, documentation of the procedures (overview, functional specifications, manuals, program specifications) and maintenance and evaluation of the system.

2.5.2 HRIS Designing Issues

Designing an HRIS department essentially requires the following issues to be resolved:

1. Level of Involvement of the people in the system: Integration of professionals from various functional areas.
2. Merger of old and new systems (for running organization): Adoptability, sequence of activities, controls to be exercised during the transition.
3. Financial Aspects like cost of people, machines, and other financial implications on the organization.

Suggestions for attention in the determination, usage and assessment of HRIS presentation, acknowledgement level and administering worthiness around the workers, is the most amazing test to be undertaken by the Organizations. With full scale exertions the administration of an enterprise needs to improve the positive organizational behavior/intervention and if needed, even get the expert consultation from the HR guides and advisors to enhance the adequacy and diminish disturbance towards the new framework. This accelerates the different issues and tests identified with the configuration of HRIS frameworks.

The expanding utilization of Human Resource Information Systems (HRIS) in these quickly changing advanced times, is a discernible pattern inside human asset administration. It has been seen that this technique has been radical in the working frameworks in the companies and promoted between the two valuable stakes, human asset and information technology. The traditional style of working, changed radically from the way Management Information System (MIS) was utilized two decades back and the possibility to significantly improve companies' capacity to gather, store and use the information pertaining to the employees.

2.6 HRIS Expectation

Critical Elements to consider when Designing HRIS Solutions :

Appropriate arrangement of the HRIS task will protect the determination of a high-worth, financially savvy framework and is an imperative in the 'Design Phase'.

The HRIS stakeholders in the organization need to consider the sum of the important components when overhauling or installing any system. Some of these components are enrolled as follows:

1. Identify the Size Range of HRIS Solution :

Organizations need to find HRIS development vendors that suit their budget and requirements rather than looking out for the most standard or the most cost-effective vendors. They need to understand the fact that the vendors come in all essences and sizes.

2. Project Approval Stage :

Every Organization will perceive this process distinctly. A few organizations will think about an HRIS speculation as a trivial overhead. This happens when the undertaking is not deliberately thoroughly considered, and the worth of a framework is not conveyed to senior administration. Think about the time funds when no more extended there is a need to copy worker information.

Some of the key questions to be asked at this juncture are :

(i) Do you need project approval?
(ii) What is the software budget?
(iii) What is the implementation budget?
(iv) By what date would you like the system installed?
(v) How long does the vendor estimate for installation?
(vi) What is the training budget?
(vii) What is the maintenance and support budget?

3. Defining of Business Objectives :

What are the key factors that are driving this decision to purchase an HRIS?

(i) No existing system.
(ii) Existing system is not performing as desired.
(iii) Existing framework is obsolete or incapable of integration.
(iv) Organization is adding more employees.
(v) More complex transactions such as benefits or attendance are required.

What would be the consequences of not purchasing a new HRIS?
(i) Loss of talented employees.
(ii) Loss of productivity.
(iii) Loss of talented applicants.
(iv) No consequences.

How will the organization benefit through the added value that the new system will generate?
(i) Ability to produce information not possible within the current environment
(ii) Ability to do the same things :
   (a) Better.
   (b) Faster.
   (c) At a lower cost.

4. **Timing of the Project :**
   - Are there any real or perceived deadlines important to the installation of the system?
   - What is the estimated date for completion of the project?
   - Will resources be available to work on the project in the allotted time?

5. **Budget Factors :**
   Have the following budget items been considered?
   (i) Implementation.
   (ii) Training.
   (iii) Licensing of Application.
   (iv) Support services and maintenance.
   (v) Customization and reports.
   (vi) Time for your staff to work on the conversion.

6. **Consideration at Time of Delivery :**
   In this aspect the Organization needs to consider how the application would be delivered? Should the HRIS application be in the form of a hosted service with a monthly processing fee or should it be an in-house development? Each approach has its own benefits and drawbacks.

7. **Involve Key Personnel in the Decision Process :**
   This process should include members of the HR, IT and Finance Departments. Each member should be responsible for evaluating his or her respective areas of the project.

8. **Hardware Considerations :**
   (i)   **Network :** Windows 2000, Windows 2003, Windows 2008, Windows XP.
   (ii) **Server :** Microsoft, Novell, Unix, Linux.
   (iii) **Report Writer :** Crystal Reports, RandR Report, Smith Access.
   (iv) **User Skills :** Basic or Advanced.
   (v)   **Email Server :** MS Exchange, GroupWise Lotus Notes.
   (vi) **Number of HR Users.**
   (vii) **Internet Connection :** Dialup Less than1Mb, DSL/ISDN Greater than 1 Mb.

9. **Current Data Sources :**

   This element is associated with identifying the current sources for the employee data, including payroll data, spreadsheets, older HRIS systems and databases that aroused to track employee information. The vendor should be easily able to put this data into the new system.
   (i)   Spreadsheets.
   (ii) Databases.
   (iii) Current HRIS.
   (iv) Payroll data.

10. **Developing an Understanding to Use the Integrated System to Save Time and Effort:**

    If data is being entered more than once, what is the frequency of errors created due to redundant data entry? Some prominent areas to consider in this context are:

    Spreadsheets, Databases, Current HRIS, Payroll Data, Manual files and information: Type of information? What is the current use? Duplicated elsewhere? (Yes/No) Are these usable for workforce reporting and analysis?

11. **Schedule :**

    A detailed project schedule is critical to insure a successful implementation. This should cover all elements of the project with target dates. Here is a sample schedule to follow :
    (i)   Week 1 Complete negotiations with vendor and sign contracts.
    (ii)   Week 3 Send specifications for benefit and attendance information to vendor.
    (iii) Week 5 Send sample ASCII files from current HR system and other sources.
    (iv)   Week 7 Specifications for reports and modifications completed.
    (v)   Week 12 Send final ASCII files for complete data load.
    (vi)   Week 13 Installation of system and initial training.
    (vii) Week 17 Advanced training.
    (viii) Week 21 Report creation training.

2.7 HRIS COST BENEFIT VALUE ANALYSIS

Cost Justifying Human Resource Information Systems Investment. An HRIS system represents a large investment decision for companies of all sizes. Therefore, a convincing case to persuade decision makers about the HRIS benefits is necessary. The common benefits of HRIS frequently cited in studies included, improved accuracy, the provision of timely and quick access to information, and the saving of costs.

Five reasons why companies should use HRIS. These are :

1. Increase competitiveness by improving HR practices.
2. Produce a greater number and variety of HR operations.
3. Shift the focus of HR from the processing of transactions to strategic HRM.
4. Make employees part of HRIS, and Reengineer the entire HR function.
5. HRIS survey, found that the top four metrics used in formal business cases supporting HRIS were improved productivity within HR organization, cost reductions, return on investment, and enhanced employee communications.

However, companies realize many of these cost reductions and efficiency gains early in the implementation of an HRIS system, so they provide compelling evidence needing to get a project up and running. In fact, the payback period, or the time it takes to recoup the investment, may be as short as one to three years.

HRIS contribute to cost reductions, quality/customer satisfaction, and innovation computerized HRIS function enable, faster decision making, development, planning, and administration of HR because data is much easier to store, update, classify, and analyze. Moreover, while it may be possible to identify many of the relevant costs (e.g., software and hardware), it is more difficult to quantify the intangible benefits to be derived from an HRIS system.

Beyond cost reductions and productivity improvements, HRIS potentially and fundamentally affect revenue channels. However, establishing direct and objective benefits measures is more difficult to achieve.

On the other hand, there are costs associated with HRIS implementation. Moreover, to capitalize on all HR possibilities, workers need to have personal computers and global Internet connections. Some companies facilitate this by providing employees computer discount programs to encourage home usage.

While many companies are adopting HRIS systems and extolling their benefits, others are reluctant in embarking on such an expensive and time consuming change. Nevertheless, some firms are adopting less complex forms before attempting to transform their HR departments. However, for those who have already adopted HRIS, many are yet to realize its full benefits.

2.8 GETTING MANAGEMENT SUPPORT

Overcoming Employee Resistance to Change :

Human capital is the true asset for any enterprise. The conduct of this most critical asset 'Human Resource' responds specially in diverse scenarios when a slight change is presented in the customary working arrangement of the company.

There has been impressive study done on "resentment from the inception", which is an inbuilt human reaction wherein the human mind rejects any new prescription or enhancement in the standard working style or framework from the very beginning and afterward acknowledges it gradually with part of positive intercessions after painstakingly comprehending the inputs.

These are modest progressions that change certain minor angles, searching for a change in the current scenario, however keeping the general working skeleton. When the idea of progress is presented in the association, the term 'imperviousness to HRIS is dissected. This safety is a marvel that influences the change methodology, deferring or easing off its starting, hindering or preventing its execution, and expanding its expenses.

The capability of enterprises to tackle the potential of HRIS and overcome imperviousness to change relies upon an assortment of components, for example :

1. The size of the enterprise, with huge firms ordinarily procuring more prominent profits;
2. The HR philosophy of the organization as well as its vision, organizational culture, structure, and systems;
3. The managerial competence in cross-functional decision making, employee;
4. The measure of top management commitment and backing;
5. The accessibility of assets (time, cash, and staff);
6. The mentoring and participation;
7. The capability and cause of people in the organization in receiving change, for example expanded computerization crosswise over and between capacities.

2.9 LIMITATIONS OF COMPUTERIZATION HRIS

An HRIS system is important for an organization be it manual or automated because it provides a sequential and structured way of storing information which can be used for better accessibility at any given point of time, this tool helps in decision making process at the operations and top management level, an HRIS is the only source of sharing the critical information at the top management level.

So there are multiple benefits of using it, it decreases the probability of errors because here you rely on the system and not on individuals. It provides reusability, accessibility and security to the processes by ensuring that the information is not redundant and remains accessible to all stake holders who are required to view it.

But with these positives, there are constraints as well of using an HRIS, the constraints normally come when we become too reliant on this system, which many a times acts like a speed breaker and decreases the speed and performance.

For an HRIS to be performing well, every layer/ stake holder has to contribute equally in making sure that the system is updated on defined interval and that the data is entered accurately else this system becomes "An Elephant in Cage" which is too costly to manage.

At last, in my opinion, an automated HRIS is normally required when you have a big manpower size normally more than 300 else it is not a wise decision to purchase an automated system which come at a huge cost. Rather, similar systems can be developed within the company and a lot of money can be saved.

In total, an HRIS is important but you need to make a choice off its form whether you want to construct an HRIS yourself (which is a real fun) or you want to purchase a tool (which comes at a cost) but provides you ready made features which are ready to use.

1. **Unauthorized Access :**

When an organization collects personal data about its employees in an HRMS, certain security risks may arise. An organization spends funds to keep employee private information secure against internal and external threats. One disadvantage of an electronic HRMS is that an organization must collect information about who accesses employee private information. This data requires follow up with an audit process, which could result in disciplining or prosecuting an employee who accesses employee data without authorization or without an official purpose.

2. **Specialized Knowledge :**

The need for data control is another potential disadvantage of an HRMS. This data control extends beyond unauthorized access of employee private information. An organization using an HRMS such as PeopleSoft must employ its own set of technical staff to program, troubleshoot, update and support the system. While an HRMS may help an organization reduce the cost of HR personnel, it could increase the requirements for technical staff with knowledge specific to the HRMS solution.

3. **Data Entry Errors :**

An HRMS is also only as good as its human programmers and end users. People with high-level access, such as people who update an HR master file, may enter the wrong information deliberately or in error. If data is improperly updated, changed or lost, an organization can face government fines and other costs associated with damage to the HR master file. Pick a system with lots of internal controls so that one employee cannot make changes to your company's master file.

HRIS is the package which has got that potential to give greatest returns on Investment provided an Organization buys that apt package after some ground research. HRIS will help an Organization in limiting its Human Resource staff to the minimum, and reducing the number of Papers and files over the Desk. Thus HRIS will definitely give greater returns on Investment when invested based upon the size of the company.

2.10 HUMAN RESOURCES (HR) METRICS AND WORK FORCE ANALYTIC

Human Resources (HR) metrics and workforce analytics have become a hot topic in organizations of all sizes. Interest is rising, and organizations are reaching out to learn more about metrics and analytics and how they can use them to improve organizational effectiveness. Although the use of HR metrics and workforce Analytics is not new, various factors have driven increased interest during the previous decade. The most important driver has been the implementation of integrated.

HRIS in response to the "millennium problem" of Y2K (Year 2000). The Adoption of these systems shifted what had been primarily paper and pencil processes To electronic processes and, as a result, greatly increased the capacity of Organizations to access and examine transaction-level data.

These new HRIS featured faster and more capable computers, improved connectivity through organizational networks and the Internet, and the earliest versions of user-friendly analytics software. These changes fundamentally altered the dynamics of human capital assessment in organizations, driving the marginal cost of assessment lower while providing the potential for near real-time analysis and distribution of information.

In addition, the quality revolution that swept through U.S. manufacturing and Service firms in the 1980s and 1990s, including Total Quality Management (TQM), Six Sigma, and lean manufacturing, increased managers' expectations about the availability of organizational data and the capability of using this data to generate analytics that could support managerial decisions. These factors, combined with recent and growing interest in evidence-based management, have produced a rapidly growing interest in HR metrics and workforce analytics.

Activities

1. Refer to the www.albany.edu/hrs and enlist the innovative skills required for HRIS Practitioners other than those provided in this chapter.
2. The sub-roles of a manager for HRIS have been discussed in this chapter. Browse the net and find information of the role of external consultants who provide HRIS Solutions to mid-range Organizations.

Summary

Effective application is the focal objective of each HRIS venture, and it starts with an extensive design for the HRIS framework. The basic knowledge that is critical to the implementation process will be emphasized here as the steps in the system development process are covered in this chapter.

A HRIS generally should provide the capability to more effectively plan, control and manage HR costs; achieve improved efficiency and quality in HR decision making; and improve employee and managerial productivity and effectiveness. A HRIS offers HR, payroll, benefits, training, recruiting and compliance solutions. Some of the most popular modules are :

1. Organization charts.
2. Employee self-service.
3. Benefits Administration.
4. Track training for employees.

A typical set of responsibilities for the HRIS Practitioner part might incorporate :

1. Performing routine managerial errands in support of the HRIS.
2. Generating standard reports for Human Resources or supervising staff.
3. Information of normally utilized ideas, practices, and methods inside a specific field.
4. Working under immediate supervision.
5. Typically reports to a supervisor.

Appropriate arrangement of the HRIS task will protect the determination of a high-worth, financially savvy framework and is an imperative in the 'Design Phase'. The HRIS stakeholders in the organization need to consider the sum of the important components when overhauling or installing any system. Some of these components are Identify the size range of HRIS solution.

Designing an HRIS department essentially requires the following issues to be resolved :

1. Level of Involvement of the people in the system.

2. Merger of old and new systems for running organization.
3. Financial Aspects.

Human capital is the true asset for any enterprise. The conduct of this most critical asset 'Human Resource' responds specially in diverse scenarios when a slight change is presented in the customary working arrangement of the company. The presentation of another human asset data framework in an organization brings in connected change in the conduct of the workers who show disturbance and reject the thought of execution.

Self-assessment Questions

1. Enlist some of the important aspects which an HRIS system generally should be capable of?
2. Describe how an HRIS system facilitates communication processes and saves paper?
3. Enlist and discuss in some of the most popular modules of the HRIS system?
4. Explain in brief the primary responsibility of the HRIS Practitioner.
5. Enlist the activities in a typical job description for the HRIS Practitioner role.

❖❖❖

Chapter **3**...

Implementation of HRIS

Objectives ...

After discussing this chapter, you will be able to :
- Enlist and Describe the Critical Requirements for Strategic HR Information Systems Planning
- Understand and Explain the HRIS Implementation Strategy
- Enlist and Explain the Tools in HRIS Implementation

Structure ...

3.1 Introduction
3.2 Implementation of HRIS
    3.2.1 Factors that Need to be Considered During Implementation of HRIS
    3.2.2 Important Requirements for Strategic HR Information Systems Planning
    3.2.3 Issues in Implementation of HRIS
    3.2.4 Issues Needed to Control and Maintain Security of Data Before Implementing a Computarized HRIS
    3.2.5 HRIS Implementation Strategy
3.3 Tools in HRIS Development
3.4 Major HRIS Solution Providers
    3.4.1 Large Scale HRIS Vendors
3.5 Case Study : Transforming HR at Novartis
- Activities
- Summary
- Self-assessment Questions

3.1 INTRODUCTION

The implementation of HRIS should be in tune with the overall business strategy of the firm since this system forms the crux of strategic HRM. The people involved in the management of these systems have to play an active role in strategic HRIS planning at a level that helps the organization to anticipate and prepare for a successful HR technology transition. The introduction of new, efficient and effective HR Information systems, programs and services come under the overall responsibility of these entities.

Seeing that new company processes are created, the actual project team customizes the HRIS about these pilot processes. Customers probably will realize that exceptional instances would call for considerable effort of the manual labor or though-process - since exemption isn't going to fit into the business enterprise course of action seeing that implemented inside the HRIS system.

The project group alters the system around the new forms of business processes as new business courses of action are designed. End-users will probably realize that exemption cases require huge manual thought or work to process – since the special case does not fit into the business transform as actualized in the HRIS. The people involved will have to do a balancing act between generalization of the methodology to fit exemptions vs. a more limited usage of the procedure to authorize information respectability and correct requisition of HR strategy. The managers and policymakers must be eager to back any considerations and skews from the normal course and to help execute them. As the group members dive into the present business forms, they might uncover that the HR clients, and some of the time the HR-Managers, don't generally comprehend or know the methodologies well. Clients might recognize what is carried out, yet not why it is carried out. Knowing the why part is basic to getting the most out of your HRIS execution.

3.2 IMPLEMENTATION OF HRIS

3.2.1 Factors that Need to be Considered During Implementation of HRIS

An HRIS implementation is an expansive venture that could be broken down into more diminutive parts, to handle one stage at once. A number of the success components distinguished underneath are concentrated on creating readiness and improving a usage plan that incorporates certain perspectives. This will lead to guaranteeing the realization of the implementation.

1. **Comprehension of Data :**

It is critical to comprehend, before an execution, where all existing HR information is constantly supported, with the goal that it can best be resolved how that same information will be followed in the new HRIS, this is because the system is information intensive. It is essential to know how the information will be changed over into the new HRIS from the present sources. HRIS worth will be improved when populace of information is arranged, and information is converted into data. This starts with a comprehension of the information.

2. **Clearly Defined Requirements :**

Since HR techniques adjust with corporate systems, and corporate methods are extraordinary the requirements are as distinct as the associations that have them. This phase comprises of incorporating any reporting needs in a concise manner. This will serve to guarantee that the HRIS is designed to take into account the following of any information that will be obliged to help.

3. **Methodology in the Implementation :**

A successful HRIS implementation needs an organized approach. Numerous distinctive distinguished usage approaches exist. What is significant is that one appropriate method needs to be adopted that it is suitable to your firm. A critical entity in this process the provider of the software application will likewise have a favored methodology.

An implementation system is not the same as the project plan, which fuses those approach parts into an arrangement of requested points of reference with due dates. An execution technique gives substance to the project plan, and the task plan conveys the strategy. Embracing an implementation procedure is an exhaustive methodology and accommodates several phases of planning.

4. **Assessment of Risks :**

It is observed in most organizations that there segments of employees that are impervious to change. Thus there are potential and unanticipated barriers in firms that can represent a danger to the implementation of a new HRIS. The critical issue of retaining the interest of the key stakeholders also needs to be ensured at the critical implementation phase.

5. **Training :**

Technical and non-technical must be distinguished and performed to assist individuals make the move to working with the new HRIS and the new association show.

The preparation needs to go past screen-prints and simple procedures to a description of how the new application fits into the company, its relationship to different forms, and the execution steps in a holistic manner. The users should know the 'why' and in addition the 'how' of the methodology. Formalized cross-project help groups are fundamental to the enduring operation of the HRIS.

3.2.2 Important Requirements for Strategic HR Information Systems Planning

Accumulation and breaking down of data in tune with the HR methodology for conversion from the existing framework to the new and enhanced ones requires the use of strategic perspective on the HRIS planning. The users of the system and the implementers should get comfortable and must not offer resistance to change. It essentially requires that, involved parties must put time and efforts to understand how new things work and how they can or cannot help the organization. It gets fundamental, accordingly, to improve programs, partnerships and procedures for successful technology transition.

Some of the important requirements for -strategic HR information systems planning are given below :

1. Overall Business Environment Assessment.
2. Strategic HR goals Assessment.
3. New technologies and process tracking.
4. HRIS resources optimization.
5. Implementation activities streamlining.

An organization needs to consider the following during implementation :

1. **Management of change :** Develop a plan to handle changes. The plan should involve communication, organizational and job design, leadership, training and support issues.

2. **Planning for emergencies :** Build in emergencies when considering overall time horizon for implementation.

3. **Specialization :** Factor in the cost of the changes today and the ongoing maintenance of those changes in the future software release.

4. **Assets :** Determine whether the company has the people and skills to implement the system. If not, the company should think of outsourcing the resources.

5. **Pledging people to the system :** Find the best people to implement the system or a full-time basis.

6. **Business process :** Do not assume that the system will do what the company does today.

3.2.3 Issues in Implementation of HRIS

It is a known fact that non-technical personnel mostly deal with HRIS, yet it requires great technical support in a computer-based environment. This support may be rendered by HR professionals HR technical staff, outside consultants etc.

Occasionally encountered, however, is an adversarial relationship between the HR and the MIS Staffs' thus careful and meticulous planning is necessary in the context of the HRIS transformation.

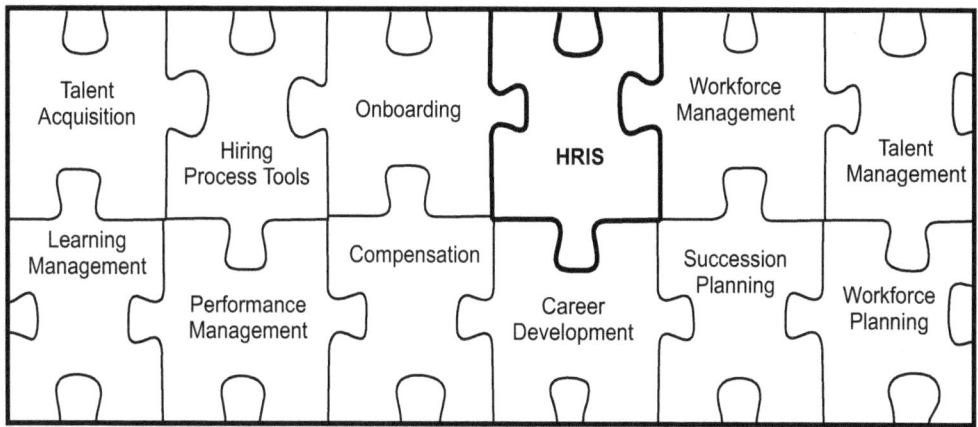

Fig. 3.1

The major issues in implementation of a HRIS are :

1. Stakeholder Contribution :

The key HRIS stakeholders need to be recognized at the inception of the implementation procedure. Implementation of an HRIS suggests change to existing methodologies, and unanticipated association of stakeholders serves to increase their forthright investment to the HRIS, collaboration and acknowledgement of that change.

2. Conflicts and Resistance to Change :

In the case of an HRIS system most of the information on HR is controlled by people possessing dominant control. Due to this ownership the HRIS Managers enjoy power and prestige which may lead to friction between the employees groups. It has been observed that there is a good amount of opposition by employees while implementation of a computerized HRIS. A prime reason for conflicts and politics may also be that the Managers possess complete information about the system. Due to human nature resistances would be encountered and lead to implementation failures. Therefore, before implementing any HRIS, it has to be resolved that, how the conflicts arising there from will be addressed.

3. Environment :

Implementation of a HRIS implies transformation from one operating environment to another and brings complex problems. The transformational problems may be in terms of :

(i) Feasibility of the new HRIS.
(ii) Hardware and software requirement and their adaptability.
(iii) Implementing a modified HRIS or altogether a new one.
(iv) Definition of user groups, controllers and implementers.

3.2.4 Issues Needed to Control and Maintain Security of Data before Implementing a Computerized HRIS

Since, the information archived on frameworks is clearly private and private, it gets crucial to keep it safe and be approachable just to the authentic people under regulated conditions.

Security issues become critical and often are posed as a threat to computerization, since in most of the firms the systems are used in combinations. There can be two methodologies to maintain the integrity of records :

1. Regulatory Access :

Where the client documents an appeal, which is steered and affirmed through some interior methodology. On the other hand, in this framework the profits that present HRIS offer viz. correspondence, speed and unexpected dissection are lost.

2. Security Technology :

Through which a PC client is constrained either in (a) What data could be entered and (b) sort of access. The indexes can, consequently, be continuous, perused just, compose just or both. Whatever blend be utilized, there must be an individual answerable for the security of HRIS. Subsequently, before executing an automated HRIS, associations may as well deliver the accompanying issues to uphold control and security of information :

(i) Information security, such as locking diskette and hard drives, documenting PC applications, backup procedures, and network safety precautions.

(ii) Physical security, such as access to PC areas, diskette handling, and secure housekeeping.

(iii) Management considerations, such as who is authorized to use PCs, user training, inventories of equipment and procedures, and procedures for special events, like power outages.

3.2.5 HRIS Implementation Strategy

An effective strategy in implementation is requires as the HRIS is highly strategic in nature. Following steps may be ideally considered :

1. Identify all clients and build a representative implementation team that must be multi-departmental and include representatives of all potential users of the system employees, executive officers, managers, heads of departments, directors, payroll, accounting, budget, computing services and components.

2. Define the objectives including project scope, time frames and resources to implement and maintain the system.

3. Define problems with the current system, listed in order of priority.
4. Document the current system - current functionality, prioritized user complaints, key problems, compliance issues, options for automating current manual processes.
5. Define necessary functions for the new system.
6. Develop a list of recommended solutions based on the implementation team's decision which includes HRIS deliverables, system requirements, training needs, and cost of implementation level of maintenance support and cost/benefit analysis.

3.3 TOOLS IN HRIS DEVELOPMENT

I.T. has changed the era completely. It is because of Information Systems today that the organizations, such as Amex, Cisco, Infosys, and many more are leveraging on their competencies to compete in such a dynamic economy. Information Technology and Information Systems (ITIS) has become a critical aspect of developing and using human resource management programs to better manage the human capital of an organization; and further evolving HR related information systems (HRIS).

A Human Resources Information System (HRIS) is the integration of software, hardware, support functions and system policies and procedures into an automated process designed to support the strategic and operational activities of the human resource department and managers throughout the organization.

HRIS enables the human resource department to make a more active role in organizational planning. Computerization can make forecasting more timely, cost effective, and efficient. HRIS will facilitate Integration and storage in a single database of all the human resource information. HRIS can accelerate the process of comparing costs and benefits of human resource activities.

Following tools are used extensively in business, applications of which are discussed in detailed in Chapter No 5.

1. **Human Resource Tracking and Reporting System :**

The ATS (Applicant Tracking System) is intended to add structure to the preparing of candidate profiles and data on aspirants. The essential work of the software application related to recruitment is incorporating all the data in a unified manner in an organization's recruitment database. Information related to candidates is either gathered from candidate forms (through the front-end), found on the organization sites or is obtained from aspirants on online job sites and forums. Some present day Applicant Tracking Systems permit candidates to be sourced from the organization's own database of previous work candidates.

2. Applicant and Employment Management :

Organizations today are in the process of utilizing expert frameworks to accelerate the process of selecting prospective candidates and guarantee that it becomes a reliable process. The Data frameworks can help the selection and recruitment procedures in a multitude of ways. The highly complicated and advanced system of automated inventory guarantees that the candidate database is refreshed constantly and could be seen by a prospective aspirant whenever. The framework can likewise be utilized to produce different facts like employments with high turnover and the normal time it takes to fill an opportunity. Profiles sent through the web and via mail could be checked for decisive words recognizing needed information, abilities, skills, and experience.

3. Recruitment Core System to Manage Complete Hiring Life-Cycle :

The recruitment module permits supervising the opportunities and competitors with the capability to allocate designated recruitment supervisors. Profiles can be obtained by the framework for individual opportunities by interfacing the organization site's vocation page to direct job openings on the system. The huge amount of capital spent in supporting an arranged recruitment exertion, candidate listing internally and through general or industry-particular job forums and sites and administering an aggressive introduction of availabilities has offered ascent to the advancement of a committed candidate tracking framework, or 'ATS', module.

4. Payroll Module :

Payroll assumes a critical attribute in an organization for a multitude of reasons. It is characterized as a system for administrating workers' compensations in the firms. In an organization, payroll is the total of all budgetary records of pay rates for a worker, compensation, rewards and findings. In accounting terms, it means the sum paid to employees for the organizational duty they furnished throughout a certain time of time. The methodology comprises of estimation of salaries and employee tax deductions, providing the retirement profits and payment of compensations to workers. It can likewise be termed as an action coming under accounts which embraces the pay organization of workers in the firm. Calculating the workers' pay rates is not a simple assignment, the Human Resource and the accounts division work together to figure and dispense the compensation to the workers.

The Application related to Payroll deals with all prerequisites concerned with administration of workers' Payroll and the accounting process. This application saves finished records of the workers, produces registers for attendance and pay-slips, figures all remittances and tax-deductions and creates all statutory forms.

5. Performance Management Module :

Performance Management is a framework and methodology that connects the enterprises objectives and systems to singular and group performance in order to expand enterprise adequacy. It is a combined procedure that includes both operational leaders and their immediate reports who together distinguish regular goals/objectives which correspond to the higher objectives of the firm. This process brings about the creation of performance related expectations and objectives in a written format (an Agreement related to Performance) - later utilized as measures for input and execution appraisals/reviews. Companies now need to investigate execution past fiscal measurements with numerous stakeholders (universal and nontraditional dissecting the proceeded execution of a company's continuous improvement).

Performance Appraisal :

A performance appraisal is a methodical and ongoing procedure that evaluates the staff's performance at work and efficiency in connection to certain pre-set criteria and organizational targets. Performance appraisals are a core part of profession advancement and comprise of ongoing assessments of staff performance inside companies. Appraising of employee performance is a system by which the occupation execution of a worker is assessed.

Attributes of distinct staff members are acknowledged too, for example company responsibility conduct, achievements, potential for prospective change, qualities and shortcomings, and so forth. To gather information on appraisals, there are three principle strategies : goal creation, staff, and judgmental assessment. Judgmental assessments are the most usually utilized with an extensive multitude of assessment techniques.

6. Training and Development :

The competitive business environment is forcing the HR professionals to optimize HR resources. Employee's training and development is the crucial tool which enhances productivity of an organization. The traditional methods of training and development are time consuming and hence ineffective, since jobs have become more sophisticated and influenced by technological changes. The success in enhancement of employee's productivity has become a thrust of HR department area, due to the fact that the employees need constant improvement and motivation to achieve organization's goals and objectives.

Most major corporations now have LMSs but some are looking to change because they are not satisfied with the ones they have. More and more medium and smaller enterprises are adopting LMSs. Like all software, LMSs evolve as the market matures.

7. Employee Self-Service Model :

Employee Self Service (ESS) is a web-based application that provides employees with access to their personal records and their payroll details. The most common features of ESS allow employees to change their own address, contact details and next of kin. Often included with ESS is the ability for employees to apply for leave and have that application directed to the employee's manager for consideration. Some applications enable employees to change their bank account details and provide details of pay slips, both current and historical. ESS can operate as a feature on an employer's intranet or via a web ASP service.

3.4 MAJOR HRIS SOLUTION PROVIDERS

HRIS Solution Providers : Indian Scenario :

The developments in the Indian industry have also seen the implementation of Enterprise Resource Planning (ERP) configuration in HRM with extensive use of manager and employee self-portals. Most critically, these changes ensure that firms can significantly advance in the use of people knowledge in managerial decision. They can access people's knowledge more rapidly with a higher degree of accuracy.

ERP integrates the human resource module with finance, production, sales and administration modules. Technology-driven automation (IT) processes certainly help reduce costs and cycle times as well as improve quality. Information System (IS) can further help decision makers to make and implement strategic decisions.

HRIS and other information systems can be used to support a Talent Management Program. The importance of talent management is uttermost to get competitive advantage. Numerous researches speak of the same. A talent management program is a part of the Human Resource Planning (HRP) function of an organization. Recruiting talented individuals by using social networks has been increasing too. Very few companies have quality Talent Management computer applications.

This includes elements like industrial relations, grievance handling, and Employees participation in Management and Employee welfare activities. There is a requirement of transformation of myopic view of organization from economic need fulfillment to enable the employee as the knowledge worker forth organization thereby considerably contributing to the development of the organization.

3.4.1 Large Scale HRIS Vendors

1. SAP HR - SAP Human Resources :

The Human Resources module (SAP HR) consists of all master data, system configuration, and transactions to complete the Hire to Retire (or, as some say, Fire) process. It includes the following information and processes.

SAP Human Resources (HR) Components or Sub-Components :

(i) Personnel Management
- Personnel Administration
- Recruitment

(ii) Organizational Management

(iii) Travel Management

(iv) Time Management

(v) Payroll

Typical Hire to retire business process associated with the SAP HR module.

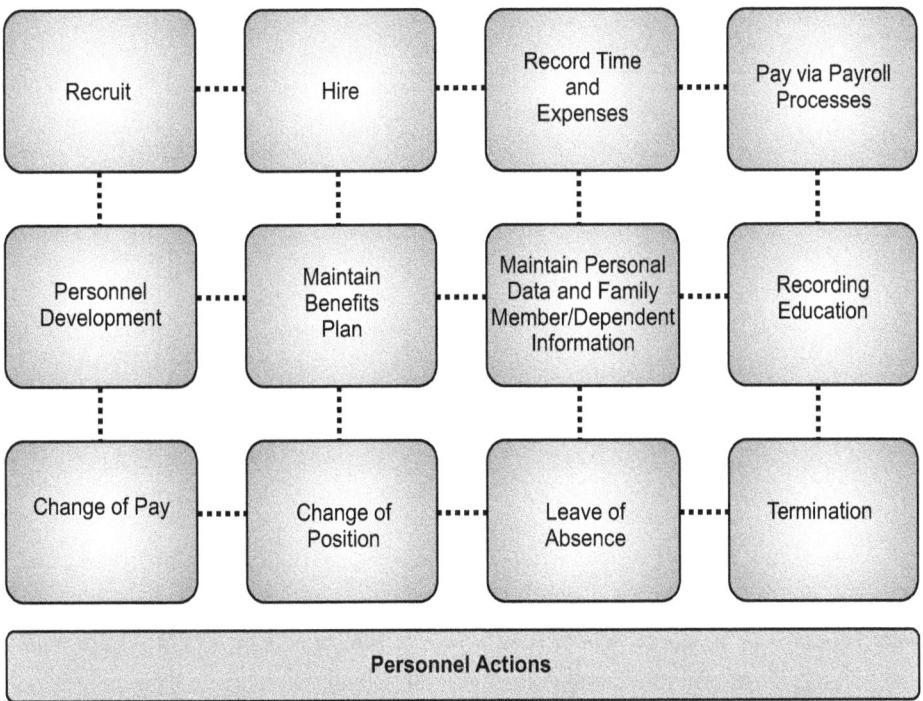

Fig. 3.2

The mySAP HR module enables companies to effectively manage information about the people in their organization. It is integrated with other SAP modules and external systems.

What are the main modules of SAP HR?

The SAP Human Capital Management (HCM) contains all the process is classified in two major scenarios :

Workforce Process Management :

That includes the following processes :

(i) Employee administration.

(ii) Personnel time management and evaluation.

(iii) Payroll calculation.

Talent Management :

That includes the following processes :

(i) Recruiting.

(ii) Career management.

(iii) Employee performance management.

(iv) Compensation management.

This is the main SAP Human Resource menu path image :

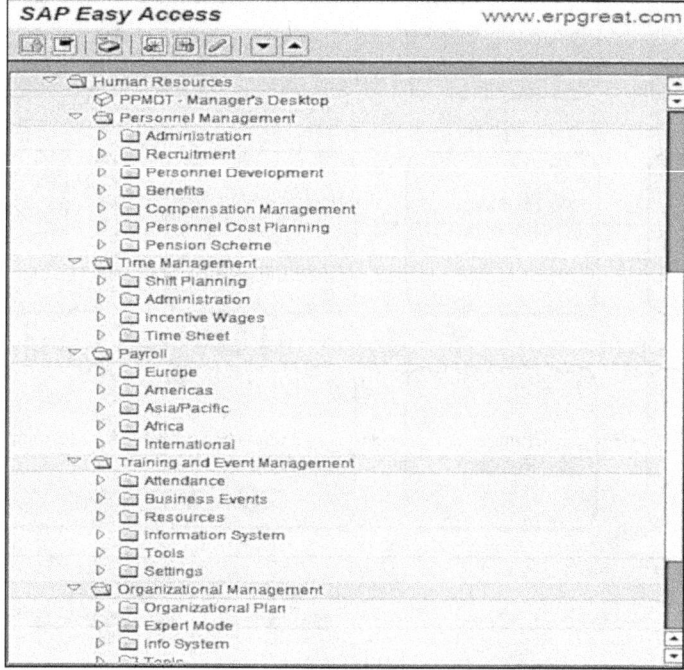

Fig. 3.3

2. JD Edwards Enterprise One :

Oracle's JD Edwards is one of today's leading Enterprise Resource Planning (ERP) software and supply chain management software solutions. An integrated applications suite, JDE E1 combines business value, standards-based technology, and deep industry experience into a business solution with a low total cost of ownership.

New Enhancements in Oracle's JD Edwards Enterprise One Release 9.0 :

The latest release of JD Edwards Enterprise One 9.0 delivers enhancements that address global market dynamics, regulatory reporting requirements, intricate transactional and contractual arrangements, and the technical changes you face every day.

(i) Includes broad based enhancements for operational efficiency and system flexibility for additional visibility and control.

(ii) Enhancement for financial management, supply chain management, and human resource management. Enhanced financial compliance capabilities are gained through new data relationship functionality for assigning correct values to entered information.

JD Edwards Enterprise One Integrations :

Designed to help you gain the most value from your business applications investment, JDE E1 integrations support your business processes by enabling you to use all the capabilities of other Oracle products and third party software with the full range of your implemented ERP processes.

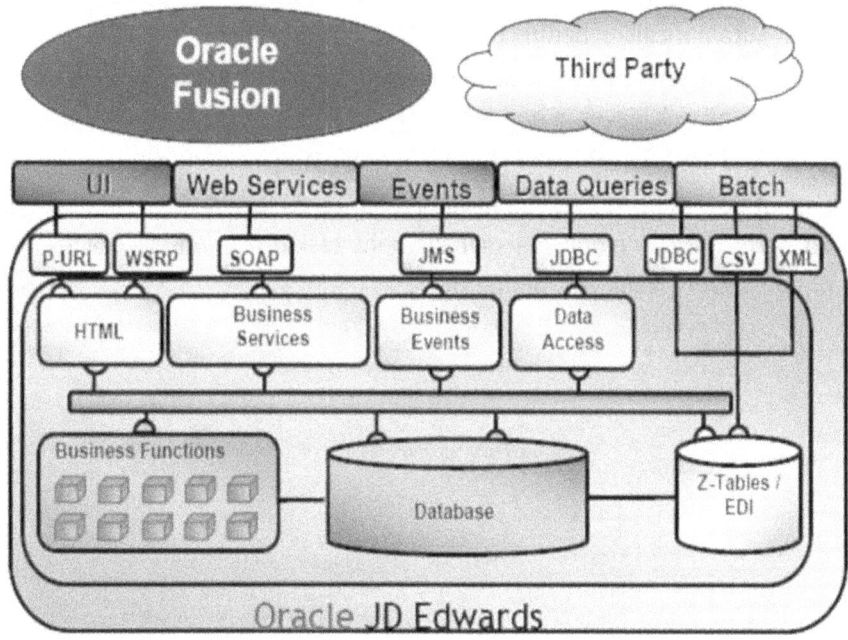

Fig. 3.4

3. Medium Scale HRIS Vendors :

There are more than approximately more than 500 medium and small scale HRIS Vendors. Some of the prominent ones are as follows :

4. SimpleHR :

Track It, Retrieve It, Document It! with SimpleHR :

Human Resources Information Systems should make your HR tasks easier. And SimpleHR will do that. This employee management system can simplify your workflow, increase your efficiency and quickly become an essential tool in your HR workday.

Here's how :

(i) Easy Installation on your computer.

(ii) **Quick Setup** as standard Human Resources codes have been entered.

(iii) **No Training Required** with the intuitive interface.

(iv) **Online Help**, Tips and Tricks and a complete User's Manual.

Features at a Glance :

SimpleHR gives you the ability to maintain all of your employee's confidential information in a single secure place.

(i) **Salary History and Benefits** : View salary and position history online or in a report.

(ii) **Performance Reviews and Training** : Select from list of performance review types. Automatically schedule next review.

(iii) **Vacations, Attendance and Sick Leaves** : SimpleHR allows you to track both vacation and sick leaves in one program.

(iv) **Health and Safety Records** : Maintain accident and incident history.

Think about how many things you have on your to-do list each day. Reduce the time it takes to perform your employee management tasks. You will save a tremendous number of hours every week with SimpleHR.

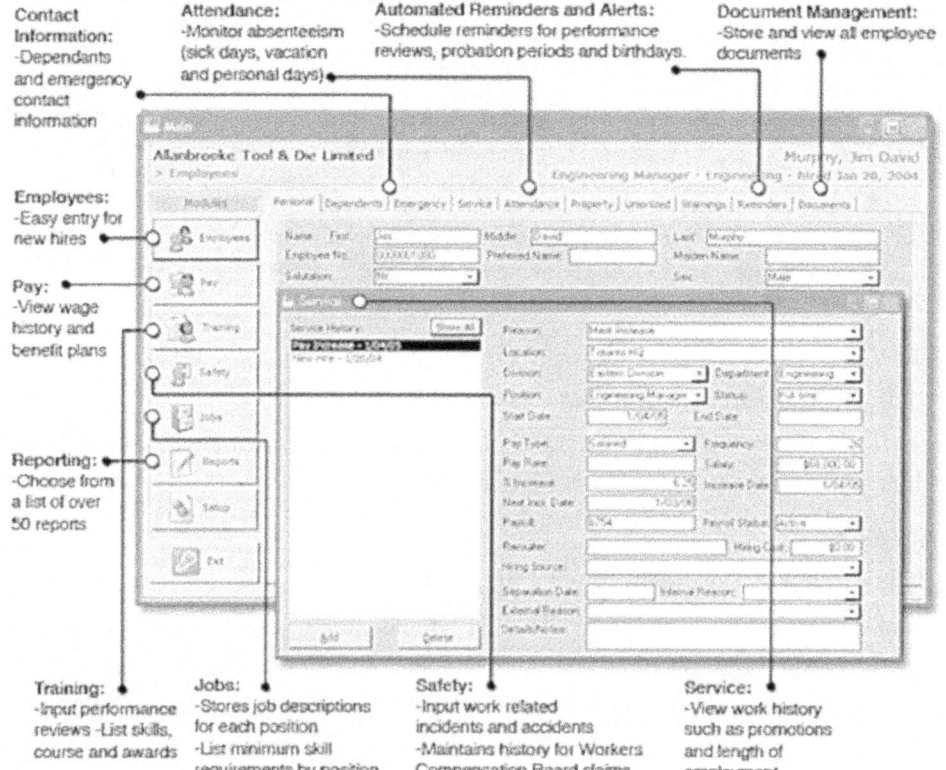

Fig. 3.5

5. Apex Software :

Powerful and cost-effective HR software.

Products from Apex :

iHR : iHR provides a full-featured, cost-effective HRIS that empowers HR professionals and supervisors to effortlessly manage critical employee information on a day-to-day basis. It provides all of the leave and time management features of iLeave, adding personal information, licensing, education, reviews, certifications, equipment, COBRA and benefits. Manage confidential information using iHR's secure, networked software. iHR includes all of our specialized software products in one package.

Add Instant Self-Serve, and employees can access leave schedules, time cards, and benefit enrollment over the Internet.

Screen shots of iHR :

Fig. 3.6

Instant Self-Serve :

Instant Self-Serve (ISS) is a Web add-on for iHR and iLeave. It gives employees and managers the ability to check leave, request leave, approve leave, change personal information, change benefit enrollment, and manage time sheets over the Internet. ISS provides secure Internet access to leave calendars, individual leave history, leave requests, individual time cards, and clock in/out features.

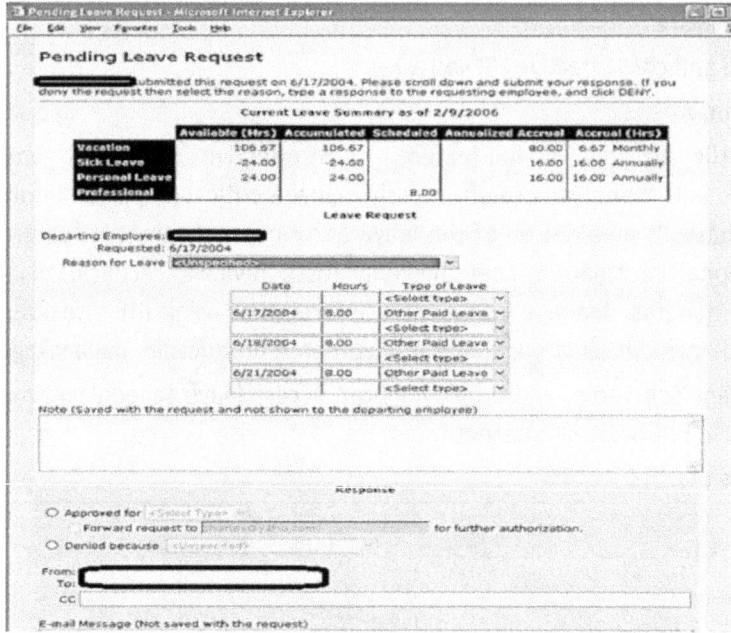

Fig. 3.7

3.5 CASE STUDY : TRANSFORMING HR AT NOVARTIS

The HRIS Challenges faced by Novartis HR Organization in Implementation of the HRIS :

The HRIS effort represented a major change in the fundamental role and responsibilities of the HR function within Novartis. There was profound impact of the new system on the relationships of HR professionals with their business partners. The Technical challenges for system implementation comprised of issues such as web enabling of critical processes.

Reasons for System Failure :

1. Problems arise when system is designed with features to add value to business but not relevant to HR.
2. Threats from Data Protection and Privacy Issues.
3. Cultural differences in communication between Global branches as a result of misinterpretation that arise due to lack of commitment in implementation of HR strategy.

Major Obstacles :

1. Resistance by Line managers in actual implementation of this system.
2. Failure to standardize the complex new HR system which increased the difficulties with subsequent implementation.

3. Risk of overselling the project in order to gain commitment which can cause problems when the system does not deliver the promised benefits.
4. After the implementation of the HRIS system it would focus more on customer service and Strategic planning with less emphasize on administration.

Solution to Overcome Obstacles :

In order to overcome these obstacles, first of all the senior leadership of the company must be actively involved in the effective implementation of this new system to resolve any disagreements regarding the system design and keep the top managers on track. The role of the HR department within the company would require a more fundamental transformation i.e. a shift from a functional expert and transaction processor to strategic partner and change event.

In its new role it will be more actively involved in the overall operations of the company with greater emphasize towards the development of its employees than its product. The competencies required for the HR professionals would be more sophisticated and people oriented.

Activities

1. Browse the web www.ihrm.org to enlist and describe more aspects related to the Feasibility studies.
2. Refer to the information available online on above site and provide more insight on the critical design tools used in System analysis.

Summary

The implementation of HRIS should be in tune with the overall business strategy of the firm since this system forms the crux of strategic HRM. The people involved in the management of these systems have to play an active role in strategic HRIS planning at a level that helps the organization to anticipate and prepare for a successful HR technology transition. Business process reengineering is becoming an integral part of many HRIS implementations in varying degrees. Some of the important requirements for - strategic HR information systems planning are given below :

1. Overall Business Environment Assessment.
2. Strategic HR goals Assessment.
3. New technologies and process tracking.
4. HRIS resources optimization.
5. Implementation activities streamlining.

It is a known fact that non-technical personnel mostly deal with HRIS, yet it requires great technical support in a computer-based environment. This support may be rendered by HR professionals HR technical staff, outside consultants etc. Occasionally encountered, however, is an adversarial relationship between the HR and the MIS

Staffs' thus careful and meticulous planning is necessary in the context of the HRIS transformation. The major issues in implementation of a HRIS are :

1. Stakeholder Contribution.
2. Conflicts and Resistance to Change.
3. Environment.

An effective strategy in implementation is requires as the HRIS is highly strategic in nature. Following steps may be ideally considered :

1. Identify all clients and build a representative implementation team that must be multi-departmental.
2. Define the objectives including project scope, time frames and resources.
3. Define problems with the current system, listed in order of priority.
4. Document the current system.
5. Define necessary functions for the new system.
6. Develop a list of recommended solutions based on the implementation team's decision.

We have also discussed the phases of HRIS, which are enlisted below :

1. Phase 1 : Need Analysis.
2. Phase 2 : Design and Development.
3. Phase 3 : Implementation and Maintenance.

Self-assessment Questions

1. Explain in brief the statement – 'Business process reengineering is becoming an integral part of many HRIS implementations'.
2. Enlist and discuss the reasons that most HRIS packages don't handle exception processing very well?
3. Enlist and discuss in detail any two factors that need to be considered during implementation of HRIS?
4. Explain in detail the 'Assessment of Risks' factor in the context of implementation of HRIS.
5. Explain in brief the functions of the Benefits Administration module of an HRIS system.

Chapter 4...

HRIS Applications

Objectives ...
After discussing this chapter, you will be able to :
- Explain the Recruitment Core System to Manage Complete Hiring Life-Cycle.
- Understand EEO and explain the Key Features of EEO.
- Understand various HRIS modules such as Compensation, Human Recourse Planning.
- Describe in detail Payroll Module.

Structure ...
4.1 Introduction
4.2 Applicant and Employment Management
    4.2.1 Recruitment Core System to Manage
    4.2.2 Job Seeker Relationship Management Application
    4.2.3 Vendor Management Application
    4.2.4 Referral Management Application
4.3 Equal Employment Opportunity (EEO) and Affirmative Action
4.4 Compensation
4.5 Benefits
4.6 Employee and Industrial Relations
    4.6.1 Introduction
    4.6.2 Key Features of Leave Management Module
4.7 Training and Development
    4.7.1 Introduction
    4.7.2 E-Learning
    4.7.3 Selecting a Learning Management System (LMS)
4.8 Human Recourse Planning
    4.8.1 Introduction
    4.8.2 Key Features of Module on Performance Management
    4.8.3 Performance Appraisal
    4.8.4 Key Features of the Human Resource Planning Management Model
4.9 OSHA
4.10 Payroll
    4.10.1 Introduction
    4.10.2 Key Components of Payroll Management Module

4.11 Short Case Studies
    Case 1 : Adrenalin Case Study
    Case 2 : Doctrina Learning Solutions
    Case 3 : Application of Multi-Rater Feedback Software in the Hospitality Industry
    Case 4 : Yaware – A Web-based Time Tracking System
- Activities
- Summary
- Self-assessment Questions

4.1 INTRODUCTION

In the present day handling of job requisitions and supervising of resume information is conducted by some kind of recruitment software or ATS (Applicant Tracking System) in essentially all types of organizations. In Large-scale organizations, recruitment applications may be offered as one of the various modules of an intricate human assets suite or HRIS (Human Resource Information System). In the case of firms of a relatively small size the applications used are spreadsheets or electronic mail messages to supervise with the HRIS recruitment efforts.

4.2 APPLICANT AND EMPLOYMENT MANAGEMENT

Aspirants that don't meet the base capability or do not pass a test can immediately be sent dismissal letters by the framework. This data can then be archived in the framework for instantaneous or future utilization. Master frameworks might be utilized to test and assess applicants' identity, learning, and abilities at diverse organization areas. This enhances precision in the selection process and decreases human transforming and lapse.

4.2.1 Recruitment Core System to Manage

Internet selection has turned into one of the essential strategies utilized by Human Resource divisions to earn potential aspirants for accessible positions inside an association. Recruitment management frameworks normally include :

1. Analyzing work force utilization inside a firm.
2. Potential candidate identification.
3. Recruiting through organizational postings.

The Applicant Tracking System (ATS) is one of the finest methods for having the ability to recapture the center of a business. Recruitment applications are utilized by both big and small organizations, yet differ in practicality and characteristics relying upon the requirements of the organization. Frameworks today have the practicality to join with all types of social and business networking sites, to post employments on the organization page.

Some of key features are :
1. Schedule feature for aspirants.
2. Archives for utilization in the future.
3. Feature of parsing to scan resumes and essential words.
4. ConFig.urable screening polls.

Following images show snapshots of Application Tracking software :

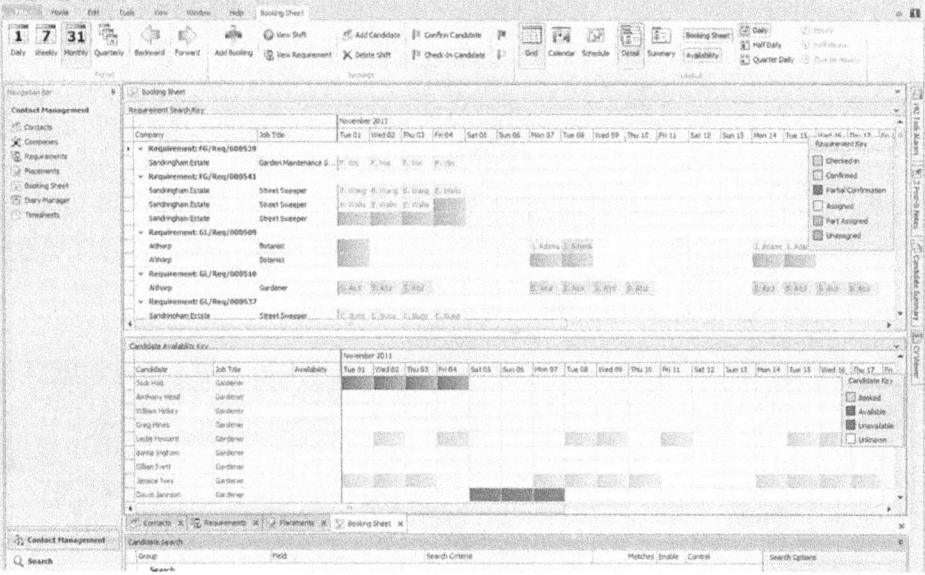

Fig. 4.1 : Recruitment Software

Fig. 4.2 : Application Tracking System

4.2.2 Job Seeker Relationship Management Application

The employees are helped by web-based portals to supervise their exercises related to workforce procurement like raising employee requirement, resume audit process, meeting booking and announcements and to track the status of every job post requirement by the concerned departmental administrators.

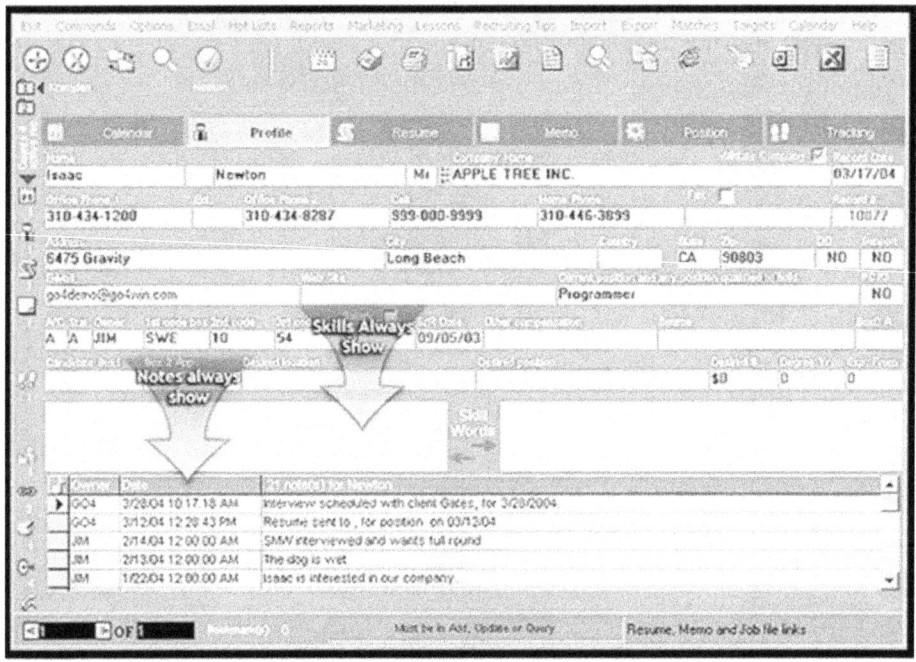

Fig. 4.3 : Interview Scheduler

Critical Characteristics of the Application are as follows :

1. Request for manpower can be raised by operational people and manage the entire lifecycle of managing the workforce request approval process cycle. The requisition gets input into the framework and tells the concerned Manager when an accepted requisition is input. Post this phase, all the exercises of every prerequisite will occur through the central framework.

2. The position of each requirement (man power request) can be traced by the operational Managers. The Managers can see the profiles screened by enrollment specialists and the same might be checked/redesigned as denied or accepted, after this procedure, selection specialists can plan talks with the selected aspirants.

3. The run-time perspective of recruitment related information like position of selection transactions, satisfaction status and the present status of the overall advancement can be monitored by member of the top Management.

4. Post the assessment; feedback might be upgraded through an online appraisal form. The selection specialists can accept electronic message notices and likewise are equipped to view the meeting calendar of each aspirant.
5. Managers from operations can additionally see the position of completion for every necessity, the progress of each applicant they have assessed and likewise appropriate reports as and when there is advancement on aspirant recruitment.

4.2.3 Vendor Management Application

The application in HRIS related to Managing vendors presents a complete framework to administer vendors and the issuing of requirements to chosen vendors; specialists can transfer the resumes and track the status progressively. Dependable vendors are seen as a prominent source of candidate profiles for on-time recruitment. The most appropriate administration of vendor affiliation requires the use of advanced technology. Thus there is an exponential increase in the efficiency as the cost is drastically reduced as the system does not require many people to input data. Some of the key features of Vendor Management System are as follows :

1. System is capable of recognizing changes in the recruitment status and sends out updates to the vendors.
2. Vendor accounts get updated on an automated basis.
3. System is capable of checking for replication for each iteration.
4. Distributing of necessities to chosen vendors.
5. Associated framework to source applicants continuously from related vendors.
6. Vendor capable of loading the profiles for every necessity.
7. Inbuilt administration of all current vendors.

4.2.4 Referral Management Application

Numerous vendors give the utility needed to accomplish your set targets like distributed prerequisites to select candidates through a web-based framework, obtain profiles from workers, a self-administration module where every representative can track the status of the applicant they have provided as references and the bonus they have earned for the referrals.

Thus, employee referrals are considered as one of the most reliable systems to obtain quality candidates based on previous experience. In situations when quality of candidates is critical to the organizational success or there is an acutely short supply of skilled professionals the process of employee referrals is one of most reliable recruitment methods that can be employed.

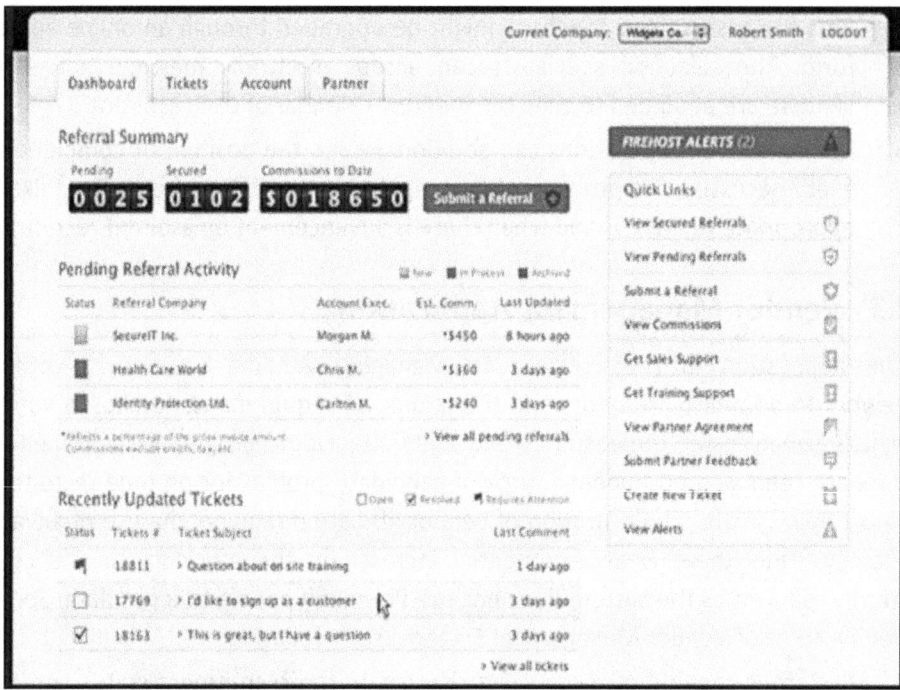

Fig. 4.4 : Referral Management Application

4.3 EQUAL EMPLOYMENT OPPORTUNITY (EEO) AND AFFIRMATIVE ACTION

This is committed to equal employment opportunity, affirmative action, and eliminating discrimination. This commitment is both a moral imperative consistent with an intellectual community that celebrates individual differences and diversity, as well as a matter of law.

Discrimination against any individual based upon protected status, which is defined as age, ancestry, color, disability, gender identity or expression, genetic information, HIV/AIDS status, military status, national origin, race, religion, sex, sexual orientation, or veteran status, is prohibited.

All persons regardless of color, national origin, race, religion, sex, or veteran status shall have equal access to positions in the public service, limited only by their ability to do the job.

Harassment :

Verbal, non-verbal or physical conduct constitutes harassment if it is based on a person's protected status and creates an intimidating, hostile, or offensive work or academic environment that unreasonably interferes with work or academic performance or negatively affects an individual's employment or academic opportunities. Harassment can occur between any individuals associated with the university, e.g., an employee and a supervisor; coworkers; faculty members; a faculty, staff member, or student employee and a customer, vendor, or contractor; or a student and a faculty member. Ohio State is committed to providing a workplace that is free of harassment based on age, ancestry, color, disability, gender identity or expression, genetic information, HIV/AIDS, status, military status, national origin, race, religion, sex, sexual orientation, or veteran status, is prohibited.

Affirmative Action :

Designed to help eliminate effects of past and present discrimination. It is a process in which employers identify areas of improvement, set goals, and take positive steps to enhance opportunities for protected class members - individuals with disabilities, minorities (Asian/Pacific Islander, Black, Hispanic, Native American Indian), qualified veterans (Vietnam era veterans, special disabled veterans, campaign badge veterans, and recently separated veterans), and women. Affirmative Action focuses on hiring, training, and promoting qualified protected class members where they are underrepresented.

Guiding Principles :

1. Recruitment processes should be designed and conducted so as to result in the most diverse and qualified applicant pool possible.
2. Selection practices should emphasize hiring the best-qualified individuals with due consideration for persons from underrepresented groups.
3. Management practices should facilitate inclusive work environments that value and seek out human diversity and reward effective human relations skills.
4. Management practices should emphasize prevention of discrimination and harassment.
5. Training and development opportunities should be made available to employees and should enhance the opportunities for individuals from underrepresented groups.
6. Promotion practices, including tenure, should be inclusive and acknowledge the contributions of individuals from underrepresented groups.

4.4 COMPENSATION

One of the earliest areas of HR to be automated was compensation, and today, virtually all organizations use technology to automate payroll processes.

Today's e-compensation systems provide much more value than the simple automation of payroll processes. E-compensation uses web enabled technology to help managers design, implement and administer compensation policies. An HRIS allows organizations to streamline and automate the compensation planning process, to model proposed changes in compensation plans, to track employee compensation history, to allocate incentive pay and bonuses, and to provide higher quality information to decision makers.

A recent survey shows that 61 percent of organizations use e-compensation systems or plan to implement them in the next year. Multiple business drivers support the growth of e-compensation technology.

Pressure to contain labor costs. E-compensation systems can help increase access to both internal and external salary and compensation information. Data can then be incorporated into sophisticated compensation models and metrics, which can help managers better plan and model the costs associated with various incentive programs. Through better access to information and better compensation models, organizations are able to gain tighter control over compensation costs.

The compensation professional's role is one of the most diverse within an organization. It touches all employees; manages the programs that directly impact an organization's performance; requires internal knowledge of the organization's culture, structure, departments and jobs and external knowledge of its industry and labor markets; and has a skill set running the gamut from analyst to negotiator to communicator to educator.

The human resource function is also quite diverse, covering a number of specializations. Over the past several years, a generalist staffing model has gained prevalence, having at its core professionals whose knowledge and skills encompass the full HR spectrum — recruiting, employee relations, training, benefits, compensation and often HRIS. An HR Generalist is typically designated to one specific group within an organization, so that he/she gains a depth of knowledge about the group and its functions, which in turn provides managers with a familiar and well-informed contact for HR-related issues.

Certainly there are many benefits to this generalist staffing model, customer service and flexibility not the least of them. But does the broadly trained HR Generalist provide your organization with the required level of expertise in each area of HR to maximize efficiency while maintaining reasonable labor costs? Alternatively, is it more efficient to have some specialists on staff for areas of HR requiring unique skills, such as compensation, HRIS, benefits?

It is difficult to answer these questions at the collective level, as an organization's HR staffing is influenced by many variables, such as the level of work completed internally vs. externally, the size and diversity of its workforce, the complexity of the organization (global vs. national, multi or single location, centralized or decentralized) and the internal role of HR. Accordingly, the appropriate HR staffing model should be determined at the organization level after reviewing each area of specialization — its key initiatives, customers and priorities - and the way the HR team interacts across specializations.

Short of conducting an organization design study, an HR executive should at a minimum have a good understanding of deliverables and expectations for each area of HR in order to align staff appropriately and provide the expertise needed to meet customer requests. This article focuses on the compensation specialization and outlines knowledge, skills and abilities expected of the compensation professional, as well as typical reports, tools and analyses that the HR department should provide to managers to facilitate pay decision-making, delivery and administration.

Compensation Knowledge :

1. **Compensation Principles :** While an effective compensation system is somewhat unique in that it is directly linked to an organization's culture and goals and objectives, a compensation professional should be knowledgeable of key principles for compensation design and administration across the organization, best practices, typical salary structure and budget movement from one year to the next, financial modeling and effective communication tools.

2. **Laws and Legislature Impacting Compensation :** Compensation professionals should have a solid understanding of the impact and application of laws and regulations covering employee compensation.

These range from long-existing laws - like the Fair Labor Standards Act of 1938 (FLSA) that establishes the minimum wage, overtime pay requirements and child labor laws - to new legislation, such as the Sarbanes-Oxley Act of 2002 that established the Public Company Accounting Oversight Board to oversee audits of the financial statements of public companies. If the organization operates on a global level, knowledge of legislation affecting employee compensation in other countries is also required.

3. **Benefits and Tax Issues :** Benefits and compensation overlap frequently, so it is important that the compensation professional has an understanding of the organization's benefit programs and legal implications that could arise related to compensation program design or decisions. In addition, knowledge of tax issues related to pay is necessary.

Internal Knowledge :

1. **Organization :** Understanding an organization's products and services, financials, compensation programs and its various departments and their interrelationships is a requisite. If the organization is very large or has a complicated structure, a compensation professional might be responsible for one or two designated areas.

In this case, knowledge of the organization's core jobs and functions is still important.

(i) Jobs : This complements organization knowledge. A thorough understanding of jobs and how they fit into the organization is critical to valuing them appropriately and advising managers. Organization structures should be kept up to date and as uncomplicated as possible. A list of market-sensitive (hard to fill) jobs, along with a strategy to address them, should be established and updated quarterly.

(ii) Systems and Databases : Proficiency with the systems and databases that the organization uses to manage its compensation programs is essential.

External Knowledge :

1. **Industry :** Each industry has its own intricacies, standards and eminent organizations that set the pace for the others. Networking and establishing contacts within the same industry are well worth the time. (But direct sharing of pay data can lead to charges of price fixing or collusion, so it is best to use third party-based compensation surveys.)

2. **Market Surveys and Data Sources :** Even if the organization's base pay system is not primarily market-based, external market data is still required to gauge competitiveness and align the internal system with external pay rates in order to attract and retain employees. Surveys vary in scope and quality; a compensation professional should know the available sources and the various methodologies used to collect and display data. Survey sources used to gauge external pay levels must be credible and relevant to the organization. In addition, several survey sources should be used to thoroughly assess changes in market pay practices.

3. **Labor Markets :** An organization competes for talent in many labor markets – geographic, industry, and organization size are the most prevalent. Labor markets will vary by employee level and job; they will also change over time. The compensation professional must be aware of labor market conditions impacting the recruitment and retention of employees throughout the organization and also understand the cost of labor for the same jobs located in different geographic areas. (This is typically presented as a geographic differential).

4. **Performance Expectations :** Understanding the organization's and specific department's business strategy, goals and performance expectations is critical to understanding the appropriate level of cash compensation investment – base pay and variable pay – required to attract, retain and motivate staff. If performance expectations are only at the 25th percentile of peer practices, for example, compensation levels would typically not need to be at the 75th percentile.

Skills and Abilities :

1. **Mathematical and Analytical :** To complete ongoing analyses and program modeling.
2. **Technical :** Spreadsheet and database proficiency (understanding of current systems and ability to readily pick up the skills and knowledge necessary to understand new systems).
3. **Communication skills :** Ability to write succinctly and for the intended audience; good presentation skills.
4. **Independent judgment :** Ability to reason through data and findings and use good judgment in making recommendations concerning internal application of such information.
5. **Negotiation :** Ability to see two sides of a situation and compromise when appropriate.

The compensation function has experienced significant change over the past 20 years. Here is a before/after analysis of compensation programs, a view from the early 1980s (before) and early 2000s (now).

ITEM	BEFORE	NOW
Administration	• Compensation administration and analyses were paper-intensive. • Reports and analyses were typically run from organisation's mainframe computer system. • Little use of online tools for managers.	• Compensation administration and analyses are typically PC-based. • A multitude of HR software systems are available that seamlessly interface with the organisation's IT system. • Online tools for managers are common.
Base Pay	• Employees tended to invest a significant amount of time at one employer. • Internal equity took precedence over external competitiveness. • Analysis of job by compensable factor and focus on equity in pay across discipline.	• Employees likely to have held a number of jobs by the end of their careers. • External pay focus is of primary importance. • Whole job review, not component-by-component review. • Equity tends to be established and maintained

		within a discipline, consistent with how the market moves.
Short-term incentive	• Incentive pay was reserved for the top tier of the organisation. • Easier to link individual contribution to results, given participant's direct influence over such results. • Communication was to select group and less formal compared to today.	• Variable pay's role in influencing performance at all levels has been elevated. • Widespread use of broad incentive plans covering all or most employee groups. • Effective "line of sight" communication to engage and focus employees on their contribution to overall goals is considered key to plan's success.
Long-term incentive	• LTI plans rarely reached below the top management level. • LTI portion of total reward was not as significant as it is today. • Less widespread use of LTI meant fewer issues related to stock dilution, underwater options and appropriate reward levels. • Less focus on sharing organisational performance objectives and practices; less education provided to eligible employees.	• Broad-based stock option programs are common. • LTI is significant portion of total reward package for executive and managers. • Organsations seek appropriate balance between LTI and other pay components. • FASB 123 stock option expensing is timely topic. • Enhanced organisational training and education to assist employees in understanding how they affect overall results.
Performance management	• Main focus was the end of the year performance evaluation and goal-setting for upcoming year. • Salary increase budgets were higher (6% of payroll and	• End of year evaluation considered a culminating event following a year-long cycle of ongoing feedback and coaching. • Annual salary increase

	above) due to inflation, as well as less frequency use of incentive pay. • Employee performance goals were not often linked to corporate goals.	budgets hover around 3.5% to 4% of payroll. • Link between employee and corporate goals and performance are typically established at the beginning of the performance year.
Executive compensation	• Executive compensation decisions and administration often made outside the HR department.	• HR typically accountable for executive compensation.

Compensation Reports and Analyses:

Reports and analyses that should be provided by a compensation department are outlined below according to the typical time period in which the report is produced.

Reports Quarterly or more Frequent:

Report	Purpose
Employee turnover analysis	Employee turnover from one time period to the next presented for the whole organization and by department/group. Follow-up analyses for high turnover areas to uncover the root cause.
Cost of turnover	Summary of expense associated with hiring employees (recruiting fees, interview time, testing, cost of job ads, lost productivity and other) multiplied by the number of new hires during the quarter.
Range analysis	Comparison by incumbent of salary range position and targeted position based on performance and other important factors to determine the gap between the two.
Diversity analysis	Comparison of pay, merit increases and incentive payouts to protected classes of employees (female, minority, age 40 or over) vis-a-vis all other employees.
Overtime analysis	Review by department of overtime hours worked by employees and the cost of such overtime to determine whether staffing additions are justified.
Market-sensitive job review	Outline of hard-to-fill jobs and special pay deals offered on a temporary basis to retain incumbents.
Incentive plan	Analysis of year-to-data performance against incentive goals

performance analysis and communication	followed by employee communication update.

Annual:

Report	Purpose
Market analysis	Update of market data for a group of benchmark jobs to determine changes in pay from year to year.
Geographic analysis	Analysis/update of the cost of labour for each location as a percentage of the national average.
Salary structure and Budget analysis	Analysis of market salary structure adjustments and salary budget adjustments followed by recommendations for the internal structure adjustment and pay increase budget.
Rating analysis/Pay adjustment analysis	Review of performance ratings and requested salary adjustments by department to ensure budget is met.
FLSA classification review	Random FLSA audit of a small group of jobs, including employee and manager interviews or desk audit to determine accuracy of job description.
Total compensation analyses	Review in growth of total compensation expense from an absolute perspective as well as per employee to assist in monitoring staffing levels; analyses should include comparisons of total compensation expense vis-a-vis revenue per employee to view the potential return on compensation investments.
Top performer analyses	Also frequently referred to as HIPO analyses; a review of pay increases, promotions, bonuses, and other compensation components for the organisation's top performers to ensure retention but more importantly additional growth in these valuable assets.

As Needed or Requested:

Report	Purpose
FLSA testing	Determination of exempt or nonexempt classification as jobs are changed or created.
Market analysis	Market analysis to determine the external rate of pay for new or changed jobs.

Special pay analysis by department group	Various pay analysis upon request (internal pay compared to market, difference between lowest and highest paid person in a select job, analysis of pay level to performance level and others)

4.5 Benefits

Benefits are a growing and expensive component of every employee's total compensation. A recent government survey suggests benefits costs now average 43.6 percent of wages and salaries. Given the continued growth in the expense associated with health care and pension plans, the costs of employee benefits likely will continue to grow as well. In addition, with the coming implementation of the new Patient Protection and Affordable Care Act, reporting requirements also will grow.

An e-benefits approach uses the web to communicate information on benefits to employees and allows them to elect and manage their benefits online. A recent survey suggests nearly all organizations are using technology to support benefits administration.

Motivations for using E-benefits include :
1. Reducing the costs for delivering benefits.
2. Improving employee access to benefits information.
3. Streamlining benefits administration.
4. Empowering employees to manage their own benefits.

Although there are multiple ways that an organization can pursue an e-benefits approach, underlying each of these is the use of Employee Self Service (ESS). Most organizations now make benefits information available via the HR portal, providing details ranging from health benefits to pension contributions and planning calculators, EAP program offerings, educational benefits, leave information, vacation scheduling, and many others.

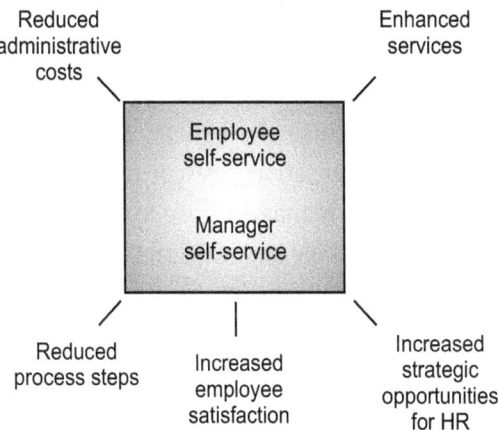

Fig. 4.5: Web-based Self-service Applications and Benefits

Outsourcing, Timeliness and Employee Management of E-Benefits:

Implementing e-benefits does not mean simply replicating paper-based forms online. Employees will only access the website when they need information, so the website should provide employees the information they need as quickly and clearly as possible. If employees are unable to find the information in a timely manner, they are likely to call the HR department. When this occurs, the goal of reducing the time and expense associated with benefits administration will not be achieved.

The most effective e-benefits websites are organized by life events such as marriage, birth and death, or by changes in work status, such as layoff and promotion.

Many organizations now link or outsource many of their benefits information support. For example, financial services organizations provide their clients' employees with financial literacy information, allow them to forecast the financial implications of their decisions, and encourage them to learn more about how to manage.

Many health care insurers provide online services to customers, allowing employees to learn about healthy eating, exercise and health management practices. Employees are empowered and encouraged to take more responsibility for their financial and physical well-being.

The importance of timely information increases dramatically when benefits go online. Indeed, if an employee makes a decision based on inaccurate information from the employer's website, the employer may be held legally liable. If timely and accurate information is not available via the website, employees will be less likely to use it and will continue to call HR for assistance.

It is now a best practice to push the management of benefits to employees.

By using Employee Self-Service (ESS), organizations encourage employees to sign up for benefits online and manage their profiles and benefits online. Each vendor's website should accurately reflect your firm's policies, and organizations also should ensure their systems interface seamlessly with vendor systems to ensure information accuracy and user-friendliness.

HR professionals make intensive use of e-benefits systems for a variety of activities, such as controlling workers' compensation costs or monitoring unemployment claims for ineligible former employees. Managers responsible for compliance with legal mandates (such as COBRA or the Family and Medical Leave Act) use systems to monitor employee status, payment and eligibility for health care benefits. Many mandated benefits programs carry significant financial penalties for noncompliance.

E-benefits applications often can have a positive ROI in a relatively short time, not only by reducing transaction costs, but also by avoiding fines and penalties.

Potential Pitfalls in E-Benefits:

Websites cannot replace skilled staff members. There is a temptation for HR policy makers to view the website as a way to reduce or eliminate HR personnel from all aspects of benefits administration. The HRIS can automate basic transactions, educate employees and create efficiencies in benefits administration. At the same time, the HRIS is not as effective in dealing with the inevitable exceptions to policy for which HR experts will need to be available. Consider the spouse who is inquiring about the benefits due him or her after a death or about the company's options for accommodating someone with a disability. Systems are not good at being empathetic, and a website can never completely replace a skilled HR professional.

An organization cannot depend exclusively on the website to communicate complex benefits information. The benefits website can be a rich source of information for employees, but it should not be the only source. Benefits are more complicated today than ever before, and pending changes in health care and pension benefits will only make the potential for confusion worse. Employees may not be able to make sense of choices and rules from the website and may need to speak with benefits experts to assist them in understanding the choices they will face.

4.6 EMPLOYEE AND INDUSTRIAL RELATIONS

4.6.1 Introduction

Leave is an entitlement provided to the employees and accumulates in an automated manner. All workers are relied upon to utilize their leaves within a reasonable way. Workers may be instructed to ask for leave a few days to some weeks ahead of time that they wish to take it with the intention that work can delegated and the leave plans of different representatives facilitated. Managers have the decisiveness to choose when and in what measure leave may be affirmed. This choice may as well weigh the necessities of the work environment with the goals of the worker.

In the event that the manager discovers that work-related necessities prevent permission for leave, or if the explanations communicated by the worker for non-attendance are not adequate, the manager might request the person to show up at the workplace. In such occasions, the manager at his or her circumspection might concede sufficient time on sanction leave to achieve the work environment. Unless overwhelmed by occasions, an employee is answerable for informing the manager and reporting a crisis that will require non-appearance in an unplanned fashion.

This application computerizes the leave requisition procedure by diligently incorporating Human Resource approaches into the framework and permits workers and their supervisors to administer their leave without interference from the Human Resource department. This application incorporates web-based electronic leave provision and approval, recording verifiable leave, including support cycles into the framework. The Leave Management Software module is an extensive application that mechanizes and streamlines the whole leave-administration workflow.

Leave management software will helps the HR department base the performance appraisals on accurate information since there is no chance of human error through the employee leave management systems.

The critical functions of assessing, screening, recording, tracking of the workers job times and exercises are seamlessly facilitated by today's Leave Management Software. With this application the schedule for segments of job activities might be set and reused throughout the organization. Instinctive client interfaces are customized to the distinct needs of operational administrators, HR experts, supervisors, Team Managers and other organizational entities.

4.6.2 Key Features of Leave Management Module

Some key features of Leave Management Module are listed below:
1. Leave privilege records might be transferred and loaded into the system.
2. No programming customization needed for leave procedures.
3. Enables HR Managers to design the leave types in the module and the leave policy.
4. Email notification feature will be integrated to alert requestor on leave approval status.

1. **Ability to Define the Types of Leave:**
   (i) Once the leave requisition is placed, Web-based leave planning modules provide the feature of decision support to verify qualification and privilege to leave provision.
   (ii) The module provides the user the capability of categorizing the type of leave required as per the organizational policies and procedures.
   (iii) Notices in the form of emails might be designed for applicants and supervisors as the leave application is tracked through the procedure.

2. **Earmarking of Leave Application:**
   (i) Employees can apply for leave online and have their requests for planned type of leaves, sent to their manager and the Human Resource department. The system creates vital reports, for example documents such as taxation forms and transfer forms letters. Workflow communicates with the leave database to display employee leave history when the employee is using the system.
   (ii) The system gathers information on absence in the run-time and also obtains the details of approved leave and applied leave.

3. **Tracking of Leave Balances:**
   (i) The supervisors can recognize which leave procedures apply to the leave request, and the leave administration result will track and manage these simultaneously with the different sorts of leave. The eligibility for leave is figured out by adaptable guidelines they also determine the leave balance calculation.
   (ii) The leave administration cycle is finished on receiving confirmation from the Manager HR on the requestor's leave status and upgrades the leave balance.
   (iii) Function of balance checking and screening of leave utilization.
   (iv) Functional queuing framework to adjust the manager's approvals workload.

4. **Cancel / Revert any Pending Leave Application Functionality:**

   Leave is proposed to permit the employee recreation, travel, vacation and rest and is duration of absence with pay from official duties in an approved manner. Leave is also proposed for the person's emergency or personal issues and also to extend the time available to the employee under some other leave programs.

   In many situations due to work related contingencies an employee might need to cancel / revert any Pending Leave. In this context today's Leave Management system should take into consideration there requirements and incorporate the feature of cancelling or reverting any pending leave application. In case paid leave being requested and approved and then cancelled upon the employees request most systems have a 'roll-back' facility.

5. **Linkage to Time Management System for Identifying Employees on Leave:**

   Many of today's Leave Management System integrates with biometric/swipe card "punch clock" terminals and Time Management Systems and manage leave and time sheets without managing all of the other HRIS information. A prominent system doing this is iLeave from Apex Business Software. This system manages vacation, PTO, sick leave, personal leave, professional leave, bereavement, annual leave, FMLA, workman's comp, and state family leave. And it supports tour of duty pay and shift differentials.

   The iLeave system automatically accrues leave over practically any period including annually, quarterly, monthly, semi-monthly, biweekly, weekly, and hourly. Its inbuilt features are able to answer employee inquiries accurately with easy access to vacation, sick leave, personal leave, and lateness.

   Thus with iLeave it is possible to replace exhaustive paper charts with quick-reference leave calendars and share leave history by printing or e-mailing leave and lateness reports.

6. Linkage to Payroll System for the Deduction of Unpaid Leave and Pay in Lieu:

The module on Leave management facilitates the building of performance appraisals with respect to precise leave data since there is no possibility of human lapse through the leave management frameworks. Consequently, blunders in the data inputs, calculation of leaves, and diligence on part of manual efforts some of the aspects that are automated by this system.

Numerous Leave Management provisions today accompany inbuilt practicality of liaising with the Payroll System for deducting the measure of leaves of the unpaid category that the worker has availed. Job times for work classifications might be set and reused throughout the organization. Intuitive client interfaces are custom-made to suit the unique needs of various important entities like HR Managers, operational supervisors, HR experts, supervisors and Team Managers.

Key Benefits of Leave Management Module:
1. Exponential decrease in HR interference.
2. Exponentially decrease the administrative load by evading manual effort spends on processing, authorization, filing of records as ordered by enactment.
3. Accessible at any time and at any location.
4. Calculates and looks after leave offsets in an automated manner.
5. Capability of identifying potential problems associated with absenteeism in advance and plan for backup coverage.

Functionality and Snapshots of Leave Management Application : iLeave feature From Apex Business Software :

Apex Business Software is a software development firm that specializes in providing computer-based management, leave, FMLA, and benefit tracking products. Apex delivers human resource software packages to a variety of companies by providing leading-edge products that cater to the multiple needs of human resource personnel. The products are strategically designed to meet the HR objectives of business owners, managers, HR administrators and employees.

If HR management is considered to be a core competency, Apex Business Software can help increase the HR productivity by providing flexible, secure, easy-to-use software packages. iLeave integrates with biometric/swipe card "punch clock" terminals and manages leave and time sheets without managing all of the other HRIS information. iLeave manages vacation, PTO, sick leave, and state family leave. Also it supports tour of duty pay and shift differentials.

Main Web Form : The Main Web Form allows employees to log in and check leave and benefits. Hourly staff clock in/out and access in/out boards.

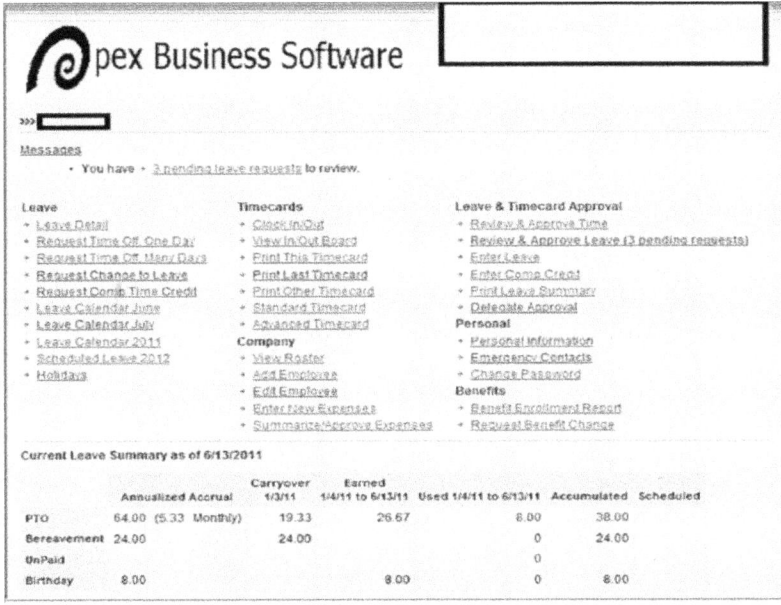

Fig. 4.6

Leave Matrix : The Leave Matrix allows you to use one window to easily look up and schedule leave for all employees. Employees are listed in the Tree View (left) by department, manager, location, etc. View the Leave Matrix to summarize used leave over any period. Open individual employees quickly to enter leave requests or update time off.

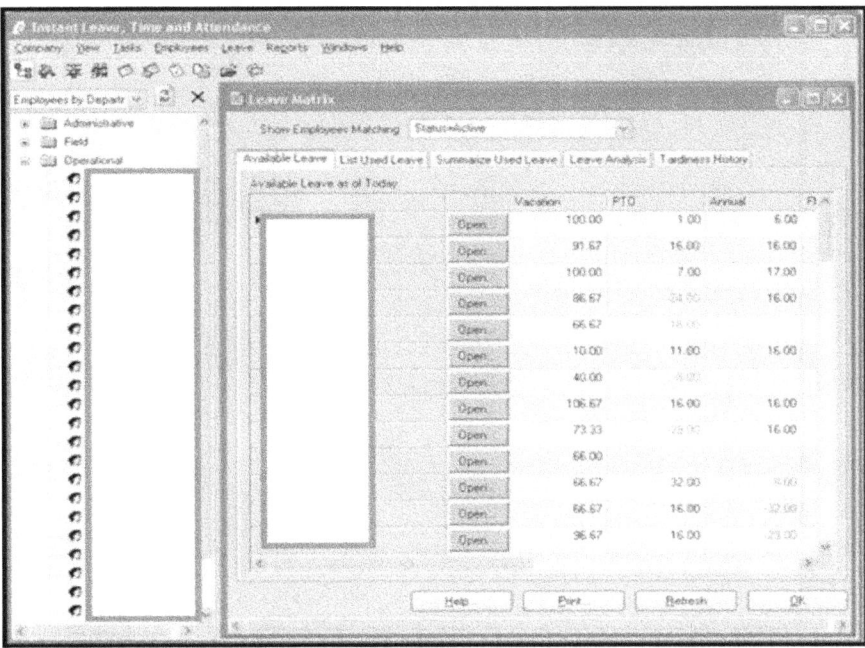

Fig. 4.7

Employee Leave:

Use the Leave tab on an employee's window to enter anything and everything about individual leave, schedule, accrue, and credit. Quickly check for an employee's unused leave. Make manual adjustments and schedule tasks regarding a specific employee.

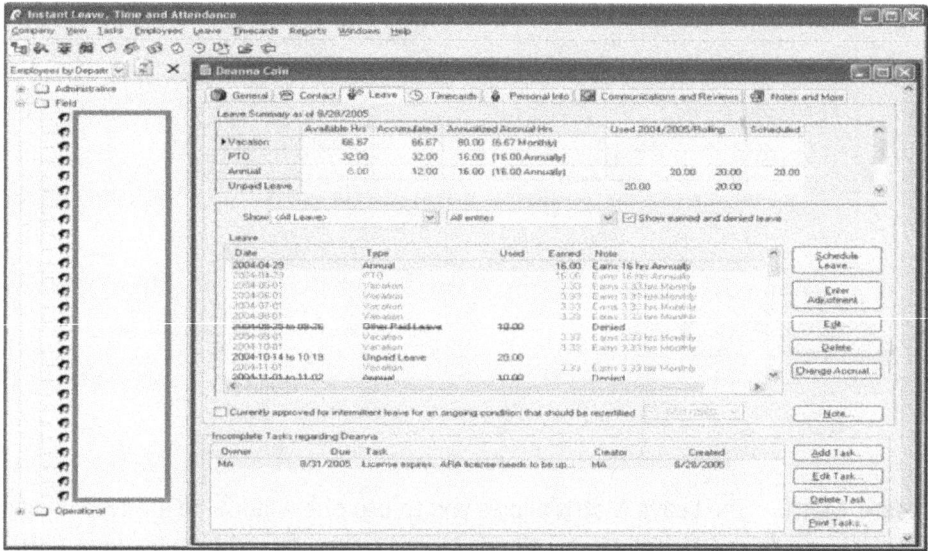

Fig. 4.8

Leave Accrual Plan: Many companies use different accrual plans for different employees. Leave accrual plans allow executives to earn more vacation, etc. than managers.

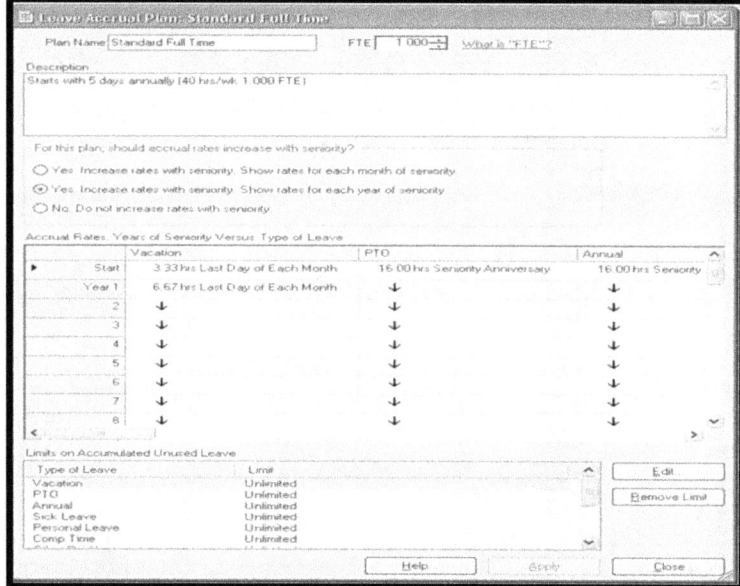

Fig. 4.9

Scheduled Leave: iLeave offers dozens of reports that focus on leave. List employees by month and date or print out monthly calendars. List covering employees on calendars as well. Run reports on denied or pending leave requests.

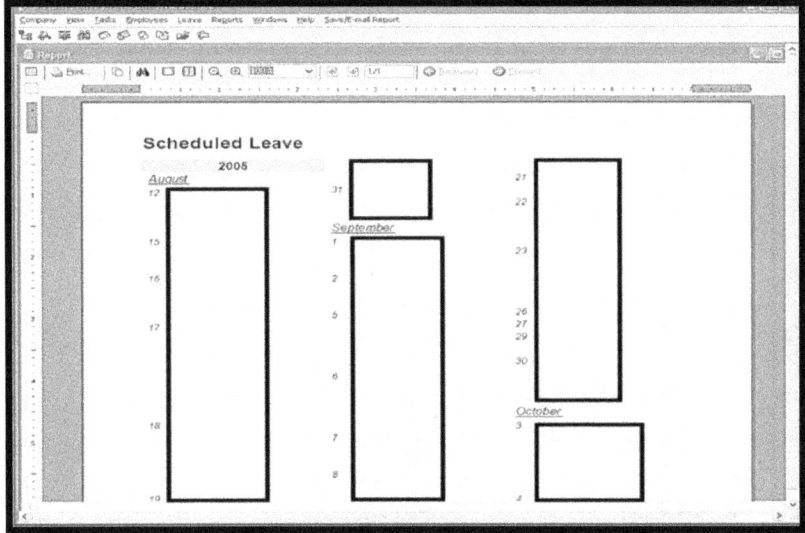

Fig. 4.10

Leave Calendar: iLeave offers dozens of reports that focus on leave. List employees by month and date or print out monthly calendars. List covering employees on calendars as well. Run reports on denied or pending leave requests.

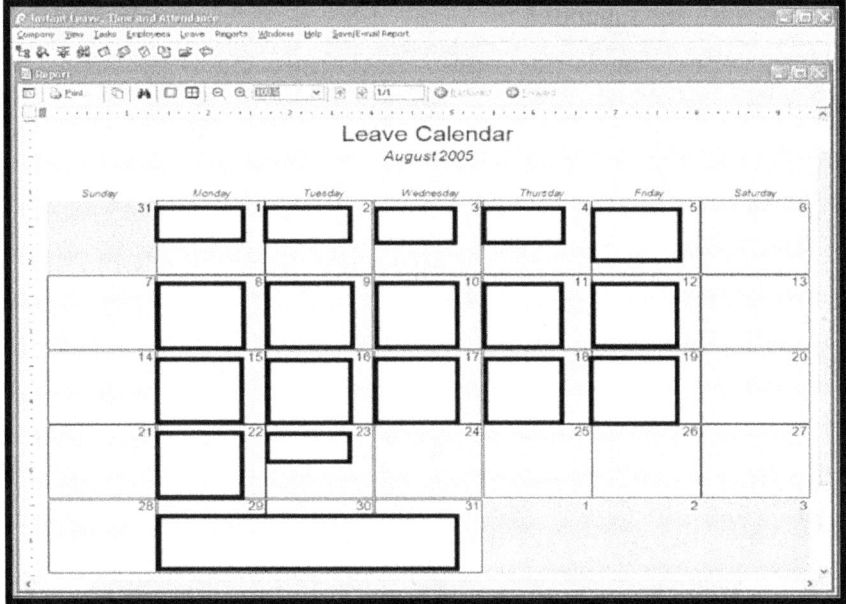

Fig. 4.11

Pending Leave Requests : Run a report for pending leave requests to help stay organized. Easily record leaves requests and track whether they are approved, denied, or pending. Track the period of absence, type, and number of hours used.

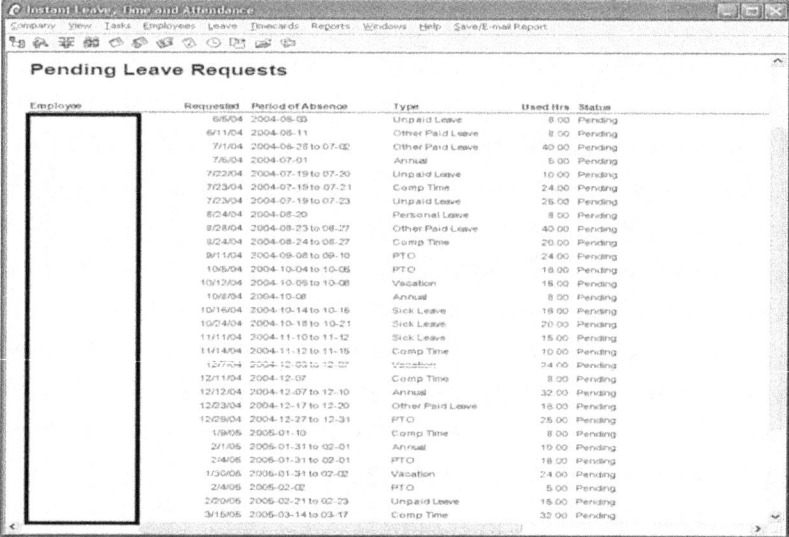

Fig. 4.12

Time Sheets : Enter time sheet entries for one employee or many employees. Select from different schemas to support hourly employees, salaried time logged against projects/jobs, and manager approval. Optionally purchase Instant Self-Serve so employees can clock in/out and enter their own time sheets over the Internet. "Punch clock" terminals are also supported.

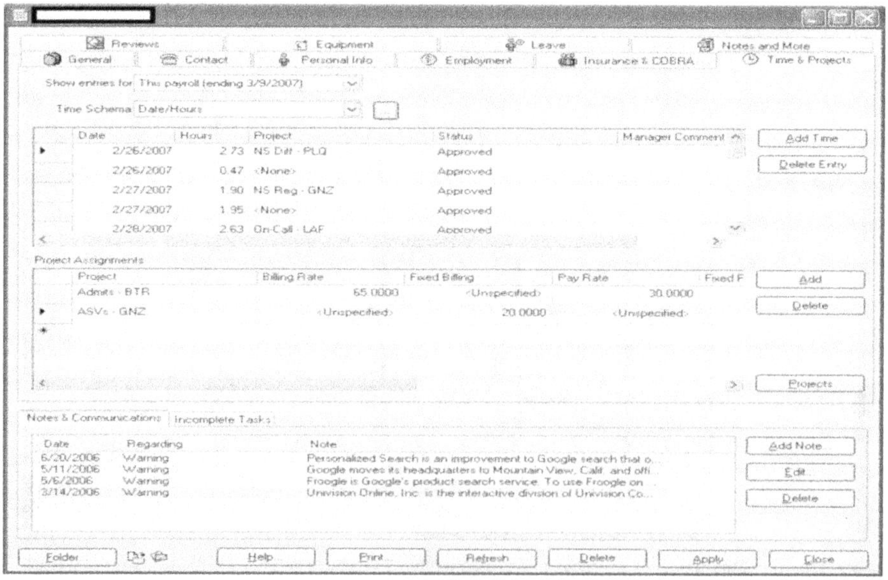

Fig. 4.13

Time Sheet Entry : Easily enter or edit in\out timesheets.

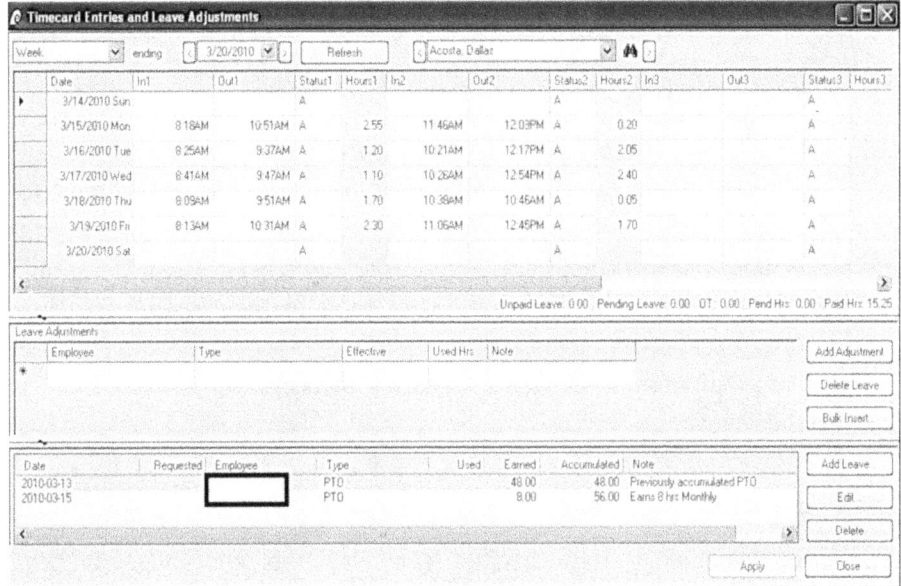

Fig. 4.14

Time Sheet Summary : Run a time sheet summary for payroll that incorporates used leave. Set up timecard options like rounding guidelines.

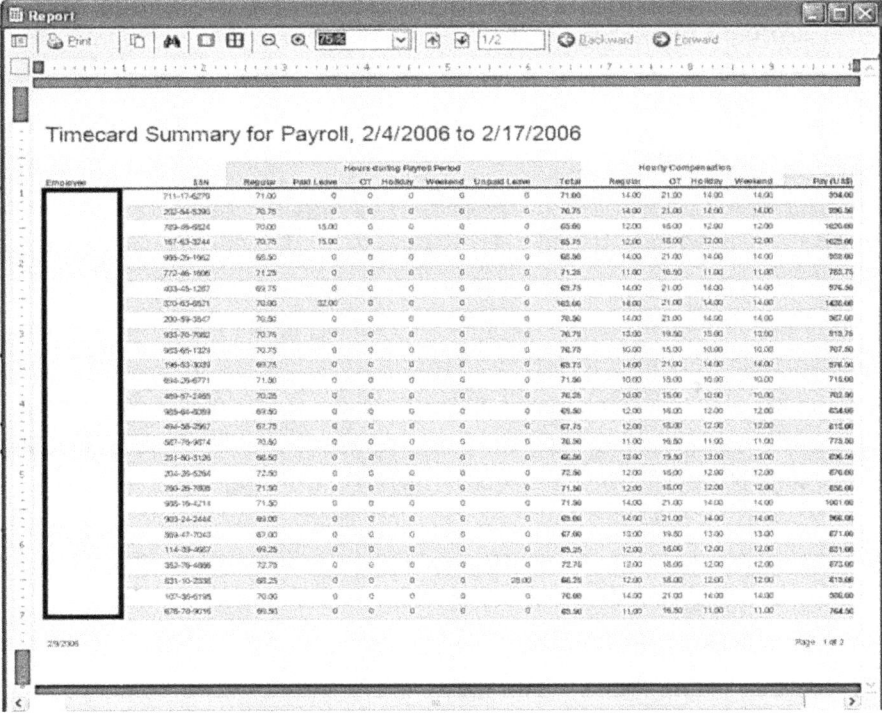

Fig. 4.15

4.7 TRAINING AND DEVELOPMENT

4.7.1 Introduction

With the popularity of Web 2.0 and social networking tools like MySpace, Facebook, YouTube, and Twitter, there has been great demand to include similar tools to help people make connections internally in companies. In spite of some unresolved issues concerning security and incorrect information, they have been widely accepted. LMS vendors have been quick to add these kinds of tools to their features by providing connections with experts, mentors, and communities of practice. This improves the efficiency of informal learning as well as creating a record which can be put into a searchable database.

4.7.2 E-Learning

Information technology has changed the way the knowledge is acquired, manipulated and disseminated among individuals. Due to open knowledge environment and easy access to information, the stress is on the critical evaluation of knowledge and access to information to the employees of an organization. The effectiveness of training and development of human resources can be enhanced by creating an open IT-enabled e-learning environment.

1. E-Learning is the use of technology to enable people to learn anytime and anywhere.
2. E-Learning can include training, the delivery of just-in-time information and guidance from experts.

If you could stop time and inexpensively bring together all of the people in your organization who need to learn and the resources to teach them, you would not need e-learning. In the real world, people have jobs to do and budgets are limited.

Open IT-enabled e-Learning Environment-learning, is the design, sequencing, and integration of all electronic and Non-electronic components of learning, to deliver optimum improvement incompetence and performance. The power of online training and knowledge management is magnified when they are used in combination. But they are even more powerful when properly integrated with more traditional classroom training programs. In following this path, the organizations are required to move from building single learning programs, courses, databases, or tools, to building an e-Learning architecture for the organizations for the development of human resource.

Feature of Computer-based Training :

A successful corporate skills development program includes components for essential learning, future learning and corporate mandates.

1. **Essential Learning :**

   Employees should be provided with training opportunities to develop the minimum skills required to perform their tasks. Training may include new hardware or software training or update training for new releases.

2. **Future Learning :**

   Often overlooked, future learning is an essential component of a successful training program. Organizations should provide clear paths to continuing education to help end users quickly get answers to their problems. Online training, embedded learning and reference cards can help reduce help desk volumes and operational costs.

3. **E-learning Modules :**

   E-learning allows students to learn independently and repeat exercises to reinforce or refresh their understanding of the content. Available 24×7 at the learner's convenience, self-paced e-learning provides an alternative to classroom teaching for students who are geographically scattered or too busy to participate in a classroom session.

The Pre-requisites of e-Learning:

Within the context of e-Learning, we have a number of choices and decisions to make about the types and combinations of online training to deploy. We will have to take care of, and where is IT-enabled learning appropriate? How should be e-Learning used to supplement classroom learning? How should the e-learning and classroom learning components be sequenced? How much time should be there between each component?

Involving Employees in an e-Learning Environment:

Getting employees involved in learning has always been a challenge. We often express frustration that company leaders do not attend courses, even courses that designed for them. Instead the organization should try to find the right course that would attract executives.

Building an e-Learning Architecture:

A learning architecture is not the same as a curriculum1 which generally refers to organization and relationship of courses to create the appropriate learning sequence Curricula important but insufficient to define a complete learning architecture. From IT-enabled learning to classroom training independent study monitoring and work experience become most important components.

Creating an Environment for Ongoing Learning:

A newly hired employee asks her manager a question. The harried manager replies that the classroom training or Web-based course will provide the answer. The worker feels disappointed and frustrated; the manager has missed an opportunity.

He's sent a message to the employee that learning begins and ends with training. From then on, she may ignore other chances for vital formal or informal learning. This is how workers start expecting learning to flow over them and stop taking a self-directed approach. Here's how.

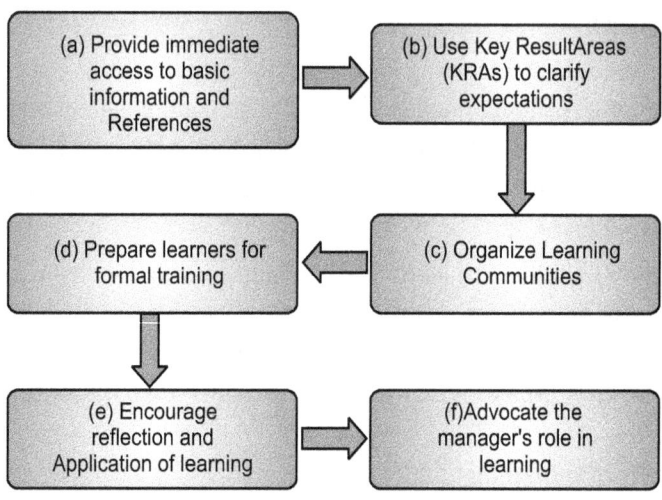

Fig. 4.16

1. **Provide Immediate Access to Basic Information and References:**

Have you ever been amazed, when a new hire asks for information that you were sure he had learned during orientation of the first week on the job? Avoid this situation by gathering the questions that new employees ask most frequently regarding the job, company, industry and market, competition, products. and soon. Categorize the answers in an easy-to-read format published on the company intranet. Whenever possible, offer links to other documents. It your company doesn't have an intranet, provide a binder to new employees with the basic facts and FAQs [link to glossary].

2. **Use Key Result Areas (KRAs) to Clarify Expectations:**

A key principle of adult education theory is relevancy. Learners are motivated to learn when they perceive that the knowledge gained will help them perform their more effectively. To ensure relevancy, all learning should be linked directly to their job expectations. Managers should provide each worker with Key Result Areas (KRAs) for the position. A KRA is made up of the tasks that work collectively towards the achievement of a goal.

KRAs help employees determine their goals. Monitor progress, and measure achievement. They also provide managers with a coaching tool to target specific areas for improvement. For example, for the position of property manager, one of the KRAs is financial management.

Use KRAs to Design Learning:

Instructional designers can use KRA's to determine appropriate content and resources to help learners achieve their goals, verify whether existing courses facilitate the learning of key tasks, and create new content where there are gaps. The end result is a checklist of self-directed activities for a learner to complete, starting from day one up to a year on the job. Learning plan checklist aspects like Timeline, Resources, Activity, Completion Status, Follow-up etc.

(i) Answering guided questions in a development workbook.

(ii) Sharing answers to guided questions in an online forum (email or discussion groups).

(iii) Meeting to discuss an issue with a small peer group Discussing reflections or questions with their manager Participating in a follow-up training session.

Performance management is the process of setting goals, self-assessment, manager assessment, peer-assessment (also called 360 degree assessments), coaching, development planning, and evaluation. Competencies are the collections of skills, knowledge, and attitudes necessary to do a specific job.

3. Organize Learning Communities:

Learning is fundamentally a social activity. Help your learners to access dynamic, rich knowledge from experts and colleagues by providing a forum to change ideas and best practices. Learner communities can form in various ways.

(i) **Online Discussion Board :** Monitored by training facilitators or a subject matter expert, a discussion board creates a knowledge base from previous postings that can be used by new hires to answer questions and review best practices.

(ii) **Synchronous Online Learning :** Using synchronous technologies, learners can meet with and learn from employees with more-developed skills.

(iii) **Face-to-Face :** Gather your learners for a summit. In addition to providing the formal learning opportunities such as, breakout sessions, presentations, and games, F2f sessions can enable learners to share war stories, learn new tips, and find resources over coffee or drinks.

4. Prepare Learners for Formal Training:

According to constructivist theory, learners approach any learning situation with their own assumptions and beliefs. To prepare workers for formal training, you can use discussion boards, email, or surveys to ask people reflective questions about their baseline knowledge or attitudes. Here are some examples, before a class on customer service, a facilitator asks learners to email their own service "delights and duds" and then posts the responses on the Intranet.

5. **Encourage Reflection and Application of Learning:**

Instructional designers are often unsure whether or how employees are applying their learning on the job. There is one simple, straightforward way to find out. Follow up and ask. By using discussion boards, email, or surveys, you can encourage learners to share, how they have used the information, best practices, war stories, and scenarios.

6. **Advocate the Manager's Role in Learning :**

Finally, we return to our disillusioned new hire. Her manager needs to appreciate has role on her learning process and help her reach her KRAs. Instructional designers can help managers be effective in that role by :

   (i) Educating them about their role in learning, especially in helping learners complete their development plan.

   (ii) Providing tips and resources for coaching employees.

   (iii) Making sure, they are aware of the content of all learning programs and have necessary resources at their fingertips.

The ideas suggested in here can help cultivate a learning culture and encourage workers to take an active role in their own learning. Keep in mind that your job is never done. Learning is a lifelong process and the fruits of your labor are in the journey, not the destination.

4.7.3 Selecting a Learning Management System (LMS)

Selecting a learning management system can be the most critical decision you make when building your company's e-learning infrastructure, Implementation can take up to a year and cost from Rs. 25000 to 50,000. To gauge the marketplace determine internal needs and issue a request for proposal (RFP). In addition to functionality, key considerations are technical infrastructure, scalability, and maintenance.

Start the search process by attending several product demonstrations, or attend the supplier's user meetings. Then, meet with companies that have installed the system your Company is considering and talk to their training administrators, IT department, and the managers, who have worked with the system. Determine the number of staff and skills required to maintain the system. It may be used differently by other customers, which can help further assess the supplier's capabilities or modify your implementation plans.

In terms of cost, the software license is only a portion of the investment. All learning management systems will require additional consulting, technical conFig.uration, and administrator training. Indeed, some training managers have horror stories of expensive, yearlong implementations caused by major data conversion and customization work.

It's possible to reduce the initial time and financial resources required by focus core functions, with plans to implement other components at a later date. To cost effective, select a system that requires minimal customization and beta adapt internal processes to fit the new system's workflow.

Negotiating WBT Courses and Costs:

There are many providers of off-the-shelf Web-based training courses. Such companies, as Smart Force, Skill Soft, and Net, market their courses directly and can either host individual courses or install the course libraries on a company's internal server.

Although comparison shopping for Web-based courses seems difficult, it isn't impossible. The Review of course catalogues, and evaluation of courses that are essential to company's core business must be done. Questions to be considered include:

1. Is the curriculum structure logical and complete?
2. Are the courses user-friendly and easy to navigate?
3. Are the courses engaging and interactive?
4. Do courses use effective instructional design?
5. Do courses meet learning objectives?
6. If needed, can the Courses be customized? What are cost and maintenance implications?

If course descriptions are in a format that's incompatible with your LMS, another option is to use hosted Web-based courses without purchasing a full-blown Lissome suppliers and course aggregators provide course launching and tracking tools that offer basic security.

Here, are some guidelines for buying other e-services.

1. **News and Information Subscriptions :** Depending on the service, companies can pay a flat rate or peruse for various levels of service. Till the company determines the actual volume of use by employees, pay-per-use is a more cost effective approach.

2. **Advisory and Reference Tools :** A one-time enterprise licensing fee plus an annual maintenance fee is recommended for this type of service. But before contracting, test the tool in the company environment and determine whether company-specific information can be added.

3. **Synchronous Learning and KM Tools :** These can also be used as the general and business tools, so look at the other departments for buy-in and Pricing can get complicated because some providers sell their services bundled, while others sell services in components. In general, it's cheaper to buy a bundled system with a single maintenance fee.

4. **Library Tools** : It is important to get someone with a background in library automation or information science to help you assess products. Typically, library systems can import catalog data and allow choosing among several catalog schemes. The new generation of tools is Web-enabled and can integrate collections from multiple libraries.

5. **Mentoring Services** : Because it takes significant marketing and buy-in to get some audiences to use this type of service, companies risk paying for an underutilized product. Before contracting a mentoring service, consider the following questions :
   (a) What are the areas of expertise and qualifications of the people offering mentoring?
   (b) Is the service available 24/7?
   (c) Does the service include phone support, real-time online combination of both?
   (d) Are there any technical barriers? For example, some companies block these of chat rooms.

6. **Custom Web-based Courses** : Projects of any size start with an RFP. Most companies tend to use the same Web-based provider for multiple projects, budding partnership with a company that understands its business. When setting terms the implementer must be sure to agree on a specific project schedule and backup plans should the project go off course. Questions to be asked before contracting with a supplier include :
   (a) Who will provide the subject matter expertise, content, and reviews?
   (b) Do the organizations want just simple content delivery with some testing, simulations, and performance support?
   (c) Based on technical considerations and course objectives, will the company use multimedia tools, such as Flash to develop the course?

7. **The Technology and Suppliers Change Rapidly:** Therefore, e-Learning managers must build scalability and flexibility into their e-learning model and strategy. By building strategic relationships with proven suppliers and technologies, as well as with internal sponsors and technology support, e-learning managers can count on a successful e-learning solution.

4.8 HUMAN RECOURSE PLANNING

4.8.1 Introduction

Performance Management consists of Planning Performance, Managing Performance, Reviewing Performance, and Rewarding Performance. Also shown in the Fig. 4.17 below.

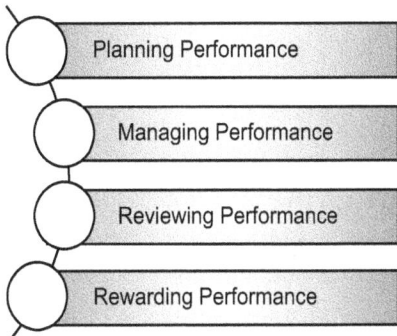

Fig. 4.17 : Performance Management

The below provided is a model illustrating the performance requirements of the organizational employees :

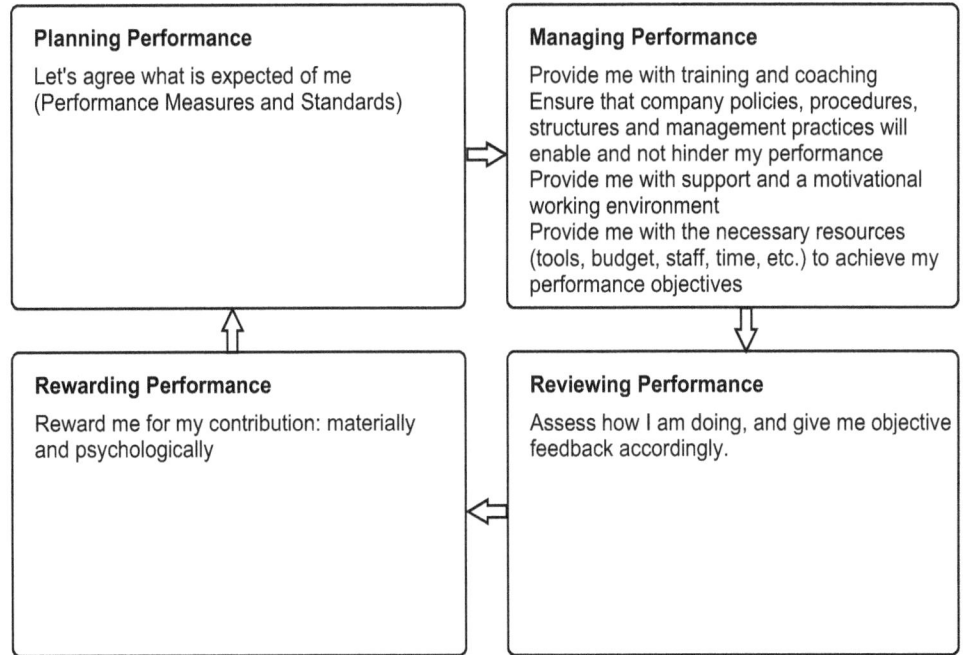

Fig. 4.18 : The Performance Requirements of the Organizational Employees

To accommodate the above requirements of organizational employees, let's reflect what needs to happen at each phase of the Cycle of the Performance Management system :

1. **Planning Performance** : Performance Measures for different levels in the organization are mutually talked over and concurred throughout one-on-one meetings with their immediate operational managers. These maybe competencies, KRAs, KPIs,

targets, objectives and so on. These are put into a formal, composed Performance Agreement for every employee. (Agreements on the factor of Performance can likewise be created for complete departments in the enterprise where collaboration is foremost).

2. Managing Performance : During this phase, staff members implement/execute their concurred objectives. Operations supervisors are additionally answerable for coordinating and facilitating the Objectives of all their sub-ordinates, checking their performance, initiating remedial action, and doing joint solving of performance related issues as and when essential.

3. Reviewing Performance : Two critical topics discussed at this phase are how well the concurred KPIs/ Objectives had been accomplished and specified competencies exhibited by the members of staff and are assessed by their operational managers. Restorative measures are set up for the identified performance related-issues, incorporating conceivable coaching and preparing that the employees need. Subject to the kind of enterprise and its style of administration, the recurrence of Performance Appraisals may be either a monthly, quarterly, half-yearly or yearly manner.

4. Rewarding Performance : The real Rating of execution (how well the competencies have been exhibited and every KPI / Objective had been attained) structures part of the Interview for Performance assessment/ review.

An organization's ability to administer and write about their business performance assumes a necessary part in the administration of their risk and improvement of operational execution. Guaranteeing that KPIs (key performance indicators) are created, conveyed, and gathered over the enterprises might be tedious to supervise. Likewise, the gathering of all the needed data from diverse divisions, areas, and execution areas could be a testing undertaking and can frequently consume a lot of time and money related assets.

The Module on Performance Management furnishes senior administrators and executives with, dependable, time-bound and correct data on performance at a location, a department, or over the whole business. When the information is gathered more assets and exertion are needed with a specific end goal to present and provide details regarding performance. Having clear perception of this is not simple without the right techniques. To meet these tests, organizations require devices which permit them to supervise, investigate, enhance, and cover their execution.

Organizational guidelines might be created to confirm activities that need to be performed when contingencies happen. This module helps staff members to realize organizational objectives, exhibit positive conducts and identify proper preparing to upgrade the staff expertise in a holistic manner.

With attributes to characterize and set performance measurements at the organizational level and screen and report execution in connection to the measurements set, the Performance Management Module guarantees that KPIs are dependable, equivalent, and relevant over the complete business. This application has impressive characteristics that furnish employees with precise and immediate visibility on execution issues and issues with performance.

The following snapshots show elements of Performance Management Module of 'iHRIS software':

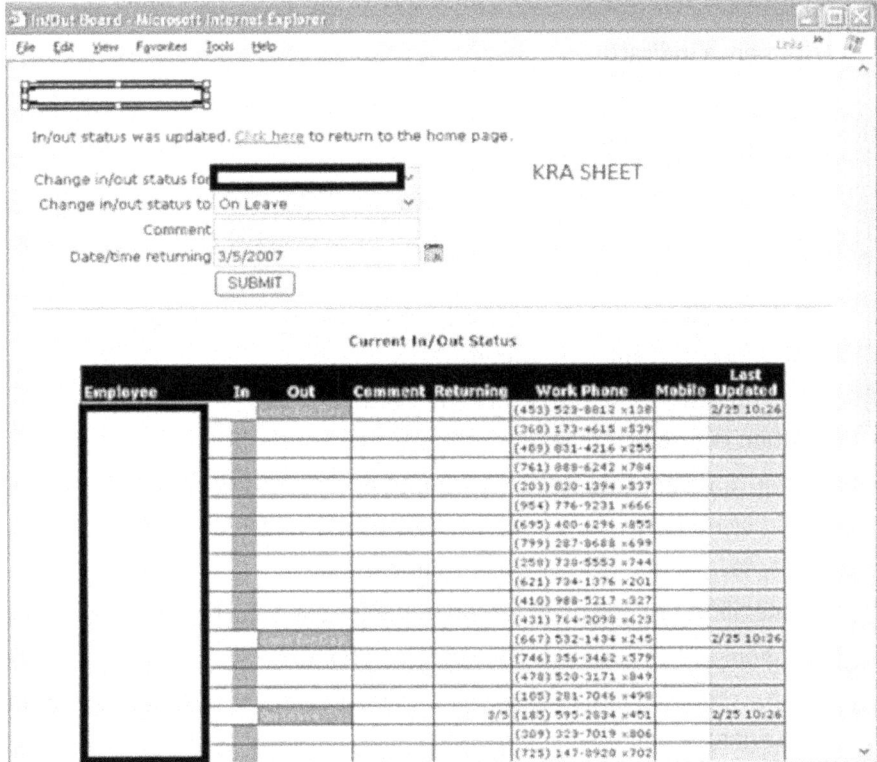

Fig. 4.19

4.8.2 Key Features of Module on Performance Management

1. Ability to communicate with personnel through different sub-modules.
2. Capability of determining the learning and aptitudes requirements of employees for successful performance.
3. Created on performance results or decisive plans performs budgeting activities.
4. Work objectives clarification.
5. Manage staff performance.
6. Provides a time sensitive dashboard and measurement tracking tool.

7. Training and development requirement determination in a precise manner.
8. Balance Scorecard utilized for tracking performance requirements.
9. Building rapport and creating open communication and feedback through positive debates.
10. Organizational and staff objectives linking tool.
11. Ability to determine the right disposition and conducts as per the organization strategies.
12. Identifying knowledge and skills for effective individual performance.

1. **Key Performance Indicators :**

A KPI is used to measure advancement towards a specified enterprise goal or objective. It can be either a monetary and non- monetary measure.

The Advantages of Computing KPIs:

(i) It might be an extremely speedy method for seeing the genuine performance of an objective or vital goal.

(ii) Organizational choice could be made much speedier when there are precise and unmistakable measures to support them.

(iii) Can permit the administration to see the organizational or departmental execution in a holistic manner.

(iv) A group can work together to a normal set of measurable objectives and this need to be uniform. This uniformity is provided by the KPIs.

(v) KPI is always linked with the organizational goals.

(vi) Staff members are personally accountable for the outcome of KPIs.

(vii) A KPI should be concise as they are action oriented.

(viii) They are simplistic in nature and are top indicators of performance desired by the companies.

(ix) Users can measure their ongoing development.

The KPI examples from diverse industries are as follows :

(i) **KPIs in HR :** These include - Compensation and Benefits, Performance Appraisal, training and development Employee Engagement, Employee Retention, recruitment etc.

(ii) **KPIs in Sales :** These include – Sale-force management, developing sales presentations, sales campaign development, sales pitch development, customer care, after sales service etc.

(iii) **KPIs in Marketing :** These include – developing PR, promotion mix completion, advertising, e-marketing etc.

(iv) **KPIs in Procurement :** These include – delivery on time, quantity bought over required, purchasing cost, cost of purchasing units, and determination of the transaction cost of units purchased vendor qualification etc.

(v) **KPIs in Manufacturing :** These include – Material management, Planning order management, inventory planning productivity, quality and maintenance etc.

The following snapshots show elements of Performance Management Module of 'iHRIS software' :

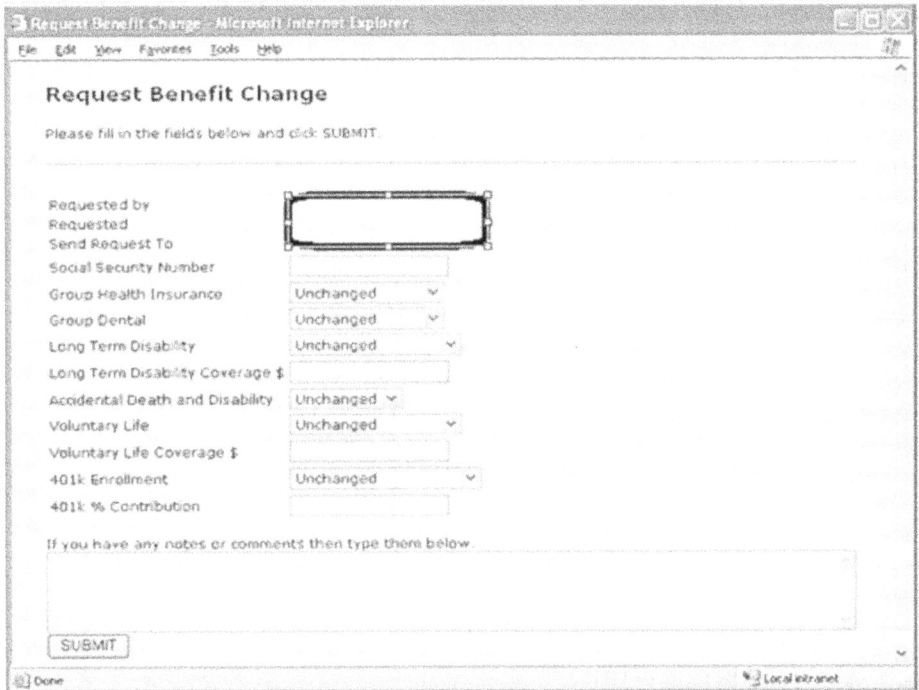

Fig. 4.20

Most organizations utilize estimations to track performance against a target; it is a part of the exact principle that makes up an organization. Some essentially decide to screen complex data, for example units sold this month or income. At the top-end of the range a few organizations decide to interlace KPIs into a more holistic business performance environment

Both methods have their divide pros and cons; however the primary issue with utilizing KPIs is not following excessively few or indeed, checking an excessive amount of, it's about utilizing the accurate KPI's. Equally critical is the development of an understanding of the correct tools to measure the appropriate KPIs.

2. Managing KPIs : KPI Software Choice

Most Business owners would admit that gathering KPI information can take an excessive measure of time, to add to that examining and writing about that KPI data.

Explore the extensive array of features :

(i) KPI Entry : The system offers a simple and intuitive 'one point' of entry for KPI Fig.ures, teams and individuals no longer have to juggle with sales spreadsheets to submit their KPI figures. It's all controlled conveniently in one place.

(ii) KPI Analysis : Drill down into performance data to determine the root cause, highlight top performers and identify areas of concern.

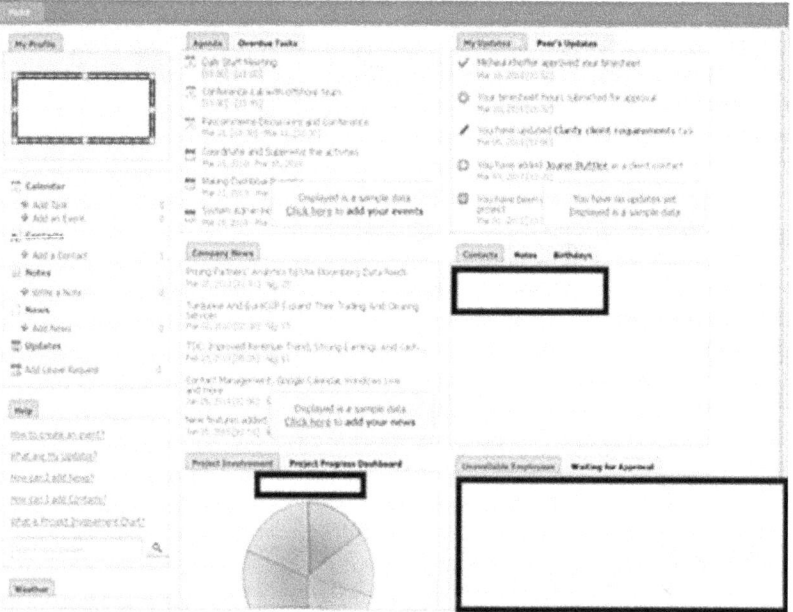

Fig. 4.21

4.8.3 Performance Appraisal

Performance administration frameworks are utilized "to supervise and arrange" the greater part of an enterprises assets so as to accomplish most noteworthy execution. How execution is supervised in an enterprise figures out to a vast degree the triumph or disappointment of the enterprise. Consequently, enhancing employee appraisal for everybody ought to be around the most noteworthy necessities of contemporary firms.

Appraisals have been directed on an annual basis, however numerous organizations are moving towards shorter appraisal cycles (like half-yearly, or quarterly), and few have been transitioning into still shorter-cycles (monthly or weekly). The meeting could pose as "furnishing feedback to staff members, directing and nurturing employees, and passing on and talking over remuneration, work status, or disciplinary choices". PA is regularly incorporated in execution administration frameworks.

Vital to any Performance Management Application (PMA) is the application on Performance Appraisal and it needs to be transparent, adaptable and client friendly. As a computerized, self-administration framework, it might as well enhance performance through continuous audits and feedback to the staff members and offers opportunity to supervisors to adjust execution in time. The process of administration of staff appraisals through ongoing employee assessments is the core component of the performance capability advancement methodology of any firm.

Benefits to the Organization:
1. Create, execute and analyze an automated, effortless and efficient performance appraisal process.
2. At-a-glance goal-setting to align individual goals to the organization's vision.

Benefits to HR:
1. Ensures secrecy of the process of employee appraisal.
2. Flexibility to choose from different performance management based systems like Balance Scorecard method, competence or KRA methods.
3. Get easy access to KRAs to keep performance on track.
4. Scan deviances in performance at a holistic level and plan course correction.
5. Save time by executing a paperless appraisal process.
6. Benefits to the Managers and the staff members.
7. File appraisal forms and get review results online.
8. Keep record of profession development for better arranging.

Online Job/Role Descriptions:

Posting job descriptions in an easily accessible place, such as the Web based management location ensures employees and other stakeholders understand what is expected of them. Everyone can also see what are the duties and requirements of managers. Why is this important? Communicating the job responsibilities to everyone helps diminish confusion arising when conflicting employees don't understand the authority, responsibility and expectations of the employee positions within the airport or airline. Managers may also use these items to assist in annual employee assessments.

Job descriptions outline the authority, responsibility and expectations of all stakeholders. When creating your job descriptions of key safety personnel, managers often overlook the authority element. To be complete, for each job description, we recommend using a template for job descriptions and responsibilities. Whichever template you choose, ensure that the authority element is present.

Functions for HR Administrators :

Most of today's HRIS Applications put the description of job duties and requirements in a module called "Duties and Requirements of Key Safety Personnel," or "Duties and Requirements" for short. Duties and Requirements allow operators to communicate clearly to stakeholders the key safety personnel SMS duties and requirements.

Key personnel are employees who fill top management positions. They make significant contributions to decisions about company direction, provide leadership to employees, and provide expertise in their assigned positions. Many of today modules are cloud-based which enable the editing and access to custom job descriptions from anywhere.

A well-developed job description will help you review employee performance, and hire the best candidates. The online Job Description Builder should be simple to use. The application today act like efficient tools, HR Managers can transform a blank page into a professionally-developed job description in minutes by following these simple steps :

1. Choose from the comprehensive library of job descriptions.
2. Check off tasks and activities as well as skills associated with the job.
3. Select from the list of physical demands or the job/ work environment or add your own.
4. Print out a complete job description in Word or in an Excel Spreadsheet—it's that easy.

The online Job Description Builder clearly and quickly defines a program and project management job role for you. Following are some screenshots of job description reports :

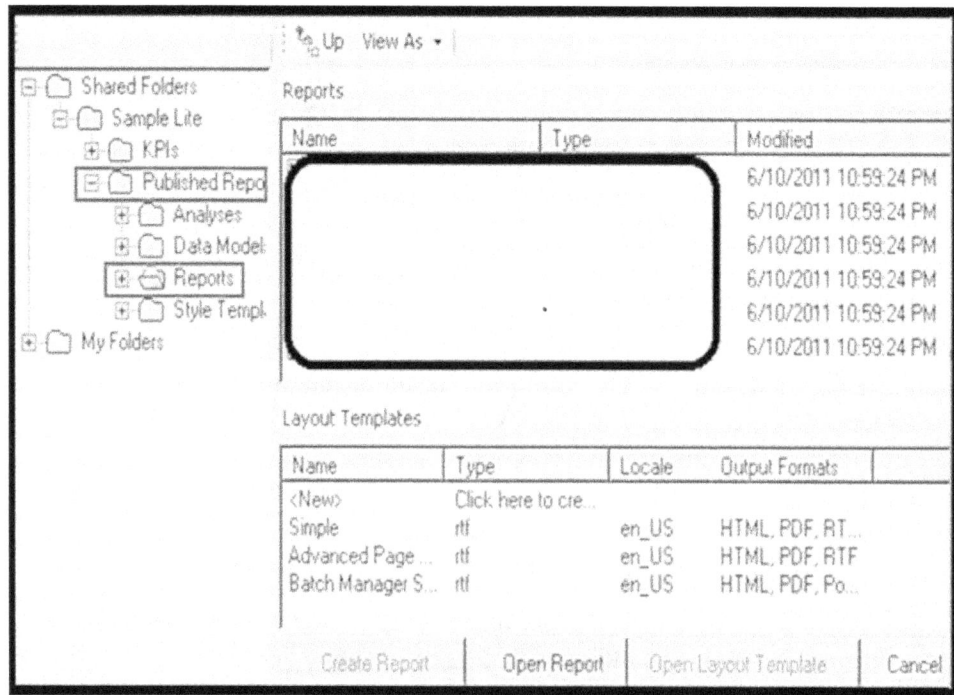

Fig. 4.22

Multi-rater (360-Degree) Feedback Module:

In human resources 360-degree feedback, also known as multi-rater feedback, multi-source feedback, or multi source assessment, is feedback that comes from members of an employee's immediate work circle. Most often, 360-degree feedback will include direct feedback from an employee's subordinates, peers, and supervisor(s), as well as a self-evaluation.

360 Degree Feedback has raised interest because of a number of organisational and working changes which have taken place over the last decade or so. The changes fuelling interest include :

1. The flatter structures which are now replacing many traditional hierarchies.
2. Fewer promotion opportunities available in flatter organisations.
3. A move to measuring the value-added element in roles, people and specific jobs.
4. A growth in project methods of working meaning that direct line managers no longer know about or have experience of all aspects of an individual's work and contribution.

Over the past 20 years 360 Degree Feedback or appraisal has been used in a variety of ways to inform and support such activities as :

1. Performance management systems.
2. Team building and development.
3. Management development.
4. Supervisory training.
5. An alternative to assessment centers.
6. Succession planning.
7. Career development.
8. Leadership development.
9. Encouraging personal responsibility for development and continued learning.

The Contribution of 360 Degree Feedback :

360 Degree Feedback is seen to offer a paradigm shift for hierarchical systems as organisations seek to adapt and improve systems of appraisal and feedback to ensure greater effectiveness and increased congruence with business aims and objectives. 360 Degree Feedback can help with :

1. Employee measurement.
2. People development.
3. Feedback.
4. Behaviour change.
5. Improved employee performance.

What is vital is that those considering the use and introduction of 360 Degree Feedback need to be very clear about the purpose of its use within their organisation. Key questions to ask are :

1. Is to be used evaluative to measure performance and to link to such issues as pay, promotion, bonuses etc.?
2. Is it to be used purely for developmental purposes with feedback indicating areas of strength and proving guidance on where improvement is needed?
3. Is the system to address both evaluative and developmental issues?

It can involve :

1. Colleagues above and below the individual.
2. Managers who have experience of part or parts of the individual's performance e.g. project team managers.
3. Customers, internal and external.

Three Multilayer Approaches : There are three different Multilayer Approaches :

1. Upward feedback.
2. 360 Degree Feedback.
3. Self-directed 360 assessments.

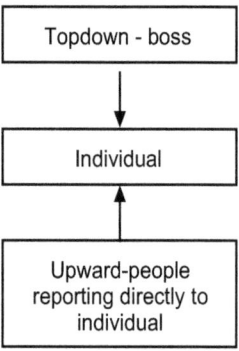

Fig. 4.23

Upward Feedback :

This is a reasonably well-established and widely used method which extends the traditional top-down appraisal'. It enables people who report directly to an individual to comment on the performance of their boss.

360 Degree Feedback :

This approach involves a number of individuals :

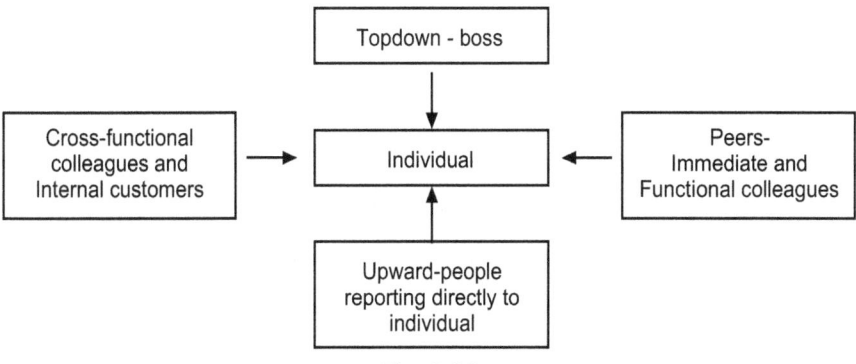

Fig. 4.24

With this approach, the individual, for whom feedback will be provided, is actively involved; they will be required to complete a self-rating questionnaire in addition to receiving feedback from a number of sources. The individual's manager, and perhaps other managers who have experience of the individual's work, will complete appropriate instruments, as will colleagues and people who report directly to the individual.

With this approach, feedback may be sought from other colleagues either from within the same team or work unit, or from different parts of the organisation. This approach is increasingly being extended to involve feedback from internal customers, although external customers are rarely included. In the main, 360 Degree Feedback is primarily intra-organisational and tends to focus on managerial input and consider managerial behaviors. It tends to be operated and initiated by the organization rather than the individual.

Self-directed 360 Assessments :

This variant extends the benefits of a standard 360 degree approach by including a process for getting face-to-face feedback directly from those who have given it. The individual can choose the performance issue on which they require feedback.

Basically, this approach is a full circle evaluation using self-evaluation and feedback from others about performance/achievements in pre-identified areas of skill or competence.

The key components of the 360 degree process all affect its success. They are :
1. The organization's climate.
2. The individual for whom feedback is being sought.
3. The people who provide feedback (the raters).
4. The instrument(s) used to collect feedback.
5. The method chosen for presenting the feedback received from the raters, this may involve outside consultants or facilitators.

Also and most importantly, for a 360 degree to work, the organisation needs to have clarified carefully :

1. What it expects to achieve by and from the 360 degree process.
2. What it will do with the results and how it will handle the outcomes.
3. The guidance and training it will provide for all individuals involved.
4. The resources, financial and otherwise, to be made available.

The organization needs to be clear about how it will handle such issues as :

1. A conflict between individual and organisational needs.
2. Individuals who are reluctant to take part.
3. Individuals who are damaged or disturbed by the process and/or the feedback received.

The Individual From Whom Feedback is being Sought :

Generally, 360 Degree Feedback, whether used for performance evaluation or for the personal development of the individual involved, makes demands on the 'central' or participating individual which extend far beyond those made by traditional Appraisal Systems. The 360 degree system requires the individual to :

There is evidence that in some organisations individuals have felt threatened by having to receive such extensive feedback.

Questions for the organization include :

1. Are the individuals involved competent to carry out effective self-assessment?
2. Will training be necessary?
3. Are arrangements to ensure anonymity and confidentiality in place? Are they thorough?
4. Is HR prepared, competent and equipped to put in place necessary development resulting from feedback?
5. Are line managers supportive and willing to aid development?
6. Are any groups or individuals likely to feel particularly threatened by the 360 system?

The People Who Provide the Feedback (The Raters) :

Those groups who can be expected to provide feedback as part of a 360 Degree Feedback system are identified. Specific individuals within these groups will need to be identified and approached for feedback. The organisation will need to decide how many views they want in order to build a comprehensive range of feedback on performance. One government department using a 360 degree approach to leadership specified that between eight and 10 colleagues, in addition to the individual's boss, would be selected by the individual and asked to provide feedback on a pre-prepared, numerically-rated questionnaire on an annual basis.

As a general rule, those requested to provide feedback should have a stake in the individual's performance i.e. their own role should be affected by the way the individual carries out their work and by the standard of their performance. Those contributing feedback will normally be line manager, peers, and direct reports, self and internal customers.

The Line Manager:

The line manager involved can be either the immediate or functional boss. Sometimes further managers may be involved, for example, in a matrix organisation or where project teams are used.

In general, the line manager can most usefully comment on work results and output, as well as have an input on leadership and team working abilities, ability to manage self and others (including upwards) organisational awareness and ability to operate effectively.

Peers:

These can be immediate colleagues or people at a similar level in other parts of the organisation. Such individuals can offer useful information on the individual's influence and negotiating ability, their openness, and their dependability.

The individual at the centre of the 360 degree process will often be required to determine who, amongst their peers, will be asked to provide feedback. The temptation for some people will be to ask 'friends' or those who are positively inclined. This may not be the best way of receiving a true range of feedback. In preparing and training people to take part in 360 degree systems the issue of choosing peers to give feedback needs to be addressed, as does the value of receiving a full range of feedback rather than just positive comments.

Direct Reports :

People who work for and report directly to the individual involved can give useful and valid information on their leadership and people management ability, the relevance of objectives agreed, levels of support and contribution to the direct reports development. The individual may have a large number of direct reports. In this case decisions will have to be made about whom and how many are to be required to provide feedback. If the organisation makes the choice it may wish to categorize the direct reports in some ways :

- new and longer serving individuals

- people who have good or less good working relationships with the individuals.
- male or female.
- Experienced or inexperienced staff.

Working with such distinctions would ensure a good range of perceptions. Where the participant is to make the final choice they will need to be informed of 'pros' and 'cons' and helped to understand the need for honest, complete feedback.

Self :

The individual also completes a questionnaire on their own performance. This helps them think through their own performance, as well as providing a basis for comparing their perceptions with those of the raters involved.

Rating of one's own performance can be difficult and if a 360 degree system is to be introduced those who will be the subject of rating and feedback need to be trained and equipped not only to use the system, but to carry out effective self-assessment.

Internal Customers :

'Off-the-shelf' questionnaires can be bought for completion by internal customers who can offer useful information on inter-group collaboration, customer focus and appropriate/inappropriate behaviors.

Selecting the Raters :

There are different opinions about and approaches to identifying those who will be asked as peers or direct reports to provide feedback. The spectrum is :

Individual selects Raters	HR and individual formally select Raters	Individual and their line manager jointly select Raters	Line Manager also selects Raters

Fig. 4.25

Each option has both advantages and disadvantages; the choice of option needs to be made based on a range of issues :

1. What the system is to achieve.
2. How prepared and competent those involved in the system are.
3. The number of raters needed to give a valid result.
4. The benefit people believe will accrue from feedback.

It is vitally important that the people identified to give feedback must be credible to the recipient if they are to act on the feedback received. It is also important that the confidentiality and anonymity of raters is maintained and their feedback delivered sensitively.

A questionnaire has most impact, and is easier to use, when it asks about the detail of a specific job. For example, one large insurance company uses a questionnaire for its sales force. It asks about the planning of sales campaigns, quality of technical advice offered to clients, use of sales support staff and other specific job-related issues. The questionnaire is 100% relevant to job performance and is written in language which is clear and relevant to the job holders and their raters.

Many 360 degree questionnaires contain generic questions based on definitions of competences rather than job tasks and the rater has to work out their relevance. One bad example of such a question is, '... fully commits him/herself to achieving according to circumstances'.

4.8.4 Key Features of the Human Resource Planning Management Model

The Resource Management Model enables companies to manage human resource deployment and capacity for project work. Resource Management empowers key project stakeholders, such as project managers, resource managers, and staffing managers, to make optimal use of their single most critical asset.

Some key features of modern Resource Management Systems are as follows :

1. Schedule automatic nomination of candidates, or nominate yourself or your staff for open requirements.
2. Rank candidates based on score and automatically notify qualified or available resources of requirements.

Define requirements for resources including competencies, availability, job levels, and location:

1. Advertise open requirements.
2. Find the right people for the right project at the right time.
3. Portal orientation for key roles and a personal staffing home page.
4. Secure functions based on project role or organization Streamline assignment process through automated approvals.
5. Borrow, lend and manage global resources.
6. View planned and actual utilization information by individual or organization.
7. Generate budgets or forecasts.

Fig. 4.26

4.9 OSHA

Occupational Safety and Health Act (OSHA) : What you need to know:

The federal Occupational Safety and Health Act (OSH Act) was designed to "assure, as far as possible, every working man and woman in the nation safe working conditions and to preserve our human resources." It attempts to achieve this end through a set of uniform national standards for workplace safety and health practices throughout the country.

The U.S. Department of Labor/Occupational Safety and Health Administration (OSHA) was given the power by Congress to administer and enforce the standards and make surprise inspections to ensure that employers adhere to the regulations of occupational safety and health established by the OSH Act.

For a Limited Time receive a FREE HR Report on the "Critical HR Recordkeeping". This exclusive special report covers hiring records, employment relationships, termination records, litigation issues, electronic information issues, tips for better recordkeeping, and a list of legal requirements.

The OSH Act governs occupational safety and health in the private employment sector (private businesses and nonprofit organizations). The OSH Act applies to all workplaces and activities involved in interstate commerce, regardless of the number of employees; in general industry, construction, maritime, and agriculture. The term "interstate commerce" is given a very liberal interpretation, making the OSH Act applicable to all enterprises, with some specific exemptions. Workplace safety and health at federal facilities are governed by each federal agency's own rules. Other public sector employers (state, county, and local government offices and operations) are governed by state rules in states that have public sector rules.

Exemptions: The following employers are not covered by the OSH Act :
1. Self-employed persons.
2. Farms at which only immediate members of the farmer's family are employed.
3. Working conditions regulated by other federal agencies under other federal statutes, including mining, nuclear energy.

Why was OSHA Created?

Congress enacted the Occupational Safety and Health Act of 1970 which created the Occupational Safety and Health Administration (OSHA). Its mission is to help employers and employees reduce on the job injuries, illnesses and deaths.

OSHA directs national compliance initiatives in occupational safety and health. Through the methods described below, OSHA helps business protect their workers and reduce the number of workplace deaths, injuries and illnesses. When employees stay safe and healthy, companies can reduce workers' compensation insurance costs and medical expenses, decreased payout for return-to-work programs, reduce faulty products, and lower costs for job accommodations for injured workers. Indirectly, additional benefits such as increased productivity, lower training costs due to fewer replacement workers and decreased costs for overtime have also been attributed to OSHA's research and guidance.

What does OSHA do?

OSHA employs the following strategies to help employers and employees reduce injuries, illnesses, and deaths on the job :
1. **Enforcement :** Making sure OSHA Regulations are followed.
2. **Assistance :** Outreach and training to employers and employees.
3. **Cooperation :** Partnerships and alliances through voluntary programs.

OSHA promotes workplace safety and health by :
1. Implementing new (or improved) safety and health management systems.
2. Completing worksite inspections. Companies failing to OSHA Regulations may be cited and/or fined.
3. Promoting cooperative programs including Voluntary Protection Programs, OSHA Strategic Partnerships, and other industry Alliances.
4. Establishing specific rights and responsibilities of employees and employers.
5. Supporting innovation in dealing with workplace hazards.
6. Establishing recordkeeping and reporting requirements for employers.
7. Developing training programs for occupational safety and health personnel.
8. Partnering with states that operate their own occupational safety and health programs.
9. Supporting the OSHA Consultation Program.

Are We Required to Comply?

The OSH Act covers private sector employers/employees in the 50 states, the District of Columbia, Puerto Rico, the Virgin Islands, American Samoa, Guam, Northern Mariana Islands, Wake Island, Johnston Island, and the Outer Continental Shelf Lands as defined in the Outer Continental Shelf Lands Act.

The OSH Act covers employers and employees either directly through Federal OSHA or through an OSHA-approved state program.

Federal Worker Coverage :

Although OSHA completes worksite inspections for federal agencies, section 19 of the OSH Act makes federal agency heads responsible for providing safe and healthful working conditions for their employees and must comply with standards consistent with private sector employees.

OSHA Approved State Plans :

Twenty two states have optioned to develop their own safety and health programs. The state plans must be at least as effective as Federal OSHA requirements. State plans covering the private sector also must cover state and local government employees. NOTE : The Connecticut and Virgin Islands plans cover public sector (state and local government) employment only.

What are OSHA regulations?

In general, OSHA regulations (also referred to as "standards") require employers :
1. Maintain conditions and/or adopt practices necessary and appropriate to protect workers on the job.

2. Be familiar with and comply with standards applicable to their establishments.
3. Ensure that employees have and use personal protective equipment when required for safety and health.

In addition, the OSH Act instituted a "general duty clause" (Section 5(a) (1) which "requires that each employer "furnish ... a place of employment which [is] free from recognized hazards that are causing or are likely to cause death or serious physical harm to his employees."

Personally, I have found it helpful to divide OSHA regulations into Six Management Centers. These centers are non-binding and of my own creation simply to help employers group general, commonly cited hazards into larger categories. Some of the sections in the Six Centers apply to OSHA specific regulations. Others may fall under the General Duty Clause; others still just make common sense and should be addressed. Please note that this list does not address every OSHA regulation and every industry. It is a general guideline only. The Six Management Centers include Administrative Safety, Exposure Control, Personal Protection, Facility Safety, Tools and Equipment, and Behaviors and Attitudes. A brief description of each center and safety topics related to each follows :

Administrative Safety :

What are the tools you need to administer a safety and health program at your workplace?

1. **Safety Program Development :** How do you set up a safety program and make sure your team buys into it?
2. **Accident Investigations :** How do you deal with an accident after the fact? How do you prevent similar accidents from occurring again?
3. **Emergency Planning :** How do you plan for the unexpected? How do you teach your employees how to handle any emergency situation that may appear?
4. **OSHA Recordkeeping :** What are OSHA's recordkeeping requirements and what must be done to comply?
5. **Safety Audits :** How do you regularly review your workplace, equipment, tools, and materials to ensure all hazards have been addressed?
6. **State and Federal Posting Requirements :** What are the Federal, State, and industry specific posting requirements that must be met at all of your work areas?

Exposure Control :

How do you prevent your employees from the exposure to hazards?

1. **Asbestos Safety :** How do you protect your employees from asbestos exposure?

2. **Blood borne Pathogens** : How do you protect your employees from blood related exposure, including needle stick injuries?
3. **Hazardous Materials** : How do you teach your employees how to read and understand hazardous material labeling? How do you put preventive measures in place so employees know how to deal with hazardous spills?
4. **Hot and Cold Working Conditions** : How do you prevent your employees from exposure to the risk of hot or cold work environments?
5. **Lead Safety** : How do you mitigate employee exposure to lead?
6. **Right to Know/Hazard Communications** : Are your employees and site visitors aware of the hazardous materials in your workplace? Do they understand how to protect themselves from these hazards?
7. **Material Safety Data Sheets** : Can your employees read and understand the MSDS forms for the materials they use?
8. **Tuberculosis** : Are your employees protected from Tuberculosis?

Personal Protection :

How do you use protective equipment to protect your employees?

1. **Back Safety** : How do you protect your employees from normal day-to-day activities that may result in back injury?
2. **Eye Safety** : Do you have sufficient protection in place to care for the eye safety of your employees?
3. **Fall Protection** : Do you and your employees understand and correctly implement OSHA fall protection standards?
4. **First Aid** : What are the requirements as prescribed by OSHA for first aid training and aid stations?
5. **Hand, Wrist, and Finger Safety** : How do you protect your employees from hand, wrist, and finger injuries while on the job?
6. **Hearing Safety** : Do you require a hearing conservation program at your workplace?
7. **Personal Protective Equipment** : Have you thoroughly reviewed all your work processes and determined if personal protective equipment is required?
8. **Respiratory Protection** : Do your employees work in environments requiring respiratory protection? Are your employees properly trained to the use and maintenance of these protection devices?
9. **Safety Showers and Eyewashes** : Do you follow OSHA specific requirements for safety showers and eyewashes?

Facility Safety :

How do you make sure your facilities are safe for your employees and visitors?

1. **Confined Spaces :** Do you require a confined space program at your workplace?
2. **Electrical Safety :** Have you established an electrical safety plan at your workplace and put preventive measures in place?
3. **Ergonomics :** Have you addressed ergonomics related injuries in both your production and office environments?
4. **Fire Safety :** Do you have the correct fire extinguishers in your office? Are they properly maintained? Do your employees know what to do in case of a fire?
5. **Indoor Air Quality :** Have you monitored your work areas for indoor air quality problems? Do you know what to look for and how to address potential risks?
6. **Lockout Tag out :** Do you have controls in place to protect workers from the accidental exposure to energy sources?
7. **Material Handling :** Do your employees know how to handle job related materials? Do they properly use/understand the tools available to aid in material handling while reducing the risk for loss or injury?
8. **Office Safety :** Do you have an office safety plan in place? Are you sure everything you need is included?
9. **Slips, Trips, and Falls :** Do you monitor walking and working surfaces for hazards that may result in slips, trips, or falls?

Tools and Equipment :

How do you ensure your team knows how to safely use and maintain the tools and equipment at your workplace?

1. **Compressed Gases :** Do your employees know/understand how to safely use compressed gas cylinders?
2. **Computer Safety :** Do you have protective measures in place to address the repetitive injury issues associated with computers?
3. **Crane Safety :** Does your team know/understand how to operate and work around your cranes? Do you have a crane safety program and checklists in place to prevent accidents and injuries?
4. **Driving Safety :** Have you adopted a defensive driving program for your drivers?
5. **Forklift Safety :** Do you have certified forklift drivers at your workplace? Have other team members exposed to forklifts been trained how to effectively work around them?
6. **Hand and Power Tool Safety :** Have your employees been trained how to safely use the hand and power tools required for their jobs?

7. **Ladder Safety** : Do your employees know how to select the correct ladder for the job?
8. **Machine Guarding** : Do you regularly inspect your workplace to ensure all machine guarding is in place and not removed? Do you follow maintenance recommendations on your equipment to ensure guarding is functioning properly?
9. **Rigging Safety** : Do your employees know/understand correct rigging procedures?
10. **Scaffolding Safety** : Do you have supported/suspended scaffolding procedures in place?
11. **Welding Safety** : Are your employees trained to the safety precautions identified by OSHA for the various types of welding activities? Do you feel your employees are safe while working around welders?

Behavior and Attitude :

How do you address the behaviors of employees and workplace visitors that may have an adverse effect on the safety and health of your team?

1. **Conflict Resolution** : How does your organization deal with conflict? Left to fester, workplace conflict can cause many problems; one of the worst is a lack of focus on the work at hand.
2. **Drug and Alcohol Abuse** : Do you have drug and alcohol prevention policies established?
3. **Fitness and Wellness** : Do you promote the fitness and health of your employees?
4. **Harassment** : How does your firm deal with employee and sexual harassment? Do you have measures in place to help protect employees from harassment?
5. **Safety Housekeeping** : Do you have a clean workplace? Have you trained your employees of the hazards of the "work around"?
6. **Safety Orientations** : Have you developed a thorough safety orientation program that addresses all the work processes an employee is responsible to perform and the safety precautions they are required to take?
7. **Workplace Stress** : Have you addressed issues associated with job stress and provide enough relief to employees to make sure stress does not expose them to other safety hazards?
8. **Workplace Violence** : Do you have a violence protection policy in place at your workplace?

What Must We do to Comply?

Employers have specific responsibilities under OSHA they must perform to ensure the safety and health of their workers. The following list is a summary of the most important ones :

1. Comply with OSHA Regulations – keep your workplace free from serious recognized hazards.
2. Monitor your workplace conditions to make sure they conform to OSHA standards.
3. Make sure tools and equipment are properly maintained prior to employee use.
4. Identify hazards for your employees by using color codes, posters, labels and signs.
5. Develop/maintain safe operating procedures and train employees follow the requirements.
6. Provide medical examinations and training when required by OSHA standards.
7. Post the OSHA Poster (or the state-plan equivalent) informing employees of their rights and responsibilities at a prominent location within the workplace.
8. Report any fatal accident or one that results in the hospitalization of three or more employees to the nearest OSHA office within 8 hours.
9. Keep records of work-related injuries and illnesses. and give employees, former employees, and their representative's access to the OSHA Log of Work-Related Injuries and Illnesses (OSHA Form 300).
10. Provide employee medical and exposure records to employees or their authorized representatives upon their request.
11. Identify authorized employee representatives who may be asked to accompany the OSHA compliance officer during an inspection.
12. Do not discriminate against employees who exercise their rights under the Act.
13. Post OSHA citations at or near the work area involved until the violation has been corrected, or for three working days, whichever is longer.
14. Correct violations by the deadline set in the OSHA citation and submit required verification documentation.

4.10 PAYROLL

4.10.1 Introduction

Payroll is core to the organization as employees are receptive to payroll blunders and irregularities : to continuously manage good spirits in employees requires payroll to be paid in a precisely and timely manner. The essential objective of the payroll branch is to guarantee that all workers are paid precisely and opportune with the right withholdings and derivations, and to guarantee the withholdings and deductions are transmitted in a time-bound way. This incorporates compensation installments, taxation, and the various deductions.

Payroll is important on the grounds that it significantly influences the net salary of most organizations and they are liable to laws and regulations. Thus it is extremely essential to an organization from an accounting viewpoint.

4.10.2 Key Components of Payroll Management Module

The computerization of payroll estimations for wages, rewards, and different manifestations of recompense, in light of client characterized views is empowered by the Payroll administration application. This Software is intended to provide solutions to the whole range of organizational payroll prerequisites guaranteeing exact, speedier and effective payroll transforming. It expedites the designing of payroll parts, for example compensation, rewards, or different types of recompense, direct taxes, and deductions. It empowers the arrangement of payroll transforming consistent with the enterprise's strategies and guarantees that payroll methodology is successful, correct and dependable.

Payroll Management Application : Core Benefits

The module for Payroll Management empowers the precise and quicker preparing of payroll data. Pick up better control over critical investment funds in both cash and time and payroll related information. Effectively support and apply payment arrangements for diverse worker segments dependent upon rank level and designation. Help them to effortlessly access payroll data with complete parts incorporating winning portions, conclusions, expenses and increasingly through ESS (employee self-service). The application facilitates the creation of pay slips for workers in helpful document designs.

Following are the critical components of this module :
1. Employee Profiling System.
2. Time Management System.
3. Payroll Management System.
4. Employee Transfer, Promotions and Increments.
5. Income Tax Management (TDS).
6. Report Generation System.

1. Employee Profiling System:

This framework empowers people in the company to upgrade their individual data by means of the software application, instead of completing hard-copy duplicates. The Employee Profile framework empowers people in the organization to view their

Appointment and Biographic data, and permits them the capacity to change their residential details and some biographic information on the web.

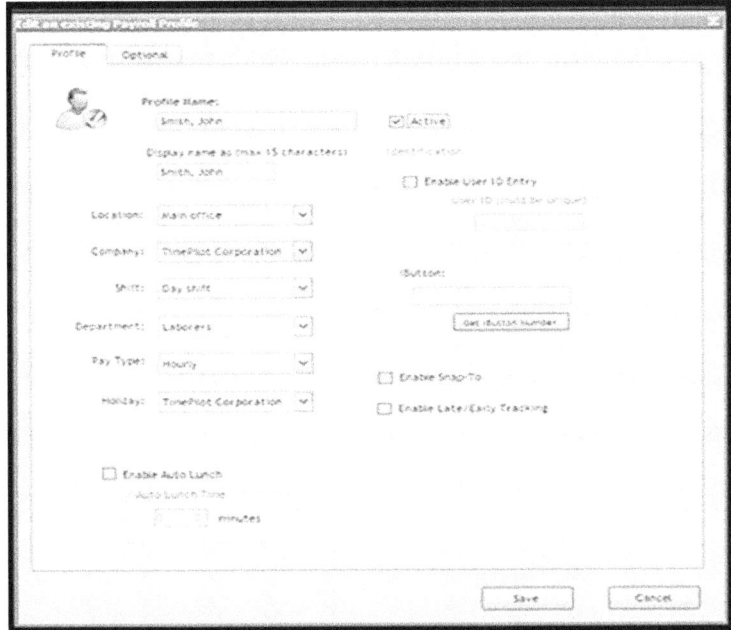

Fig. 4.27 : Screenshot of editing an existing payroll profile

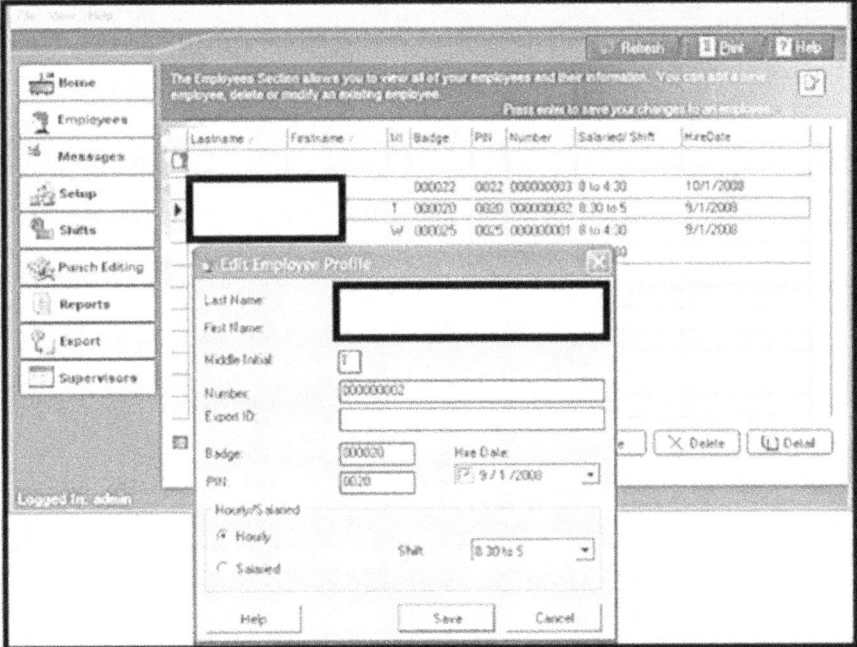

Fig. 4.28 : Screenshot of editing an existing payroll profile for attendance purpose

2. Time Management System:

Today's organizations demand requisition related to attendance and time-keeping that takes care of industry-particular and worldwide time and participation needs. To empower better proficiency, the software should go about as a solitary storehouse of time-keeping that courses of action all manage necessities while joining to the diverse branches, for example the Sales and Marketing, RandD, Technology, Procurement, Distribution, assembling, and Marketing frameworks.

Productive Time Management Application might as well Empower Enterprises to :

(i) Streamlining drawn out procedures and enhancing worker productivity.

(ii) Merging dissimilar old applications to decrease organizational expenses.

(iii) Support better choice making with organizational investigation of work information.

(iv) Automating complex time pay-rate calculations and capture in-turn reducing gross payroll costs.

(v) Increase client fulfillment in a cost-effective manner.

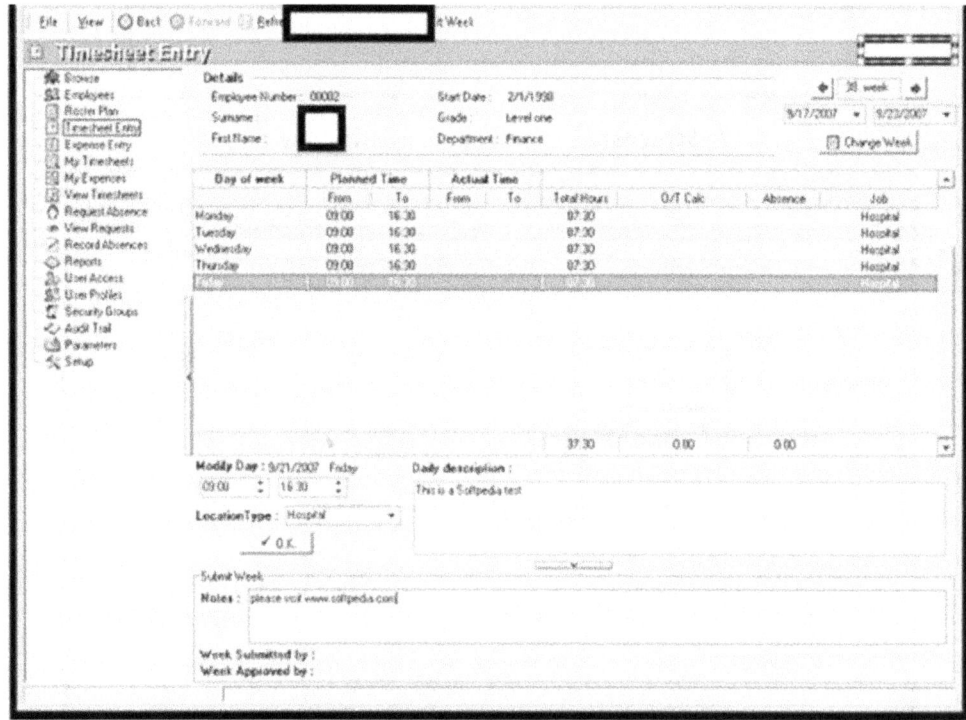

Fig. 4.29 : Snapshot of Time Sheet Entry

3. Payroll Management Systems:

Payroll software ought to be intended with the end goal of keeping up items of different remittances and deductions that should be given to the workers of the enterprise. It might as well offer exceptionally high adaptability in characterizing different remittances, derivations, and leave tenets and so on for the workers and all calculation parameters for P.F.; Tax etc. are perceptible and variably at users end. Additionally, it may as well create the compensation sheet that supports the accounts division from various perspectives.

Some of the Key features of Payroll Management Software are provided below :
 (i) Configure Payroll Components
 (ii) Create Payroll Templates
 (iii) Assign Payroll Templates
 (iv) Generate Payroll
 (v) View Payroll Reports
 (vi) Employee Self Service

4. Employee and Industrial Relations :

The modules for Payroll Management Software also should define the sub-modules related to the requirements of the employees in the enterprise such as Transfer, Promotions and Increments. Some of the key sub-modules that need to be included are:
 (i) **Annual Increment :** Should enable the calculation of Annual increment
 (ii) **Performance Increment :** Should enable the increment based on Performance.
 (iii) **Ad hoc Increment :** Increment that can be given any time.
 (iv) **Promotion :** Give Promotion to Employees. Facility to define Promotion Date.
 (v) **Re-designation :** Facility to re-designate an Employee.

5. Income Tax Management (TDS):

The modules for Payroll Management Software also should define the sub-modules related to the Income Tax Management requirements of the employees in the enterprise. Many predefined reports should be generated available for use; In addition, option is also available to configure and generate user defined reports. The reporting formats should also cater to income tax and other legal reporting requirements like generation of Monthly/ Yearly Statements, Tax Challan, Salary Certificates, and more.

6. Report Generation System:

The Payroll Software can generate different reports as per the user requirements. The three groups that cover these reports are Employee Reports, Pay related Reports and General Reports. The following is the list of some of the reports generated by most of the HRIS applications :
 (i) H.R. Reports, Employee list, Employee detail.
 (ii) Taxation Reports, P.F Reports, P.F/ PT Statement, Challan Report.
 (iii) Salary Reports, Pay Slip, Monthly Summary Report, Salary Summary.
 (iv) P.F. Challan Report, P. F. FORMS Form 5a, 5, 10.

4.11 SHORT CASE STUDIES

Case 1 : Adrenalin Case Study

HDFC HDFCSL was a 4 year old company in January 2004, when the decision to buy an HCMS was taken. This was done keeping in mind the expansive growth plans the company had in terms of employee strengthwww.hdfcinsurance.com and geographical spread, to drive the company's business targets for the next few years. The expectation from the HCMS was a value proposition to support HDFCSLs plan in terms of real time and correct data availability across locations, process consistency with minimal turn-around time, transparent communication, clear accountability of process owners and driving process efficiency for a fast increasing workforce.

Their processes on Lotus, Excel and paper had been serving them well for the start-up employee strength in the past 4 years but an HCMS was imperative for the future business plans to fructify. The Adrenalin Solution Basic HRMS, Selection & Recruitment and Performance Management module to suit HDFCSL processes Benefits Adrenalin was installed in a phased manner, one module at a time, across the organization starting March 2005. In the last 3 years 18 modules were installed, each one aligning to and considerably enhancing the organization's existing processes to align to the best in the industry.

Some of the benefits accrued are as follows :
1. Effective talent planning.
2. Decentralized offer making to regional offices – Reducing TAT's from 5 days to 3 minutes for offer generation, consistency and control over Role based CTC structure, online employee creation, appointment letter generation and extensive data on recruitment.
3. Enables the completion of appraisal exercise for a 9000+ strong population in less than 15 working days Confirmation, Leave, Attendance, Nominations for benefit schemes, Role player and cluster framework, Automated OUs and Calendar mapping were some of the other main modules that brought about better and easy management of HDFCSL's huge workforce.

Today Adrenalin is used by 12000 employees spread across 374 locations.

Case 2 : Doctrina Learning Solutions:

The Client:

Located in the UK, Doctrina is learning solutions companies specializing in creating unique solutions that help improve performance through better learning. With primary focus on learning management, its portfolio includes custom learning, mobile learning and blended learning solutions, maintenance and support services plus a managed service for start-ups and SMEs.

The End Client:

Jangro is a dynamic force in the cleaning supply industry and has the largest network of independent janitorial distributors in the UK and Ireland. It provides excellent service and the highest levels of quality, choice, training and technical support attainable including up-to-date Safety data sheets.

Business Need:

For one of its clients, Jangro, Doctrina needed a unified learning system which had the capabilities of both – a Learning Management System (for desktop delivery) and a Mobile Learning Platform (for mobile delivery). The need for the unified system stemmed from a genuine challenge that Jangro faced.

Given the large network of independent distributors and dealers, one of the biggest challenges that Jangro faced was training its employees and dealer executives, and keeping them updated with its latest products.

Solution:

To address the mixed structure of Jangro's user base, Doctrina and Upside Learning together devised a unique approach – integrating Upside LMS, Upside Learning's multi award-winning Learning Management System, with Upside2Go, Upside Learning's revolutionary mobile learning platform. This integrated solution, branded in line with the company's name – 'Jangro', proved to be the right fit for Jangro's needs.

For its internal employees who were typically in an office environment, Jangro used the Learning Management System end (Upside LMS) to deliver training on desktops. While for its dealer executives, Upside2Go was used to deliver training in the form of HTML courses, videos, podcasts flashcards etc. on mobile devices.

To offer a complete and a unified experience to administrators and users vis-à-vis separate backend management of content, delivery and reporting, additional integrations were done in the administrator interface and the system backend.

The Jangro app is available in iOS, Android and Blackberry versions so that it can be deployed across various mobile operating systems. This also ensures that Jangro can target a wide cross section of its users irrespective of the mobile devices they use.

Business Benefits:

1. **Increased operational efficiency** : The Jangro app ensured that the administrators could deliver and manage all training (be it on desktops or mobile devices) via a single unified interface
2. **Performance enhancement** : Just–in–time performance support brought in by the QR code module ensured that the learners could access all resources (PDFs/

courses/ videos/ podcasts) related to a product at the time of need leading to improvement in performance.

3. **Informed decision making :** Comprehensive reporting including a user's complete training profile with web and mobile training records in the unified transcripts enabled the admin to make informed decisions about the learner's training/learning.

Case 3 : Application of Multi-Rater Feedback Software in the Hospitality Industry

Regent Resorts and Holidays is one of the most well-known brands in the hospitality industry. With over 500 properties Regent is one of the world's largest holiday companies and one of the well-respected in the industry.

Industry Problem:

Regent wanted to provide a valuable developmental offering for all leaders across the global organization. The organization had considerable experience with Multi-rater feedback in the past but over the years had decided to refine their approach and had developed specific criteria for this initiative :

The senior management team accepted that to achieve the above goals, they needed to partner with a vendor who not only had extensive experience working with large global organizations but also had a very flexible technology and consulting experts who could advise along the way, (both in terms of Multi-rater survey design, as well as system customizations). Regent chose Tri-Axiom Solutions for this global Multi-rater feedback initiative.

Solution:

Tri-Axiom Solutions worked closely with Regent to clearly understand their objectives for this project. Most importantly, Regent wanted to provide leaders with valuable insight in terms of their unique strengths and development areas.

Tri-Axiom Solutions and Regent implemented a three-step process to achieve these objectives :

1. Design Multi-rater Survey Content
2. Configure a Customized, Multi-Lingual Solution
3. Provide Individual and Aggregate Reporting

Phase 1 : Design Multi-rater Review Applications

The first step in the Multi-rater feedback implementation process was to ensure the Multi-rater survey items not only included core leadership skills but also those constructs such as critical thinking, emotional intelligence and global perspective. Multi-rater Feedback is an incredible developmental opportunity, however balancing the leader's time commitment as a part of this process is crucial to maintaining leadership buy-in and sustaining an effective annual feedback process

Phase 2 : Design a Specialized, Application Catering to Multiple Languages

To ensure that the system was conFig.ured to best meet the needs of the management population, a pilot Multi-rater feedback program was conducted. This also allowed Regent to choose from a variety of Tri-Axiom Solutions system features which met their needs and would later serve as the settings for the global launch. Accuracy enhancers to ensure more variability in the data and the ability for raters to highlight specific items as strengths and development areas were some of the features chosen.

Step 3 : Provide Individual and Aggregate Reporting

Providing individuals as well as division leaders with actionable talent data were the most important objectives for Regent in this process. After all ratings were captured, Tri-Axiom Solutions generated individual Multi-rater feedback reports that provided each individual with their strengths and areas for development.

Results:

The Human Resources team at Regent wanted this Multi-rater feedback data to provide their leaders, and the overall organization, with a solid foundation for making leadership development decisions. The Multi-rater feedback data allowed the team to address a variety of individual and organizational aspects including :

Individual Benefits :

1. A simple, easy-to-use Multi-rater feedback tool
2. A "self-paced" Multi-rater feedback report complete with targeted questions to guide the leader through the process of uncovering strengths and development areas.
3. Specific interpretive tables and graphs in the feedback report which helped leaders analyze their data.
4. A downloadable discussion guide for report recipients and their managers – what to focus on, how to lead and focus the discussion, and how to deal with emotions/defensiveness.

Organizational Benefits :

1. Competency/skill strengths and development areas across division and employee level
2. By better understanding the skill mix across the organization, Regent was able to more effectively leverage the leadership strengths and refocus efforts where developmental opportunities may exist.
3. In addition, having specific data for each division allowed Regent to target local training efforts thereby saving precious resources.
4. Each divisional leader received an analysis of their division's results so they can take specific actions on the data and have a better understanding of the team strengths/development areas.

Case 4 : Yaware - A web-based Time Tracking System

Introduction

Yaware is a web-based time tracking system for controlling your employees' productivity on the computer. The company is mainly targeted at Russian-speaking countries.

Yaware is a web-based time management and analytics tool. It allows you to control employees' productivity on the computer, track their work time, uncover working trends in separate departments, define the productivity of each work day, etc. You can effectively motivate your personnel and significantly increase your company's output.

Business Challenges:

Yaware is a quite new service. Yaware team was inclined to explore the market, investigate user preferences, identify the course of user-program interaction, and define the most utilized features. They needed a smart tool for collecting all the essential information in one place. It was important to see what countries the customers come from and what sections are used the most. We liked to have all the information about software usage in one place ready and organized.

"Software Statistics Service provides me with a complete overview of my software usage. It allows identifying main problem areas and finding opportunities for program improvement. It also helps to anticipate user's behavior and create effective marketing campaigns".

Serge Savchyshyn, Technical Director of Yaware.

Solution:

Yaware team started using Software Statistics Service, a tool that collects software usage details and transforms them into a range of graphs and diagrams. "We needed to have all the data about our product collected together. By that time, customer feedback and some other semi-automated procedures were the only sources of this type of information. Now we get detailed statistics about the software usage in no time," says Serge Savchyshyn.

Benefits:

With Software Statistics Service Yaware team has discovered the actual user location. It turned out that quite a bit of their users came from the United States, while all promotion campaigns were focused on Russian-speaking countries. "With SSS we learned which software functions were the most and the least "popular". We implemented a few timings to determine which program areas need improving. At this point, there are a lot of things to address," says Serge Savchyshyn.

Influence on Business:

Software Statistics Service helped Yaware team not only to identify the main program issues, but to change the overall priorities in the company. "Now we have the perfect solution to identify our major problem areas and we are definitely going to use it for all our software products."

Activities

1. Some of the benefits of the HRIS in the context of selection have been displayed through the use of a diagram. Enlist and describe at least five more benefits by surfing the Internet.
2. Refer to the information available online and provide more insight on the key features of Vendor Management System. Also research on systems used in medium scale manufacturing in this context.
3. By surfing the internet resources www.chrt.com, research for Leave and Attendance Manager HRIS Software which provides flexibility to the small-scale Organizations.
4. Refer to the information available online on above site and provide more insight on the key benefits of Leave Management System.
5. By surfing the internet www.peoplesoft.com, resources research for any two HRIS Software which provides the functionality of Key Performance Indicator processing to the mid-scale Organizations.
6. Refer to the information available online on above site and provide more insight on the advances in the field of the 360 degrees module of Performance Management System.
7. By utilizing the web-based resources www.acm.org, study three Time Management applications in the Sales and Marketing domain in medium-sized enterprises.

Summary

In this chapter, we have discussed about requirements Leave Management System (LMS) in HRIS and also its key features. Leave is an entitlement provided to the employees and accumulates in an automated manner. Hence, errors in the work input, leave count, and diligence in the work of an employee are a few less things you don't need to worry about keeping track of.

Some of the key features of LMS are :

1. Leave privilege records might be transferred and loaded into the system.
2. No programming customization needed for leave procedures.
3. Email notification feature will be integrated to alert requestor on leave approval status.
4. Online requisition for leave without any hard copies or files.

Employees can apply for leave online and have their requests for planned type of leaves, sent to their manager and the Human Resource department. The system creates vital reports, for example documents such as taxation forms and transfer forms letters. Workflow communicates with the leave database to display employee leave history when the employee is using the system.

Leave is proposed to permit the employee recreation, travel, vacation and rest and is duration of absence with pay from official duties in an approved manner. Leave is also proposed for the person's emergency or personal issues and also to extend the time available to the employee under some other leave programs. Numerous Leave Management provisions today accompany inbuilt practicality of liaising with the Payroll System for deducting the measure of leaves of the unpaid category that the worker has availed. Job times for work classifications might be set and reused throughout the organization. Intuitive client interfaces are custom-made to suit the unique needs of various important entities like HR Managers, operational supervisors, HR experts, supervisors and Team Managers. Some of the Key benefits of Leave Management Module are :

1. Exponential decrease in HR interference.
2. Accessible at any time and at any location.
3. Capability of identifying potential problems associated with absenteeism in advance and plan for backup coverage.

In this chapter we have discussed about HRIS Systems for Performance Management Module. Performance Management is a framework and methodology that connects the enterprises objectives and systems to singular and group performance in order to expand enterprise adequacy.

The Module on Performance Management furnishes senior administrators and executives with, dependable, time-bound and correct data on performance at a location, a department, or over the whole business. When the information is gathered more assets and exertion are needed with a specific end goal to present and provide details regarding performance. Some of the Key Features of Module on Performance Management:

1. Ability to communicate with personnel through different sub-modules.
2. Created on performance results or decisive plans performs budgeting activities.
3. Manage staff performance.
4. Training and development requirement determination in a precise manner.

Most Business owners would admit that gathering KPI information can take an excessive measure of time, to add to that examining and writing about that KPI data. What's more once this is carried out the KPI information is obsolete, it doesn't permit you to act in an opportune way on the data, restricting chances and intense advantage.

A performance appraisal is a methodical and ongoing procedure that evaluates the staff's performance at work and efficiency in connection to certain pre-set criteria and organizational targets.

With the assistance of the Employee execution administration programming the HR can overhaul Job/role Descriptions at whenever so supervisors and employees have the most recent forms at the click of the mouse in the framework, staff members can get access their own particular work related descriptions along these lines in the framework, while supervisors can see and print out those of all their immediate reports.

The employees are most often reviewed only by their managers.360 Degree Feedback is seen to offer a paradigm shift for hierarchical systems as organizations seek to adapt and improve systems of appraisal and feedback to ensure greater effectiveness and increased congruence with business aims and objectives. 360 Degree Feedback can help with :

1. Employee measurement.
2. People development.
3. Feedback.
4. Behaviour change.
5. Improved employee performance.

In this chapter, we have discussed about the HRIS Systems for Training and Development Functionality. The competitive business environment is forcing the HR professionals to optimize HR resources.

Getting employees involved in learning has always been a challenge. We often express frustration that company leaders do not attend courses, even courses that designed for them. And if they do, they often cannot participate fully, sometimes leaving early due to the pressing nature of business.

All learning management systems will require additional consulting, technical conFig.uration, and administrator training. Indeed, some training managers have horror stories of expensive, yearlong implementations caused by major data conversion and customization work. There are many providers of off-the-shelf Web-based training courses.

In this chapter we have also discussed about the Employee Profiling System and Time Management System and also the key features of Payroll Management System.

The critical components of payroll management module are
1. Employee Profiling System.
2. Time Management System.
3. Payroll Management System.
4. Employee Transfer, Promotions and Increments.

5. Income Tax Management (TDS).
6. Report Generation System.

The Employee Profile framework empowers people in the organization to view their Appointment and Biographic data, and permits them the capacity to change their residential details and some biographic information on the web.

The Payroll Software can generate different reports as per the user requirements. The three groups that cover these reports are Employee Reports, Pay related Reports and General Reports. The following is the list of some of the reports generated by most of the HRIS applications :

1. H.R. Reports, Employee list, Employee detail.
2. Salary Reports, Pay Slip, Monthly Summary Report, Salary Summary.

Self-assessment Questions

1. Performance Management is a framework that provides what type of functionality?
2. Enlist the steps involved in the process of Performance Management?
3. The Module on Performance Management furnishes senior administrators and executives with which kind of functionality?
4. Identify the organizational entity that have the discretion to decide when and in what amount leave may be approved?
5. Enlist some of the important critical functions which are seamlessly facilitated by today's Leave Management Software.
6. Enlist some of the key features of Leave Management Module?
7. Identify three important reasons why the Payroll function is considered core to the organization?
8. The Payroll Management Module is intended to provide which type of solutions to organizations?
9. Explain in brief how the module for Payroll Management empowers the precise and quicker preparing of payroll data?
10. Describe in a brief manner about the origin of the Learning management systems (LMSs)?

Chapter 5...

Other HRIS Applications
(Ancillary Modules in the HRIS System)

Objectives ...
After discussing this chapter, you will be able to :
- Define the Key Features and Benefits of Employee Self-service System
- Explain the Features of Key features of Policy and Procedures Model
- Explain the Key Features of Employee Self Service Intranet to Manage Hiring Lifecycle

Structure ...
5.1 Introduction
5.2 Key Features of Policy and Procedures Model
    5.2.1 Introduction
    5.2.2 Key Features of the Employee Self-Service Model
5.3 Employee Self Service Intranets to Manage Hiring Lifecycle
5.4 Short Case study: A Viva Goes Third-Generation
- Activities
- Summary
- Self-assessment Questions

5.1 INTRODUCTION

Recently, a second wave of ESS shifted the focus from these purely efficiency based applications towards empowering employees and managers to take more responsibility for their jobs and development. Career planning, skills profiles, learning, objective settings, appraisals and more and more analytics are increasingly popular ESS applications. This development is driven by improved technology, a better understanding of Human Resource Management (HRM) with a more hands off role of the HR department and by an increasingly web savvy workforce.

Fig 5.1

ESS is increasingly popular in the tertiary sector where there is a high proportion of the workforce with computer and internet access. The principal advantage for employers providing ESS is that it is a more efficient means of collecting changes to employee's details and distributing payroll related details to employees.

Examples of employee self-service uses include electronic pay stubs, electronic W-2s, emergency contact forms, employee policy signoffs and many more. HRM professionals increasingly value ESS as a means of empowering employees and reducing paperwork errors and cost. ESS is becoming increasingly popular as more companies 'go green' in an effort to reduce paper waste.

5.2 KEY FEATURES OF POLICY AND PROCEDURES MODEL

5.2.1 Introduction

There are a number of valid reasons for an employer to have written workplace policies and procedures in place. Such policies and procedures are useful documents to rely on when a legal dispute arises between the employer and an employee. In many cases, where the employer can point to a policy to show that the employee ought to have known what his or her responsibilities were in relation to the disputed matter, the employer is likely to be in a much stronger position before a court or tribunal, particularly relating to an unfair dismissal matter.

Legislative Requirements:

Some employment-related laws include a requirement for a policy to be in place and that the policy fulfills certain specifications. For example, occupational health and safety laws require an employer to put in place a rehabilitation policy outlining the responsibilities of the employer. No having such a policy constitutes an offence under WHS statutes.

Codes of Conduct:

Many companies have policies relating to matters that are not regulated by law, but which are based on standards set by the employer in an effort to ensure a high standard of behavior in the workplace.

Conditions of Employment:

There are a number of different conditions of employment that may not be prescribed by law, but which are agreed to by the employer and the employee at the commencement of the employment contract. Some companies issue policies on such matters so that employees are clear on what their rights and responsibilities are.

Employee Entitlements:

It is useful to develop policies on employee entitlements which are prescribed by an industrial instrument or employment legislation so that employees and human resources staff are able to ascertain what the entitlements are.

Employee Benefits:

An employer may provide a number of different benefits as part of their contract of employment. These are often not prescribed by legislation or an industrial instrument but are provided by the employer for the benefit of employees — sometimes as incentives aimed at increasing productivity and with the intention of attracting and retaining competent and qualified employees. Employee benefits that fall into this category include: company car, mobile phone (including private use), employee assistance programs, salary packaging, career breaks, and study assistance.

iHR provides a full-featured, cost-effective HRIS that empowers HR professionals and supervisors to effortlessly manage critical employee information on a day-to-day basis. It provides all of the leave and time management features of iLeave, adding personal information, licensing, education, reviews, certifications, equipment, COBRA and benefits.

The HR department becomes paperless with integrated Windows folders and organized with automatic reminders. Documents can be attached to employee records including MS Word files, e-mails, and scanned-in authorization forms. Mail merges MS Word form letters and e-mails. Individualize iHR by adding and renaming data fields so that you can track information that is specific to your organization.

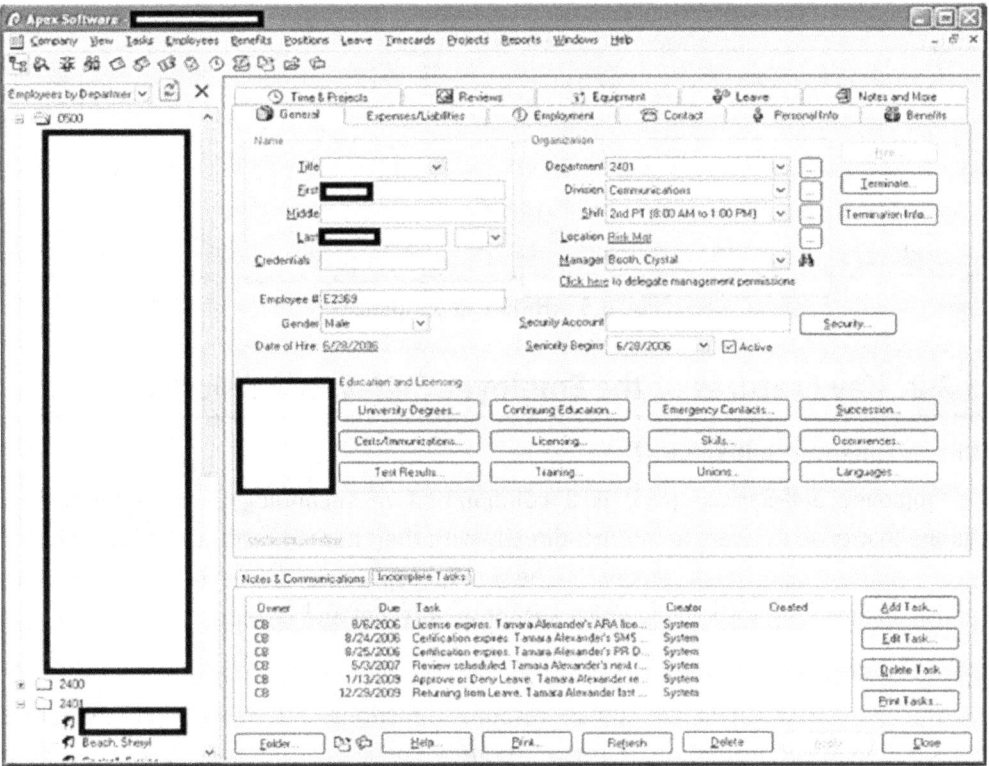

Fig 5.2 : iHRIS ESS Snapshots

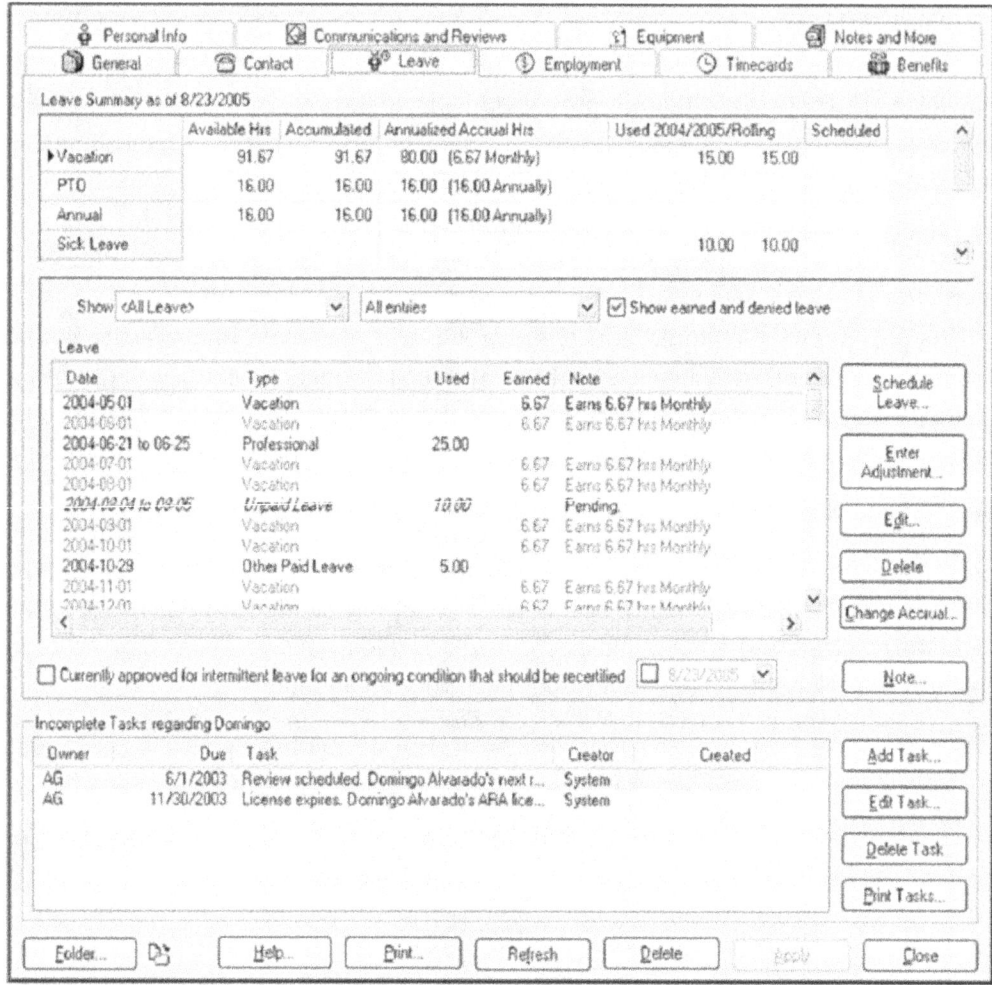

Fig. 5.3 : iHRIS ESS Snapshots

5.2.2 Key Features of the Employee Self-Service Model

What is Employee Self-Service?

Employee Self-Service (ESS) is a combination of technology and organizational change that enables users to interact directly with their human resource data to inquire, review and act upon transactions in the workplace. There are several types of self-service applications: Interactive Voice Response, Internet and Intranet.

What Features are Usually Used?

You can break down all human resource functions into four basic categories: organizational administration, human resource, benefits and payroll. Within each category, various functions can be performed "on demand" by employees using ESS.

Organizational Administration	Human Resource	Benefits	Payroll
Forms Request	Personal Information Maintenance	Benefits Inquiry	Time and Labor Reporting
Employment Verification	Emergency Contacts	Benefits (medical, dental, etc.) Enrollment	Duplicate W-2
Corporate Policies	Dependent/Beneficiaries Maintenance	Flexible Spending Account Selections	Federal and State Exemption Maintenance
Corporate Communications (newsletter, survey, annual report, company calendar, announcements, etc.)	Job Postings and Applications	Primary Care Physician Selections	Direct Deposit Set-up and Maintenance
Employee Directory (searchable by department)	Employee Development (training and skills improvement	Retirement Plan Transactions	Electronic Pay Statement Inquiry
Organizational Chart (embedded pictures)		Summary Plan Descriptions	Paid Time Off Inquiry and Request
		Stock Purchase Plan Transactions	

Self-service includes a range of administrative services (employee communications, benefit services, and personal data updates for employees), management productivity services (employee change actions, salary actions and approvals) and recruitment-oriented applications (job postings and job requisitions for managers).

When a company implements ESS, HR may choose to give employees the ability to view and update information. The ability to update information is dependent upon two factors: (a) if the information is the employee's own personal information and/or (b) if the employee is given management rights. Otherwise, the employee will have the ability to view the data only. Additionally, managers can be granted the right to view and update information about their employees and to perform manager-specific tasks.

Self Service	User Information	Action
Employee	Personal data (address and phone numbers)	View and Update
Employee	Emergency Contacts	View and Update
Employee	Education and Skills	View and Update
Employee	Licenses and certifications	View and Update
Employee	Direct Deposit	View and Update
Employee	Federal and State Withholding	View and Update

According to a recent Self Service Survey, the leading applications for employee, manager, and strategic self-service in use today are:

Employee Self Service Applications:
1. Personal data maintenance
2. Employee communications
3. Benefits inquiry
4. Open enrollment
5. Family status changes
6. 401k/pension inquiry

Manager Self Service Applications:
1. Management reports (e.g. headcount)
2. Employee change actions
3. Time card approvals
4. Leave of action management
5. Travel and expense management
6. Leave management

Strategic Self Service Applications:
1. Job posting review (Employee)
2. Job requisitions (Manager)
3. Job applications (Employee)
4. Salary actions (Manager)
5. Staff development (Manager)

Accessing Employee Self Service: Intranet or Internet?

A company can provide access to employee self-service in two ways, via Intranet or Intranet. With a corporate intranet, employees access the self service features from computers connected to a computer network within the company. Access from the "outside" world is not permitted. Concerns about intruders (commonly known as hackers) are diminished. Employees with desktop or laptop computers can use self-service at their desks. In companies where employees do not have computers, computer kiosks can be set up in convenient locations and shared by employees.

If a company chooses to open access via the Internet, employees can access self-service from anywhere in the world by using a computer, a browser and a phone line connection to the Internet. Companies with employees geographically dispersed in one country or in many countries find this to be an economical way to communicate with their employees. Typically, these companies use a "firewall" to prevent intruders from accessing the rest of the computer network. When establishing access via the Internet, many companies also implement security protocols such as Secure Sockets Layer (SSL) to encrypt and protect confidential data.

Benefits: Saving Costs and Improving Employee Satisfaction

Regardless of whether employees access self service via a corporate Intranet or the Internet, the benefits are the same. The benefits of implementing employee self-service fall into three categories: cost savings, cost avoidance, and revenue generation. In terms of cost savings, the primary gain is in reduced costs for delivering human resource and payroll services to employees. When employees have access to self-service, they are able to answer many questions independently, thus lowering the number of phone calls to the HR and payroll departments. When employees and managers are able to update information online, less money is spent on paper forms. Because employee information is captured electronically and sent to the appropriate approver or database, less time is spent processing employee transactions. There is no rekeying of data from paper forms.

Where can a Company obtain Employee Self Service Software?

Companies have several options for obtaining employee self-service software. The table below identifies the options and potential advantages and disadvantages of each approach.

Option	Advantage	Disadvantage
Vendors who sell HR and/or payroll systems with ESS	Integrated with HR and/or payroll database.	May not offer desired functionality.
Vendors who sell ESS systems only	Depth of functionality, "best of breed" approach.	Not integrated with HR, payroll, or other systems.
Vendors who sell highly specialized software (e.g. benefits education and enrollment)	Rich functionality in a single area.	Not integrated with HR, payroll or other systems.
Develop in house	Built specifically to a company's needs.	Software development may not be a core competency Resulting system may not keep up with latest innovations.

Hire a consulting firm to develop	Built specifically to a company's needs.	May be most expensive option Ongoing maintenance may be an issue.
Application Service Provider (ASP)	Minimal initial investment Quick start up.	May not offer desired functionality Not integrated with HR, payroll, or other systems Complete dependence on Internet connection.

Instant Self-Serve (ISS) is a Web add-on for iHR and iLeave. It gives employees and managers the ability to check leave, request leave, approve leave, change personal information, change benefit enrollment, and manage time sheets over the Internet. ISS provides secure Internet access to leave calendars, individual leave history, leave requests, individual time cards, and clock in/out features.

5.3 EMPLOYEE SELF SERVICE INTRANET TO MANAGE HIRING LIFECYCLE

The Employee Self Service Portal is an important HRIS application. It enables employee self-service and provides access to a comprehensive employee database. The employee database acts a centralized repository of vital employee related information available to not HR, employees and managers. Its inherent employee self-service capabilities ensure that this data remains current without tedious data entry by HR.

The Employee Self Service Portal is the base on which all other functional modules can be added in a "plug-and-play" to create a comprehensive employee self-service based HR system.

5.4 SHORT CASE STUDY: AVIVA GOES THIRD-GENERATION

Self-service is moving into artificial intelligence. Early adopter Aviva took the decision to launch an automated Ask HR response service for its 23,500 employees back in 2006.

Aviva employees type in a question or browse the most frequently asked questions in each of 23 categories, and with the help of the language search engine, suitable answers are brought up instantly from the web-based knowledge base.

Head of HR advice services at Aviva explains: "It didn't feel like a gradual process to us as this was such a big project. If I could go back, the one thing I would do is use more communication and my advice to others would be to invest heavily in communication and not just explain what a new system is, but why you are doing it."

Now staff questions are answered quickly - and, if necessary, specialist HR staff is around to answer specific questions, for example, about reward.

Since installing Ask HR, 69% of all HR enquiries are now handled through the system, reducing telephone calls and allowing HR staff to focus on more complex queries. During 2009 more than 202,000 questions were submitted and more than 90% of staff said they were satisfied with the answer they received.

Why use Self Service?

Employee self-service provider Cascade asked firms how they had benefited from having self-service:

1. Improved efficiencies 69%.
2. Ease of accessibility 69%.
3. Staff empowerment/autonomy 42%.
4. Adaptability 29%.
5. Reduced absenteeism 9%.
6. Improves staff retention 1%.
7. Other 23%.

Companies Reaping the Benefits:

- Dell Computer Corporation saved $2.5 million in the first year of implementation of a fully web-native, self-service system. Today, employees are able to access virtually every HR process via the web and the system has been rolled out to 23 countries throughout the Americas and Asia-Pacific regions.
- In 2009 fleet provider Master lease reported it saved 80% of HR administration time through the launch of a self-service system.

The speed of releasing this type of information through self-service also improved, freeing up more administration time. Another clear example of benefits to the business is the dramatic improvement of data integrity, with the number of queries around incorrect personal details decreasing substantially and automatic updating of organisational charts to reflect the true stance of the company.

Because of these benefits organizations are planning to expand the self service capability into more areas of the business in the future.

Activities

1. By surfing the internet resources www-adm.pdx.edu, research for any two applications from the IT industry which provides the functionality of Employee Self-Service.
2. Refer to the information available online on above site and provide more insight on the key features of the Resource Management Model.

Summary

In this chapter we have discussed about the key features and benefits of Employee self-service system. Employee Self-Service (ESS) is a web-based application that provides employees with access to their personal records and their payroll details. The most common features of ESS allow employees to change their own address, contact details and next of kin.

Also while discussing about Key features of Policy and Procedures Model we have seen that, There are a number of valid reasons for an employer to have written workplace policies and procedures in place. Such policies and procedures are useful documents to rely on when a legal dispute arises between the employer and an employee.

According to a recent Self Service Survey, the leading applications for employee, manager, and strategic self-service in use today are:

Employee Self Service Applications such as Personal data maintenance, Benefits inquiry, Family status changes, Manager Self Service Applications such as Employee change actions, Leave of action management, Leave management Strategic Self Service Applications such as Job posting review (Employee), Job applications (Employee), Staff development (Manager)

A company can provide access to employee self-service in two ways, via intranet or Intranet. With a corporate intranet, employees access the self service features from computers connected to a computer network within the company.

The Employee Self Service Portal is an important HRIS application. It enables employee self-service and provides access to a comprehensive employee database.

The Employee Self Service Portal is the base on which all other functional modules can be added in a "plug-and-play" to create a comprehensive employee self-service based HR system.

We have also seen that, the Resource Management Model enables companies to manage human resource deployment and capacity for project work. Some key features of modern Resource Management Systems are as follows:

- Schedule automatic nomination of candidates, or nominate yourself or your staff for open requirements.
- Rank candidates based on score and automatically notify qualified or available resources of requirements.

Self-assessment Questions

1. Enlist some of the important aspects of an ESS generally should be capable of?
2. Explain why an ESS is increasingly popular in the tertiary sector?
3. Enlist and discuss the reasons for an employer to have written workplace policies and procedures in place?
4. Explain in brief the conditions which may fall into the category of policies for rights and responsibilities.
5. Enlist the aspects in that fall into the category of Employee benefits.

Chapter 6...

Emerging Trends in HRIS

Objectives ...

After discussing this chapter, you will be able to :

- Explain the Application of Cloud computing Technology in the Overall HRIS Framework
- Understand and Explain the Increasing Complexity of HRIS Solutions and Choosing the Right Solution
- Describe in Detail the Application of Social Computing to HRIS

Structure ...

- 6.1 Introduction
- 6.2 Emerging Trends in HRIS
   - 6.2.1 2014 Global Assessment Trends Report
- 6.3 Application of Cloud Computing Technology
- 6.4 Networking, Internet, Intranet Technology Implications
- 6.5 Application of Social Computing to HRIS
- 6.6 Information Security and Privacy in Human Resource Information System
- 6.7 Short Case Study: Human Resource Information Systems and Payroll Consulting
   - Activities
   - Summary
   - Self-assessment Questions

6.1 INTRODUCTION

For a long time, "managing" HRIS has been synonymous with managing projects to implement and then enhance the packages we purchased from vendors, and our discipline has developed a set of pretty good tools and practices for use in these "project" situations. Get ready for the 21st century, because the same kinds of projects and tools just won't work anymore. Part of the reason for this shift is external to HR and HRIS-globalization, complex and interlinked systems, and the freedom that comes along with the Internet is examples of forces we can't control.

But part of the shift stems from things that we can sometimes control and almost always influence.

The following topics have been part of recent discussions within the HR market:

Innovations in Mobile Employee Self-service: An estimated one-third of the U.S. workforce is mobile. Therefore, software vendors can expect to see an increase in demand for mobile HR applications, including employee self-service for mobile devices. ADP, a leading vendor for HR, payroll and benefits administration software and services, released the industry's first mobile iOS payroll app in October 2010 so users can manage employee information, direct deposits and other payroll processing tasks from mobile devices. ADP expanded that functionality in July 2011 with a free app for Android, Blackberry and Apple device users. ADP Mobile Solutions gives employees direct access to pay stubs in addition to 401K and retirement savings information and time clock/attendance functions.

Acquisitions of Cloud-based HR Software Vendors: The move toward strategic HR is apparent. In addition to core practices such as payroll and benefits administration, businesses both large and small understand the importance of strategic HR, including talent management and employee evaluation, to recruit and retain talented employees. Best-of-breed providers, like cloud-based talent management vendors and Success Factors, have been popular solutions for strategic HR applications. Large ERP and talent management vendors, which have traditionally offered on-premise solutions, are beginning to acquire SaaS-only providers in an effort to integrate industry-leading strategic applications into their existing human resources platforms in the cloud. Most recently, on March 8, 2012, Cornerstone On Demand acquired Sonar6, a web-based HR vendor that takes a unique approach to talent management and employee evaluations.

As you prepare your management agenda for the first part of this new decade, you may want to address some of the issues identified here:

1. **Disintegration of the old HR "turf":** What used to be a stakeholder base comprising a few management users and a handful of HR professionals at headquarters is gone. In its place, we have demands for customization that make every employee and prospect a separate customer. Indeed, virtual teams and groups add another separate layer to the old HRIS business space.

2. **Commoditization of Input/Workflow/Basic Transaction Processing:** Vendors, projects, and payback analyses have focused for a quarter century on the value of basic "data processing". As we enter the new century, there's no significant profit margin left in the three areas. The more we focus on this part of the system, the more we look like techie "nerds" tinkering for the sake of tinkering, nothing more.

3. **Dramatic increases in the perceived Value of System Information:** Put another way, "input is out, but output is in". The next generation or two of HRIS will rise and fall-and we'll rise and fall at the same time-according to how valuable, personal, and actionable we make the reports and analyses that come out of our systems. Forget

report libraries: they are useless. Start to focus on custom reporting, and discontinue any "standard" output after six months of use.

4. **Devaluation of Past Experience as a Basis for Planning and Decision-Making:** Change is so rapid and all-consuming that linear projections of yesterday's trends and issues are not even close to tomorrow's realities. Except for a very few standard regulatory reports, tomorrow's HRIS output needs to focus on painting the picture of future impact of today's policies, according to a variety of different environmental conditions. It becomes our job to bring to the light of day HR tactical and strategic questions, not to deliver answers to them.

5. **On-going Miniaturization of all Aspects of HR and IT:** Even though large systems will continue to be purchased, installed, and operated everywhere in the business environment, the real point of contact (and downstream, perhaps the portal) between stakeholder and system will be a hand-held device with data, voice, and many other capabilities. Working with "the system" will become a series of self-contained, highly personalized interactive episodes-with all the data and tools we need for interaction present when the activity begins. It's likely that no two individuals in a company will have identical hand-held environments; they will each be personalized to fit the roles and experiences of the user.

6. **Constant Learning and not just "Distance Learning":** We will see every official communication covered with virtual "yellow post-its" and voice annotations, as people read, then dialogue and debate, what in the past were top-down communications. HRIS needs to find a way to capture, summarize, and distribute these "conversations" as a part of supporting organizational learning everywhere in the organization.

7. **Deterioration of "Best Practices" as a Tool for Systems Design and Enhancement:** Since, every system in every organization will become increasingly customized as a result of the forces already noted in this article, "best" will be limited to the system and environment where it exists-we can still look outside our experience for ideas, but we will become responsible for adapting them to our own way of working.

8. **Information Avalanches:** We are generating more and more information each year, almost all of it of great value to someone in the organization. The problem we face is matching the information to the target stakeholder, and then getting him or her to notice what we've developed and delivered when it arrives at desk or palmtop device. This implies a completely new competency in HRIS: information design. In terms of system output, we have gone in a decade from trying to deliver the data-packed, hard-to-read Times of London, to today's delivery of the factoid, graphic-rich format of USA Today.

9. Vanishing Boundaries-between Departments, Divisions, other Businesses in our Industry Cluster, etc.: Whether it's in accommodating information-sharing between two erstwhile competitors or facilitating the give-and-take of salary negotiations according to "market" rules rather than Compensation's salary grades, we are finding all boundaries to be both permeable and artificial. We need more exposure to the real worked, to sense and feel change as it occurs, not more artificial internal groupings developed to assist old finance and accounting practices. This means reworking organizational structures, reporting, and many, many "local" reports and analyses.

10. Changing the Metaphor of Organizations them selves: The 20th century was the heyday of the view of organizations as finely tuned machines in stable, closed environments. What's emerging is a new view - a metaphor of organizations as biological forms, living, growing, and evolving in response to changes in the environment. This shift will prove to be most important of all, since the old view was command and control oriented and allowed us to believe that good, timely, accurate information was the prerequisite to controlling the business. Now we have to resign ourselves that we can use our information to influence what the organization does, but central control of fast-moving day-to-day activity is beyond our scope entirely.

Can we do it? Not if we stay tied to artificial constructs of what an organizational "machine" is supposed to look like and how it is supposed to operate. But if we allow things to evolve, become personalized, and reflect the diversity in tomorrow's business world-it will just happen naturally.

6.2 EMERGING TRENDS IN HRIS

Virtual HR uses technology to provide HR programs via an employee self-service platform. Typically includes use of such items as voice response systems and virtual media. HR-XML is a new development in the application of Internet technologies specific to HR processes. HR-XML is an effort by a group of vendors and service providers to formulate a standard for data communication between companies, for adoption by the entire HR community. It can best be explained by comparing it to a related language, HTML. All the HRIS is learned and practiced through a software application Learning Management Software and System for the administration, documentation, tracking, reporting and delivery training programs.

Updated Professional Roles:

Hr Generalist is the person with responsibility for performing end to end of HR activities and HR Specialist means person with in-depth knowledge and expertise in a limited area of like recruiting, planning, selection, payroll, back office etc. Finally Hr Audit is a formal research effort that evaluates the current state of HR management in an organization.

Influence of Social Media:

Social Media plays a major role in the HR field. Where in Social HR the online social media platforms are used to fulfill the HR functions likewise in recruiting also most notably recruitment, but also including employee engagement and internal discussions etc and Social recruiting falls into two different categories.

The first is internet sourcing using social media profiles, blogs, and online communities to find and search for passive candidate data and information. The second is social distribution. This involves social networks as a means to distribute jobs either through HR vendors to share job openings through online social networks. Example: LinkedIn, Face book, Twitter, Google+ etc.

Planning Trends:

Work-force Diversity: In the past HRM was considerably simpler because our work force was strikingly homogeneous.

Today's work force comprises of people of different work force.

One means of achieving that is through the organization's benefits package leads to the family friendly organization.

HRM must train people of different age groups to effectively manage and to deal with each other and to respect the diversity of views that each offers.

Employee Assistance Programme: Providing counseling and other help to employees having emotional, physical, or other personal problems. A work-based intervention program designed to identify and assist employees in resolving personal problems that may be adversely affecting the employee's performance.

6.2.1 2014 Global Assessment Trends Report

How the world does's largest and most successful organisations, (those recognized as Global Fortune 500 organisations in the past three years) anticipate budget shifts in the coming year? Understanding how they plan to spend their money in 2014 provides some context for budget shifts for organisations at large.

As you might expect, these leading organisations are more likely to anticipate budget increases in 2014 for all HR areas, compared to the overall sample, but with a similar rank ordering of importance compared to the global sample (See Table 6.1).

Notably, Fortune 500 organisations are substantially more likely to plan a budget increase related to the use of competency models (27%) than the global sample (9%). As implementing a competency framework is an important first step towards a cross-organisational talent measurement and analysis strategy, this suggests a rising understanding among leading organisations of the business benefits of a 'big data' approach to talent.

Fig. 6.1: Anticipated Budget Increases: Comparison of Worlds Leading Organisations to Global Sample

HR initative / Area	Rank	Percentage F500 Endorsing Budget Increase	Rank	Percent Global Sample Endorsing Budget Increase
Training.	1	48%	1	32%
Identification of high potential talent.	2	42%	2	28%
Performance management.	3	38%	6	26%
Engagement/retention.	4	37%	3	27%
Leadership development.	5	36%	3	27%
Career development.	6	35%	3	27%
Succession planning.	6	35%	9	24%
Workforce planning/talent analytics.	8	34%	7	25%
Internal hiring (including promotion).	9	32%	12	19%
External hiring.	10	29%	10	22%
Creating/implementing competency models.	11	27%	15	9%
Change management.	11	27%	7	25%
Onboarding.	13	25%	13	18%
Restructuring.	14	23%	11	20%
Outplacement / redeployment of talent.	15	15%	14	11%

Connecting Priorities to Processes:

We examined the relative formality of HR processes as an indicator of the extent to which organisations currently support and invest in core HR processes. Respondents were asked to indicate the formality of 14 HR processes within their organisations (Table 6.2). Results show that the most common areas for which formal processes and programmes are in place (namely, external hiring, performance management, internal hiring) are not necessarily among the top HR priorities, indicating that those areas that are considered strategically important may not currently have the right HR processes and investments in place to support them.

For example, engagement/retention (the top HR priority for 2014) appears near the bottom of the list of formal processes, with only one in five respondents indicating formal programmes designed to engage and retain talent. This disconnect may reflect ambiguity over how best to develop programmes to support this area. Such efforts can start with measuring/monitoring employee engagement, aligning employee motivation and competencies to career paths, and developing plans to identify sources of employee dissatisfaction and take steps to improve underlying issues.

Fig. 6.2: Formality of Process by HR Area

HR Initiative/Area	Percentage indicating Formal Process	
	2013	2014
External hiring (including recruitment).	69%	65%
Performance management.	64%	64%
Internal hiring (including promotion).	55%	53%
Onboarding.	60%	48%
Training.	51%	47%
Creating/implementing competency model(s).	29%	36%
Restructuring.	31%	33%
Succession planning.	23%	31%
Leadership development.	21%	30%
Outplacement/redevelopment of talent.	30%	24%
Workforce planning/Talent Analytics.	17%	23%
Career development.	16%	22%
Engagement/retention.	17%	19%
Change management.	14%	17%

Challenges and Opportunities in 2014:

Given what our respondents indicate are the top priorities for 2014, in particular the focus on identifying, developing, and retaining top talent, what challenges and opportunities lie ahead?

Table 6.3 summarizes findings related to contextual components of HR practice.

Consistent with the diminished priority placed on external hiring compared to recent years, we see an increase in respondents reporting that their organisations are focusing more on developing talent internally than on hiring externally (from 49% in 2013 to 57% in 2014). Perhaps anticipating reductions in external hiring, fewer respondents indicate potential challenges with recruiting and hiring talent individuals (from 73% in 2013 to 64% in 2014). Similarly, fewer respondents indicate that they are recruiting for more open positions organisation-wide as compared to last year (from 39% in 2013 to 35% in 2014).

What opportunities are on the horizon that could help HR reach its goals in 2014?

While engagement/retention was noted as the single biggest HR priority across respondents and for most regions, only about two-thirds of respondents say they use career development as a retention strategy (63%, up from 55% in 2013).

Fig. 6.3: Challenges and Focus of HR in 2012 – 2014

Survey Statement	Percentage Endorsing		
	2012	2013	2014
In general, my organisation is focusing more on developing talent internally than on hiring externally.	53%	49%	57%
We are currently recruiting for more open positions organisation-wide as compared to last year.	39%	39%	35%
We expect it will become increasingly challanging of recruit and hire talented individuals for key positions in the coming year.	64%	73%	64%
Our organisation's competency model is being used effectively as part of our overall employee lifecycle (from hiring to development to promotion)	-	34%	42%
We use career development as a retention strategy.	58%	55%	63%

Assessment Trends Summary and Recommendations:

Based on the results of the 2014 Global Assessment Trends survey, we see four key areas for consideration by HR professionals looking to improve how they measure talent in the coming year.

Identifying high-potential (HiPo) talent is a new global top priority and the top future use of assessments:

1. Organisations focus more on developing talent internally than hiring externally (57%, up from 49% in 2013).
2. Most organisations have programmes to identify (53%) and develop (52%) high-potential talent. While most do not currently use assessments for such programmes, 30% report HiPo as the top future use of assessments.
3. Most organisations have programmes to develop future leaders (56%) and 60% use assessments as part of those programmes.

Most do not Monitor Candidate Reactions and Fail to Link the Candidate Experience to Business Outcomes.

1. 82% of organisations see a positive candidate reaction to their hiring process as important, yet only 40% actually monitor such reactions.
2. Few organisations see the value of positive candidate reactions beyond the recruiting process (such as in influencing candidates' future purchasing decisions).

Most Respondents Assess Indicators of Engagement/Retention, but 40% do not, Risking the Loss of Key Talent.

1. Engagement/retention remains top priority, endorsed by 56% of HR professionals.
2. 40% indicate they do not use or plan to use assessments as part of efforts on engagement and retention.

Big Differences in Talent Management Priorities Globally, with External Hiring only Dominant in the Americas.

1. Only 35% of organisations are recruiting for an increased number of open positions, down from 39% in 2013.
2. External hiring is a top priority (46%) in the Americas compared to 34% globally.
3. Identification of high-potential talent more likely to be seen as a top priority in Middle East/Africa (60%) compared to 51% globally.
4. Budgets associated with external hiring as likely to increase as decrease, indicating dramatically different strategies and economic conditions around the world.

Employees Who Promote their Employers' Products and Services are much more likely to Work in Organisations with Strategic HR Functions.

1. Of those who are highly favorable about their organizations' products/services, 80% view HR as a strategic function and 89% indicate that their organisations consider people decisions in the context of business objectives.

2. Organisations, whose employees highly endorse their companies' products / services (promoters) priorities ALL HR areas higher, compared to organisations whose employees do not endorse their products/services (detractors).
3. Promoters also report their companies make greater use of information on talent to make business decisions (58%) compared to detractors (37%).

Talent Dashboards can Transform Organisations, but only via Infrastructures that Integrate rich Data and Robust Measurement Tools.

HR professionals can usher in the big data era for their organisations by setting up an infrastructure for the efficient collection, use, and integration of data to support people processes. Our findings show there is considerable room for improvement in the data systems, data policies and use of objective measurement required for this.

The benefits of such an infrastructure extend far beyond the HR department. Ultimately, organisations should be able to demonstrate the same degree of control over, and return on investment, from talent that they routinely expect from their finance departments. Moreover, access to rich data on current talent, talent gaps, and, through external benchmarking, how it compares by geography and industry, will give business leaders the dashboards they need to steer their organisations to success.

Organisations should Remember that Candidates are often Customers too.

Most HR professionals agree it's important that candidates are left with a good impression of the organisation, and are very conscious of the impact this can have on their employer brand – and their ability to attract the best talent in the future.

However relatively few organisations actually measure candidate perceptions, and less than a quarter recognise any link between client perceptions and business results.

Talent measurement usage and budget allocation needs to be aligned with HR priorities HR priorities are clear and consistent over several years, with organisations increasingly emphasizing the effective identification, development, and retention of their internal talent. The priorities are often at odds with how organisations allocate budget and the use of objective talent measurement. Assessments are used substantially more in pre-hire than post-hire, even though our respondents priorities the post-hire realm.

Innovations in Hiring Tools and Methods:

Proceed with caution Our findings indicate heightened interest in technology-based hiring tools and technology-enabled assessment, although their use is often characterized by inconsistent or inappropriate justification or processes, or without demonstrable job relevance.

6.3 APPLICATION OF CLOUD COMPUTING TECHNOLOGY

Cloud Computing and HR:

Cloud Computing has been gaining momentum over the last few years, in HR it is getting some significant airtime and how could it not with the success of a multitude of cloud vendors.

Basics of Cloud Computing: Cloud computing is the use of computing resources (hardware and software) that are delivered as a service over a network (typically the Internet). The name comes from the common use of a cloud-shaped symbol as an abstraction for the complex infrastructure it contains in system diagrams. Cloud computing entrusts remote services with a user's data, software and computation.

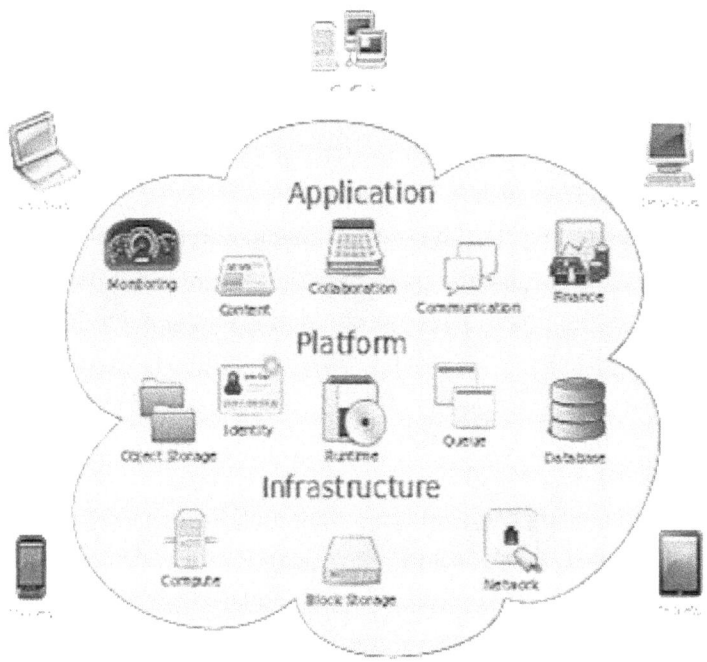

Fig. 6.1 : Cloud Computing

End users access cloud-based applications through a web browser or a light-weight desktop or mobile app while the business software and user's data are stored on servers at a remote location. Proponents claim that cloud computing allows companies to avoid upfront infrastructure costs, and focus on projects that differentiate their businesses instead of infrastructure. Proponents also claim that cloud computing allows enterprises to get their applications up and running faster, with improved manageability and less maintenance, and enables IT to more rapidly adjust resources to meet fluctuating and unpredictable business demand. In the business model using software as a service, users are provided access to application software and databases. Cloud providers manage the infrastructure and platforms that run the applications. SaaS is sometimes referred to as "on-demand software" and is usually priced on a pay-per-use basis. SaaS providers generally price applications using a subscription fee.

Proponents claim that the SaaS allows a business the potential to reduce IT operational costs by outsourcing hardware and software maintenance and support to the cloud provider. This enables the business to reallocate IT operations costs away from hardware/software spending and personnel expenses, towards meeting other IT goals. In addition, with applications hosted centrally, updates can be released without the need for users to install new software. One drawback of SaaS is that the users' data are stored on the cloud provider's server. As a result, there could be unauthorized access to the data. Cloud computing relies on sharing of resources to achieve coherence and economies of scale similar to a utility (like the electricity grid) over a network. At the foundation of cloud computing is the broader concept of converged infrastructure and shared services.

Chances are you've heard of the cloud by now, or even used the term yourself, but haven't really stopped to give it a lot of thought. If you've logged into Google, bought a book on Amazon, "liked" an article on Facebook or updated your resume on Monster, you've seen cloud computing in action -- yet probably weren't even aware of it.

In simple terms Cloud Computing is basically off-premise computing, essentially where you, the customer, do not have the computing environment located physically in your offices. In reality things are far more complex than this.

Essentially there are three relevant "flavors" of cloud computing each operating at a different level in the technology ecosystem. First Infrastructure as a Service (IaaS), then Platform as a Service (PaaS) and finally Software as a Service (SaaS) (there are two additional layers around the network and communications infrastructure but do not really influence the application landscape).

What is IaaS? At a basic level this is where a vendor provides you a virtual server to deliver a specific application usually a web site. Essentially all of my web sites and applications run on an IaaS model provided by Rack space Cloud. Rack space provides me with a virtual server and I do the rest, install software, and complete maintenance and upgrades. Other examples of IaaS include Amazon EC2, DynDNS and Joyent. There tend to be two types of IaaS; public and private. As part of an HR technology strategy public IaaS would usually only be included when it's part of a broader organizational-wide IT strategy to use public IaaS.

PaaS is when a cloud provider delivers a computing platform where applications and services can be built on top of, resulting in developers being able to focus on building cool software solutions instead of worrying about managing the hardware, operating system and databases. Example PaaS providers include Google App Engine, Force.com and Windows Azure Compute. We are starting to see a number of HR offerings being delivered on top of these platforms, specifically on the Force.com platform where you can access full-functioning HR systems, recruitment solutions and learning management systems along with smaller apps that can site onto of Sales force to providing LinkedIn information as part of the sales process.

Finally, SaaS is the layer in which most people interact with Cloud Computing. Here the provider offers their application to you the user across a network, usually the Internet, and you do not need to worry about installing and running the application on your own computers or those of IaaS providers. Most of the time you gain access to the software via a subscription model, but not always. It is at the SaaS level we see the most impact on HR Technology Strategy. Today you can run your entire HR Systems environment "in the cloud" through solutions such as Workday, SAP (Cloud Global Payroll and Employee Central), Oracle Fusion to just a specific HR process using one of the vast range of point solutions.

In summary from an HR perspective we are seeing cloud computing infiltrate at the bottom layer through private-IaaS and at the top layer through SaaS. If you do not have some form of cloud computing in your HR technology landscape today you will in the very near future.

The Uses of Cloud Computing in Human Resources:

The benefits of cloud computing for businesses are obvious, but for human resources professionals cloud computing applications may be particularly useful. In larger corporations, HR teams can be spread out over different areas of a building, or even different areas of the country and in different time zones. This is likely to result in a lack of communication, where recruiters cannot easily talk to team members working in payroll or benefits, or vice versa, and HR team members do not always have ready access to information monitored and updated by another department.

As it relates to the typically multi-functional field of human resources, having a cloud application, such as Shift iQ for example is invaluable. This is in no small part due to the fact that the many areas of HR, traditionally kept quite separate in some companies, can all be accessed in one central place, the cloud, allowing departments to 'talk to each other' more easily. This only serves to increase the quality of communication in a company, which, of course, can only result in positive changes in an organization. A good cloud computing system can, among other things, track applications, search résumés, generate reports, calculate payroll, track performance appraisals and maintain data on employees. Putting the HR department 'on the cloud' facilitates a mobile workforce and should also allow flexibility as well as being more cost effective than traditional software.

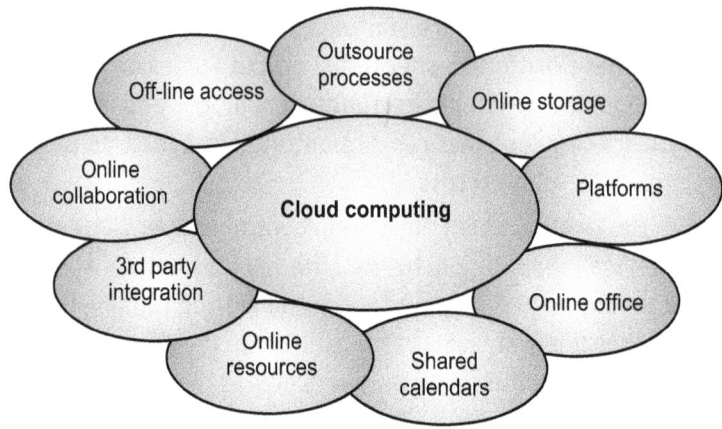

Fig. 6.2

Cloud computing also ensures that companies have instant and continual access to the latest advances and legal issues as they may affect human resources issues. All information is automatically updated, meaning team members can be confident their information is current. Security is another concern for HR professionals, who deal with sensitive information; virtual services have some of the most sophisticated security systems imaginable, assuring peace of mind to the HR department and the entire workforce. Additionally, access to sensitive information can readily be limited to certain individuals within a company. Cloud computing offers multiple advantages with no apparent downside; it's a win-win solution for businesses' HR needs.

List of Vendors providing Cloud Solutions:

1. Access a Cloud - Cloud Business Solutions.
2. ArkHRMS is a cloud based HRM solution.
3. Cavintek develops cloud-based business process automation software for enterprises of all sizes.
4. EmployWise is available as a Software-as-a-Service (SaaS).
5. Fairsail Cloud-based Human Resource Management System.
6. HeartBeat HRIS / HRMS software Cloud-based Human Resource Management System.
7. HRM Direct offers an entire toolset to screen and track applicants and on-board new hires; HRM Direct is a SaaS HR solution for small to mid-sized companies. It also offers tools for social media integration and referral management.
8. Kronos Workforce Ready is a simple, SaaS-based HR solution for small to midsize organizations seeking an affordable solution to manage employee information, including time and attendance, payroll and more.
9. OrangeHRM Cloud and Web-based Human Resource Management System.

10. Workable.com is a cloud-based applicant tracking and candidate recruiting solution for hiring teams. Their advanced profiles and comprehensive features streamline the process and give users a clear picture of their pipeline.

6.4 NETWORKING, INTERNET, INTRANET AND TECHNOLOGY IMPLICATIONS

The Computer Network (CN) is nothing but a set of computers connected to each other, mainly for Sharing information, data, programs & resources.

Networking reduces the cost of doing business since resources are utilized to optimum extent.

The evolution of newer business models such as the ITES/BPO, the offshore Software etc are an outcome of the Networks be it in Telephony or in terms of computer networks.

Benefits of Networking are :

1. Interaction and communication between various people at locations and perhaps using different types of hardware and software different.
2. Sharing of data so that there is consistency of data.
3. Sharing of expensive devices such as printers.
4. Created newer and previously unthinkable ways of doing business such as telecom, BPO etc.

Integrating Intranets with IT Initiatives:

The explosion in Web-based applications has been fueled by concepts such as client collaboration and real-time, anywhere access to firm information for the road warrior. Client requirements have pushed Web-based technology and its implementation in law firms.

IT departments need to embrace and expand intranet usage, servicing the firm's employees as their own clients. Through the use of the intranet, IT departments stand to gain accuracy, efficiency and reliability.

When the primary users are located external to the firm's network, then the website should be hosted in isolation of the firm's Local Area Network (LAN) in a demilitarized zone (DMZ). When the primary users are internal, then hosting the Web services within the LAN is an efficient choice. With either hosting strategy, isolation of TCP/IP network and open ports within the firm's firewall need to be carefully considered for secure browsing and updating the content of the pages.

Many Intranet products will communicate with your existing database applications; requiring a constant connection to your live database environment. When the connected database is within the LAN and the website is located in a DMZ, then secure communications between the Web server and the database need to be established. Web hosting has become second-nature to most IT departments; however, once the external world is allowed to make attempts at the firm's private data, one can never be too prepared to secure the environment and lock-down any potential "back doors."

Eight Areas for Intranet Development:

The concept of the intranet can be expanded and developed to aid both the IT department and the client/attorney relationship.

Eight areas that deserve attention are: communication, self service helpdesk, trouble-ticket tracking, remote assistance/administration, systems monitoring, project rollouts, staff training and new employee intake. Each of these is examined in more detail below.

1. Communication:

The first and most common use of intranets is communication.

Even the basic HTML Intranet site has an IT page. It is likely that there are announcements regarding upcoming training classes or brown bag-lunches; however the communication is usually one-way, much like a department bulletin board.

Communication of events, schedules, IT choices and bulletins continues to be the core content of the intranet; however innovative IT staff can use it to move beyond one-way distribution of information.

2. Self-Service Helpdesk:

As the example above suggests, many aspects of helpdesk support can be automated. This approach lessens the burden of basic support calls and delivers a faster first-tier response to the end-user. Other examples of self-service features that can be added to the IT department intranet include a method for end-users to apply quick fixes and hyperlinks to scripts that re-establish connections to mapped drives or printers.

3. IT Helpdesk Ticket Tracking:

A myriad of helpdesk ticket software packages are available, and many other products have been developed internally by firms. It is key that a firm determine goals for a helpdesk ticket system before choosing a product to service its needs.

Some firms utilize an e-mail address that receives all user requests. A delegated IT staffer then tracks incoming requests and takes action. Three limitations of this method are:

(i) it is labor-intensive to provide an ongoing status report to either the end-user or other IT staffers;

(ii) base e-mail systems provide no ability to search, trend or categorize the helpdesk issues in order to categorize requests into common subjects; and

(iii) if the user problem involves the e-mail system, this service method will be affected.

4. Remote Assistance/Administration:

As an extension of the helpdesk trouble-ticket system, the IT staff may respond remotely to a trouble ticket rather than sending someone out to the user's location to look at the problem. A local visit is especially inconvenient when the end-user is in a remote office.

An example of this functionality is the invisible Web-enabled remote control of application clients through Citrix or Terminal Services in Windows 2003 or the use of third-party remote control tools such as WebEx or VNC.

5. Systems Monitoring:

The use of monitoring systems has also expanded greatly and is an example of another Web-enabled application that currently floats in the IT department. Integrating system status metrics and indicators with the firm's intranet and extranet combines real-time monitoring information along with warnings, alerts and notices. Systems monitoring tools combine status, troubleshooting and repair utilities into one location. Remote access or extranet capabilities complement that information by making it more accessible to IT staff when they are far from the server room.

6. Project Rollout Tool:

The intranet's power and efficiency are impressive when used as part of the workflow to rollout workstations and software applications. Simple concepts, gathered into a single location then used as a project guide, increase deployment productivity and improve accuracy. A few illustrations of project and workstation deployment information delivered through the IT department's intranet include mapped shortcuts to the CABS file; automated software installation shortcuts; and links to.

7. Staff Training:

Web-enabled software training is an area that has had much success in the online realm. The popularity of webinars and online training programs on the Internet can easily be translated and integrated with the firm's intranet. Some IT departments have used the intranet as an advertising medium designed to announce training opportunities.

8. New Employee Intake Workflow Process:

Regardless of firm size, moves/adds/changes to attorneys and staff are often a surprise to the IT department. One tool that can improve communication between administration and IT is merging the IT department's Intranet with the new employee intake workflow process.

6.5 APPLICATION OF SOCIAL COMPUTING TO HRIS

In 2013, the traditional resume will be replaced by the breadth and depth of your personal brand this is just one aspect of HR related practices about to evolve and there are almost a complete multitude of modules in HRIS which will transform and Social Computing will be applied to HRIS.

We're moving from a "knowledge economy" to a "social economy," and as we do so, as a recent Fast Company article noted, "The line is quickly blurring between the value of what we know and who we know." In 2013, prospective job applicants will be much more deliberate in creating their "elevator pitch" and posting this promotional blurb on Facebook, LinkedIn and in their Twitter bios.

Many HRIS software providers have included the social aspect of computing in their solutions. Some of the prominent examples being:

1. TribeHR which is a new breed of HRIS. It combines the best of HR information management with innovative social features like peer and public recognition, shared goals and values, an interactive corporate news feed, and an engaging social interface that employees love. TribeHR's talent management suite shines, engaging employees in a uniquely social way. With a wide variety of tools to support personalization, engagement, feedback, collaboration, cultural alignment and employee growth, TribeHR helps build a culture of success and enhances employee satisfaction.

2. OpenHire's ATS from Silk Road has Social Recruiting Media Toolkit that provides internal and external tools for recruiters, job seekers and employees, enabling them to apply, connect, and share with hundreds of social media sites, including LinkedIn, Facebook, Twitter, and many others.

If personal branding seems shallow, think again. Putting value on candidates' networks and spheres of influences makes perfect sense in an age where crowd sourcing the right solution to a problem is just as good as coming up with it yourself.

Before you're interviewed by a potential employer, expect the recruiting manager or hiring manager to check out one or more of the following sources about you:

(i) the top ten searches on your name on either Google or Bing,

(ii) the number of Twitter followers you have and last time you tweeted,

(iii) the size and quality of your LinkedIn community,

(iv) the number and quality of recommendations you have on LinkedIn.

Also as candidates catch on to employers' focus on their Internet presence, they will shift their methods accordingly. Already, entire businesses are cropping up to streamline the process for them. Start-ups like Entelo and TalentBin help companies find eligible applicants by scanning social networks and spotlighting certain candidates. Their search tools consider the experience and history mentioned in users' profiles, but also their use of the social network. These companies can pinpoint those who have updated their bios lately or often, to determine which candidates are getting ready to get back on the job market. Getting this head start on head hunting is crucial as top corporations' search for top candidates becomes ever more competitive.

6.6 INFORMATION SECURITY AND PRIVACY IN HUMAN RESOURCE INFORMATION SYSTEM

Definition of Personal Data :

The definition of personal data is data which relates to a living individual who can be identified:

- From that data, or
- From that data and other information which is in the possession of, or is likely to come into the possession of, the data controller.

Sensitive personal data concerns the subject's race, ethnicity, politics, religion, trade union status, health, sex life or criminal record.

The HRIS Security Environment

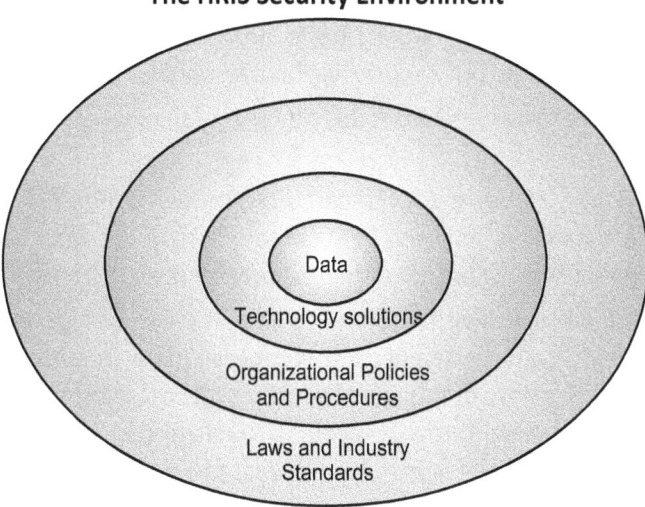

Fig. 6.3

Subject Access:

Personal data which is normally held for under 40 days may be legitimately denied in subject access requests under the Act. This is a consequence of the time limit data controllers must meet in making their response. If the data has been deleted by the normal procedures of the business by the time the data controller responds to a request, that data cannot be supplied. For data such as closed-circuit television images which are routinely overwritten, it may be impossible for a subject to exercise their data access rights.

The next consideration is technology. A number of technologies have altered the current privacy debates. The technologies in question into 4 groups.

There are technologies used for surveillance, the technologies for forming agreements (contracting) about the release of private data, the technologies for labeling and trust, and Privacy-Enhancing Technologies (PETs).

The technologies for surveillance and for data capture are used by companies for business purposes, but they have the side effect of endangering personal privacy. These include generating data trails, data warehousing and data mining, and biometrics. Many of these technical mechanisms can lead to consumer profiles that "are no longer based only on the individual's dealings with a single organization, because their data is shared by multiple merchants.

Balancing these tracking mechanisms are Privacy Enhancing Technologies (PETs), which attempt to defeat or neutralize the surveillance or tracking technologies. Basic PETs include cookie managers and personal firewalls.

Other PETs attempt to provide genuine anonymity, and include anonymous remailers (e.g., Mixmaster) and digital cash (e.g., E Cash). An active area of research and development are systems to provide non-traceable identifiers.

In addition, privacy seals (e.g., from TRUSTe or the Better Business Bureau) indicate that the company follows the privacy practices stated on their web site.

A new area of research includes the so-called labeling protocols, such as the MIT/World Wide.

Web Consortium's Platform for Privacy Preferences (P3P). P3P allows sites to describe their data handling policies (P3P statements) and permits users to describe their preferences for releasing private data (P3P preferences).

As sites label themselves with P3P and as user clients (such as Internet Explorer) handle P3P statements and preferences, it will be possible to create technologies to form contracts for the release of private data. Other technologies, such as those to help users understand contractual terms or even contract-related fraud, will also emerge. Their browser-based agents watch for privacy violations, privacy scams, and the like on behalf of the user.

Fig. 6.4

Data Protection Principles:

1. Personal data shall be processed fairly and lawfully and, in particular, shall not be processed unless:
   (i) at least one of the conditions in Schedule 2 is met, and
   (ii) in the case of sensitive personal data, at least one of the conditions in Schedule 3 is also met.
2. Personal data shall be obtained only for one or more specified and lawful purposes, and shall not be further processed in any manner incompatible with that purpose or those purposes.
3. Personal data shall be adequate, relevant and not excessive in relation to the purpose or purposes for which they are processed.
4. Personal data shall be accurate and, where necessary, kept up to date.
5. Personal data processed for any purpose or purposes shall not be kept for longer than is necessary for that purpose or those purposes.
6. About the rights of individuals e.g. personal data shall be processed in accordance with the rights of data subjects (individuals).
7. Appropriate technical and organisational measures shall be taken against unauthorised or unlawful processing of personal data and against accidental loss or destruction of, or damage to, personal data.
8. Personal data shall not be transferred to a country or territory outside the European Economic Area unless that country or territory ensures an adequate level of protection for the rights and freedoms of data subjects in relation to the processing of personal data.

Personal data should only be processed fairly and lawfully. In order for data to be classed as 'fairly processed', at least one of these six conditions must be applicable to that data.

1. The data subject (the person whose data is stored) has consented ("given their permission") to the processing;
2. Processing is necessary for the performance of, or commencing, a contract;
3. Processing is required under a legal obligation (other than one stated in the contract);
4. Processing is necessary to protect the vital interests of the data subject;
5. Processing is necessary to carry out any public functions;
6. Processing is necessary in order to pursue the legitimate interests of the "data controller" or "third parties" (unless it could unjustifiably prejudice the interests of the data subject).

Offences:

The Act details a number of civil and criminal offences for which data controllers may be liable if a data controller has failed to gain appropriate consent from a data subject. However 'consent' is not specifically defined in the Act; consent is therefore a common law matter.

- **Sub-section 21(1)** : This sub-section makes it an offence to process personal information without registration.
- **Sub-section 21(2)** : This sub-section makes it an offence to fail to comply with the notification regulations made by the Secretary of State (proposed by the Information Commissioner under section 25 of the Act.)
- **Section 55** : Unlawful obtaining of personal data. This section makes it an offence for people (Other Parties), such as hackers and impersonators, outside the organisation to obtain unauthorised access to the personal data.
- **Section 56** : This section makes it a criminal offence to require an individual to make a Subject Access Request relating to cautions or convictions for the purposes of recruitment, continued employment, or the provision of services. This was brought into effect by the Data Protection Act 1998 (Commencement No. 2) Order 2008.

Security Attacks and Treats:

A big problem with the Internet is that data is transmitted using telephone technology, which means unauthorised users can intercept the data relatively easily. Which is a bit of a pain, really?

1. On-line shopping or e-commerce has got much more popular recently.
2. The basic idea is that the retailer puts details of their products on a web site. Customers can put the stuff they want into an electronic basket (by clicking on a button). They then pay using a credit card, and the goods are delivered soon after.
3. Some people don't like on-line shopping because they're worried that their credit card details might be intercepted and used to make unauthorised purchases. Encryption software can reduce this risk.
4. Sensitive information — like credit card details — is encrypted by the web site into a code which can only be decoded with the right software and a special password called a key.

Passwords give Restricted Access to some Web Sites:

Some web sites restrict access to authorised users only. Schools allowing pupils and parents to access material on their intranet might do this to prevent other people accessing the information. On-line magazines also do this, so they can charge people for access. The usual way to restrict access is to issue user names and passwords.

Get Protection from Hackers and Viruses:

- Hacking means accessing a computer system and its files without permission. It's totally illegal, and once inside a system, the hacker might be able to view, edit copy or delete important files or plant a virus.
- A virus is a program deliberately written to infect a computer, and make copies of it. They often corrupt other files — and even operating systems. They move between computer systems by attaching themselves to harmless computer files and e-mails.

DNS Poisoning:

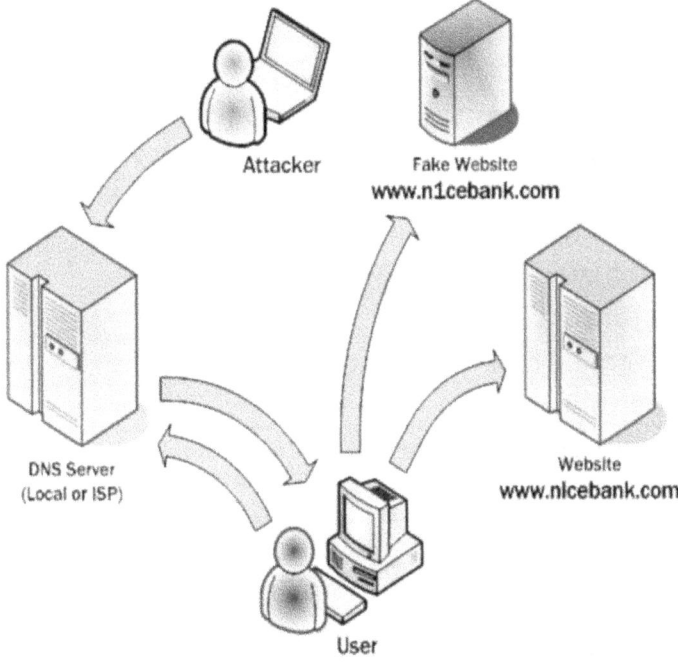

Fig. 6.5

Pharming is a derivate from phishing. Phishing mean fishing (the act of catching fish). In computer slang, fish means user name and password. Both word use "ph" instead of an "f" in this slang.

Phrasing's purpose is to obtain personal information through domain spoofing as is illustrated above. In phishing (stealing passwords) you are spammed with malicious e-mail requests for you to visit a malicious computer - spoof Web sites- which appear "nice and friendly sites". Pharming on the other hand attacks a DNS server and introduces false information into the DNS server. So if you ask the server what IP matches the nicebank domain, it will send you to n1cebank.com. (Introduce your personal bank details and you are lost).

What is Phishing?

Phishing occurs when criminals (phishers) pretend to be legitimate organisations, like banks and credit card companies in order to trick you into giving them personal details such as bank account numbers or PIN numbers.

Phishers usually send you an email in which they may ask you to 'verify' or 're-submit' personal information by return. They could ask you to complete an online form and may offer you something attractive like money or a holiday if you do so.

Be alert for anyone requesting your bank account details, credit card numbers, passwords, PIN numbers, Personal Public Service number (PPS) or National Insurance number. Phishers can use this information to impersonate you and make unauthorised withdrawals from your bank account or use it to pay for online purchases. They can even sell on this valuable information to third parties.

How will I know if I've been 'phished'? Trust your instincts. If an email looks suspicious, delete it immediately or if it offers something that looks too good to be true, it probably is. If it appears to come from your bank or credit card company, inform their customer services department immediately.

Here are some phrases that may be used in a phishing e-mail:
1. 'Verify your account'.
2. 'Respond within 48 hours or your account will be closed'.
3. 'Dear valued customer'.
4. 'Click the link below to gain access to your account'.

How can I avoid Phishing Fraud?

Trust your instincts. Remember, no reputable company will ever ask you to give out personal details by email. Never give out personal details by email, fax or in response to a pop up advertisement or unexpected website address. Always check your credit card and bank statements for any irregularities. Use up-to-date anti-virus and anti-spyware software to keep unwanted or malicious software at bay. A phishing filter can help protect you from web fraud by warning or blocking you from reported phishing web sites.

Deliberate Software Attacks :

Malicious software (malware) designed to damage, destroy, or deny service to target systems. Includes viruses, worms, Trojan horses, logic bombs, back doors, and denial-of-service attacks. Access of protected information by unauthorized individuals.

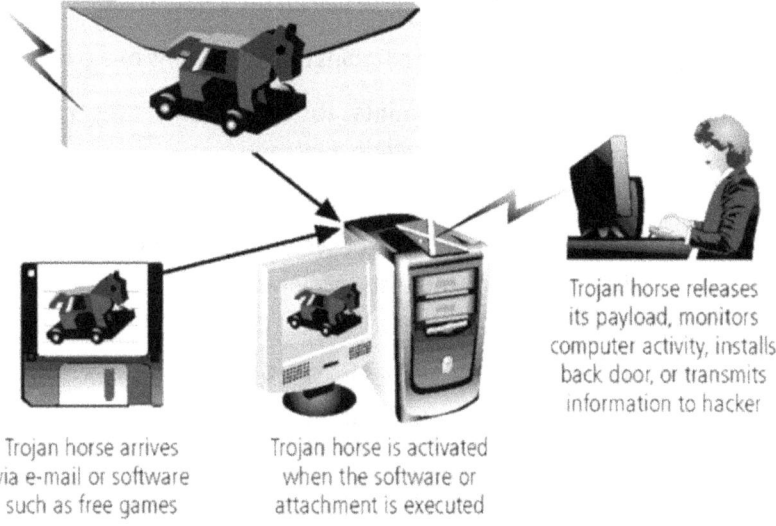

Fig. 6.6 : Trojan horse Attack

Competitive intelligence (legal) vs. Industrial espionage (illegal) Shoulder surfing occurs anywhere a person accesses confidential information! Controls let trespassers know they are encroaching on organization's cyberspace. Hackers use skill, guile, or fraud to bypass controls protecting others' information.

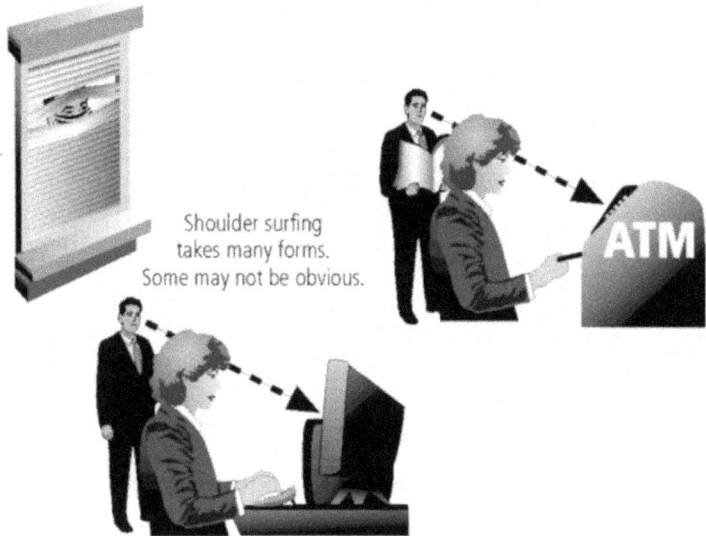

Fig. 6.7: Shoulder Surfing

1. **Malicious code:** Includes execution of viruses, worms, Trojan horses, and active Web scripts with intent to destroy or steal information.
2. **Backdoor:** Gaining access to system or network using known or previously unknown/newly discovered access mechanism.

3. **Password crack:** Attempting to reverse calculates a password.

4. **Brute force:** Trying every possible combination of options of a password.

5. **Dictionary:** selects specific accounts to attack and uses commonly used passwords (i.e., the dictionary) to guide guesses.

6. **Denial-of-Service (DoS):** Attacker sends large number of connection or information requests to a Target. Target system cannot handle successfully along with other, legitimate service requests. May result in system crash or inability to perform ordinary functions.

7. **Distributed Denial-of-Service (DDoS):** Coordinated stream of requests is launched against target from many locations simultaneously.

In a denial-of-service attack, a hacker compromises a system and uses that system to attack the target computer, flooding it with more requests for services than the target can handle.

In a distributed denial-of-service attack, dozens or even hundreds of computers (known as zombies) are compromised, loaded with DoS attack software and then remotely activated by the hacker to conduct a coordinated attack.

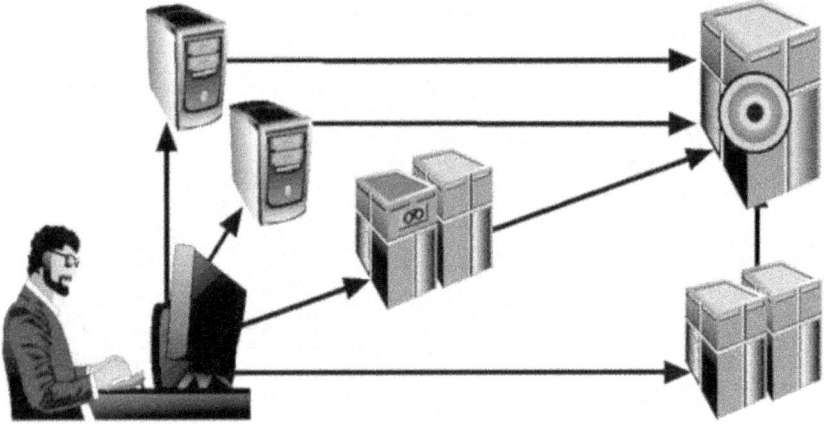

Fig. 6.8 : Denial of Services

8. **Spoofing:** Technique used to gain unauthorized access; intruder assumes a trusted IP address.

9. **Man-in-the-middle:** Attacker monitors network packets, modifies them, and inserts them back into network.

10. **Spam:** Unsolicited commercial e-mail; more a nuisance than an attack, though is emerging as a vector for some attacks.

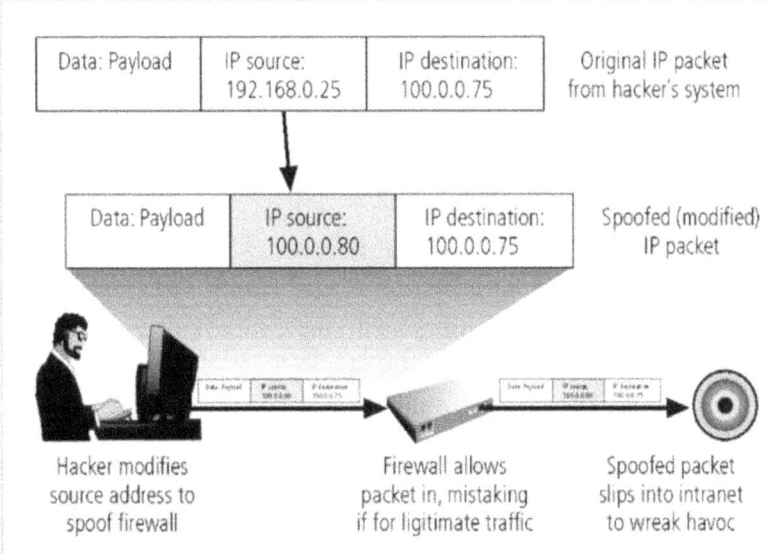

Fig. 6.9 : IP Spooling

11. **Mail bombing:** Also a DoS; attacker routes large quantities of e-mail to target
12. **Sniffers:** Program or device that monitors data travelling over network; can be used both for legitimate purposes and for stealing information from a network!
13. **Social engineering:** Using social skills to convince people to reveal access credentials or other valuable information to attacker!
14. **Buffer overflow:** Application error occurring when more data is sent to a buffer than can be handled!
15. **Timing attack:** Explores contents of a Web browser's cache to create malicious cookie Side-channel attacks: secretly observes computer screen contents/electromagnetic radiation, keystroke sounds, etc.

Information Security:

Information security is the process of protecting data from unauthorized access, use, disclosure, destruction, modification, or disruption. The terms information security, computer security and information assurance are frequently used interchangeably. These fields are interrelated and share the common goals of protecting the confidentiality, integrity and availability of information; however there are some subtle differences between them. These differences lie primarily in the approach to the subject, the methodologies used, and the areas of concentration. Information security is concerned with the confidentiality, integrity and availability of data regardless of the form the data may take: electronic, print, or other forms.

Heads of state and military commanders have long understood the importance and necessity of protecting information about their military capabilities, number of troops and troop movements. Such information falling into the hands of the enemy could be disastrous. Governments, military, financial institutions, hospitals, and private businesses amass a great deal of confidential information about their employees, customers, products, research, and financial status.

Most of this information is now collected, processed and stored on electronic computers and transmitted across networks to other computers. Should confidential information about a business's customers or finances or new product line fall into the hands of a competitor, such a breach of security could lead to lost business, law suits or even bankruptcy of the business. Protecting confidential information is a business requirement, and in many cases, it is also a legal requirement, and some would say that it is the right thing to do. For the individual, information security has a significant effect on Privacy, which is viewed very differently in different cultures.

The field of information security has grown and evolved much in recent years. As a career choice there are many ways of gaining entry into the field. The field offers many areas for specialization including Information Systems Auditing, Business Continuity Planning and Digital Forensics Science to name a few.

Basic Principles of Information Security:

Any introduction to the subject of information security must include a discussion of confidentiality, integrity, and availability. These three are also known as the CIA Triad.

Confidentiality: It is virtually impossible to get a driver's license, rent an apartment, obtain medical care, or take out a loan without disclosing a great deal of very personal information about ourselves, such as our name, address, telephone number, date of birth, Social Security Number, marital status, number of children, mother's maiden name, income, place of employment, medical history, etc. This is all very personal and private information, yet we are often required to provide such information in order to transact business. We generally take it on faith that the person, business, or institution to whom we disclose such personal information have taken measures to insure that our information will be protected from unauthorized discloser, either accidental or intentional, and that our information will only be shared with other people, businesses or institutions who are authorized to have access to the information and who have a genuine need to know the information.

Information that is considered to be confidential in nature must only be accessed, used, copied, or disclosed by persons who have been authorized to access, use, copy, or disclose the information, and then only when there is a genuine need to access, use, copy or disclose the information. A breach of confidentiality occurs when information that is considered to be confidential in nature has been, or may have been, accessed, used, copied, or disclosed to, or by, someone who was not authorized to have access to the information.

For example: permitting someone to look over your shoulder at your computer screen while you have confidential data displayed on it would be a breach of confidentiality if they were not authorized to have the information. If a laptop computer, which contains employment and benefit information about 100,000 employees, is stolen from a car (or is sold on eBay) is a breach of confidentiality because the information is now in the hands of someone who is not authorized to have it. Giving out confidential information over the telephone is a breach of confidentiality if the caller is not authorized to have the information.

Confidentiality is a requisite for maintaining the privacy of the people whose personal information the organization holds.

Integrity: In information security, integrity means that data cannot be created, changed, or deleted without authorization. It also means that data stored in one part of a database system is in agreement with other related data stored in another part of the database system (or another system). For example: a loss of integrity can occur when a database system is not properly shut down before maintenance is performed or the database server suddenly loses electrical power. A loss of integrity occurs when an employee accidentally, or with malicious intent, deletes important data files. A loss of integrity can occur if a computer virus is released onto the computer. A loss of integrity occurs when an on-line shopper is able to change the price of the product they are purchasing.

Availability: The concept of availability means that the information, the computing systems used to process the information, and the security controls used to protect the information are all available and functioning correctly when the information is needed. The opposite of availability is Denial of Service (DoS).

Risk Management:

A comprehensive treatment of the topic of risk management is beyond the scope of this article. We will however, provide a useful definition of risk management, outline a commonly used process for risk management, and define some basic terminology.

The CISA Review Manual 2006 provides the following definition of risk management:

"Risk management is the process of identifying vulnerabilities and threats to the information resources used by an organization in achieving business objectives, and deciding what countermeasures, if any, to take in reducing risk to an acceptable level, based on the value of the information resource to the organization."

There are two things in this definition that may need some clarification. First, the process of risk management is an ongoing iterative process. It must be repeated indefinitely. The business environment is constantly changing and new threats and vulnerabilities emerge every day. Second, the choice of countermeasures (controls) used to manage risks must strike a balance between productivity, cost, effectiveness of the countermeasure, and the value of the informational asset being protected.

Risk is the likelihood that something bad will happen that causes harm to an informational asset (or the loss of the asset). Vulnerability is a weakness that could be used to endanger or cause harm to an informational asset. A threat is anything (man made or act of nature) that has the potential to cause harm.

The likelihood that a threat will use a vulnerability to cause harm creates a risk. When a threat does use a vulnerability to inflict harm, it has an impact. In the context of information security, the impact is a loss of availability, integrity, and confidentiality, and possibly other losses (lost income, loss of life, loss of real property). It should be pointed out that it is not possible to identify all risks, nor is it possible to eliminate all risk. The remaining risk is called residual risk.

A risk assessment is carried out by a team of people who have knowledge of specific areas of the business. Membership of the team may vary over time as different parts of the business are assessed. The assessment may use a subjective qualitative analysis based on informed opinion, or where reliable dollar figures and historical information is available, the analysis my use quantitative analysis.

The ISO-17799:2005 Code of practice for information security management recommends the following be examined during a risk assessment: security policy, organization of information security, asset management, human resources security, physical and environmental security, communications and operations management, access control, information systems acquisition, development and maintenance, information security incident management, business continuity management, and regulatory compliance. In broad terms the risk management process consists of:

1. Identification of assets and estimating their value. Include people, buildings, hardware, software, data (electronic, print, and other), and supplies.
2. Conduct a threat assessment. Include Acts of nature, acts of war, accidents, and malicious acts originating from inside or outside the organization.
3. Conduct a vulnerability assessment, and for each vulnerability, calculate the probability that it will be exploited. Evaluate policies, procedures, standards, training, physical security, quality control, technical security.
4. Calculate the impact that each threat would have on each asset. Use qualitative analysis or quantitative analysis.
5. Identify, select and implement appropriate controls. Provide a proportional response. Consider productivity, cost effectiveness, and value of the asset.
6. Evaluate the effectiveness of the control measures. Insure the controls provide the required cost effective protection without discernable loss of productivity.

For any given risk, Executive Management can choose to accept the risk based upon the relative low value of the asset, the relative low frequency of occurrence, and the relative low impact on the business. Or, leadership my choose to mitigate the risk by selecting and implementing appropriate control measures to reduce the risk. In some cases, the risk can be transferred to another business by buying insurance or outsourcing to another business. The reality of some risks may be disputed. In such cases leadership my choose to deny the risk. This is itself a potential risk.

Three Types of Controls:

When Management chooses to mitigate a risk, they will do so by implementing one or more of three different types of controls.

1. **Administrative controls** are comprised of approved written policies, procedures, standards and guidelines. Administrative controls form the framework for running the business and managing people. They inform people on how the business is to be run and how day to day operations are to be conducted. Laws and regulations created by government bodies are also a type of administrative control because they inform the business. Some industry sectors have policies, procedures, standards and guidelines that must be followed - the Payment Card Industry (PCI) Data Security Standard required by Visa and Master Card is such an example. Other examples of administrative controls include the corporate security policy, password policy, hiring policies, and disciplinary policies.

Administrative controls form the basis for the selection and implementation of logical and physical controls. Logical and physical controls are manifestations of administrative controls. Administrative controls are of paramount importance.

2. **Logical controls** (also called technical controls) use software and data to monitor and control access to information and computing systems. For example: passwords, network and host based firewalls, network intrusion detection systems, access control lists, and data encryption are logical controls.

An important logical control that is frequently overlooked is the principle of least privilege. The principle of least privilege requires that an individual, program or system process is not granted any more access privileges than are necessary to perform the task. A blatant example of the failure to adhere to the principle of least privilege is logging into Windows as user Administrator to read Email and surf the Web. Violations of this principle can also occur when an individual collects additional access privileges over time. This happens when an employees' job duties change, or they are promoted to a new position, or they transfer to another department. The access privileges required by their new duties are frequently added onto to their already existing access privileges which may no longer be necessary or appropriate.

3. Physical controls monitor and control the environment of the work place and computing facilities. They also monitor and control access to and from such facilities. For example: doors, locks, heating and air conditioning, smoke and fire alarms, fire suppression systems, cameras, barricades, fencing, security guards, cable locks, etc. Separating the network and work place into functional areas are also physical controls.

An important physical control that is frequently overlooked is the separation of duties. Separation of duties insures that a single individual can not complete a critical task by themselves. For example: an employee who submits a request for reimbursement should not also be able to authorize payment or print the check. An applications programmer should not also be the server administrator or the database administrator - these roles and responsibilities must be separated from one another.

6.7 Short Case Study: Human Resource Information Systems and Payroll Consulting

Fortune 500 builder ready to migrate their HRIS to cloud computing

Client Need:

Our client, a $14B builder, made the decision to migrate from a client server-based HRIS (ADP HRizon version 9) to a cloud computing solution (Enterprise version 5 upgrade). They needed assistance in completing the project successfully, primarily in designing the right testing program to ensure the system met all user requirements. Simultaneously, the company's payroll processes needed to be examined to determine where changes would be required to accommodate the new system. Because of our strong reputation in HRIS and Payroll technology and processes, this company turned to Hudson to manage both of these needs.

Hudson Solution:

To begin, the Hudson Project Manager performed a preliminary analysis to identify gaps in current payroll processes, as well as gaps in relation to the new system. From our years of experience, we knew that moving from a decentralized environment to a Shared Services environment required new processes and procedures, and in some cases, new staff levels. Hudson worked closely with the client team to ensure the highest quality of findings. After conducting a thorough analysis and gaining consensus on a plan, we implemented the business process reengineering for the Payroll department.

On the technical side of the project, Hudson designed a comprehensive testing program. The company relied upon our expertise to determine the areas which needed to be tested, create test scenarios, conduct the tests and compile the results. Using our methodology, we conducted two user acceptance tests on the new application and one parallel test before moving to the next phase of the project.

Next, Hudson assisted in testing the interface for the time and labor management systems, third party benefits administrator, flexible spending administrator, and retirement vendors to ensure each of the interfaces worked properly. Finally, a new security tree was built to accommodate the more robust security features and give the company more flexibility when assigning roles. Hudson aided the client's Sr. HRIS Analyst in building, implementing and testing this process.

Results:

Throughout the project, the company was pleased with our ability to create process improvements along the way as a natural part of how we manage projects. Our specialized expertise in the HRIS and payroll areas allowed us to minimize the overall project scope and timeline to focus on exactly the areas that needed attention. At the conclusion of the year-long implementation process, our client enjoyed the benefits of a single standardized system that would meet the goals of a corporate shared services environment for years to come.

Activities

1. In this chapter the innovations in mobile employee self-service have been covered in a brief manner. Enlist and describe at least five benefits of this technology by surfing the Internet.
2. Refer to the information available online and provide more insight on the key features provided by any three Indian SaaS providers.

Summary

In this chapter, we have discussed about the innovative (emerging) trends in HRIS such as cloud computing. Here we have seen that, as you prepare your management agenda for the first part of new decade, you may want to address some of the issues below:

1. Disintegration of the old HR "turf".
2. Commoditization of input/workflow/basic transaction processing.
3. Dramatic increases in the perceived value of system information.
4. Devaluation of past experience as a basis for planning and decision-making.

Cloud computing is the use of computing resources that are delivered as a service over a network. The name comes from the common use of a cloud-shaped symbol as an abstraction for the complex infrastructure it contains in system diagrams.

Across the globe there are an ever increasing demand and a huge marketplace of SaaS vendors covering the whole spectrum of HR and Payroll management. If you are a global business looking at cloud computing for HR there is no reason you should not be able to find a solution to suit your requirements and most likely that solution will be made for the global catering.

Cloud computing also ensures that companies have instant and continual access to the latest advances and legal issues as they may affect human resources issues. All information is automatically updated, meaning team members can be confident their information is current.

Many companies use a formal request for proposal (RFP) process when shopping for HRIS software. A good RFP provides enough detail that vendors can craft replies with more substance than their basic marketing material, without getting so granular that responding is a burden. Try to send RFPs to at least three but no more than ten vendors, and then pick a few from that set to investigate further.

The HRIS market consists of both software publishers that sell their systems directly, and resellers who provide consulting and installation services to go with third-party software. Neither approach is inherently better than the other, but you should be aware of which you're dealing with.

A basic HR information package for a 20-person business is not in the same ballpark as a customized enterprise-level HRIS for a 2,000-employee corporation. Even two fairly similar businesses can wind up with very different prices for HRIS software — and both be getting a fair deal. The scope of HRIS implementation will have a big impact on the price. A basic transactional system can provide significant benefits to your business — but won't cost nearly as much as a system that includes talent management and other strategic functionality

Many HRIS software providers have included the social aspect of computing in their solutions. Some of the prominent examples being:

1. TribeHR which is a new breed of HRIS.
2. OpenHire's ATS from Silk Road has Social Recruiting Media Toolkit that provides internal and external tools for recruiters, job seekers and employees.

Self-assessment Questions

1. Identify the reasons behind Cloud Computing gaining momentum over the last few years?
2. Write a short note on the methods the end users access cloud-based applications?
3. Enlist and describe the relevant "flavours" of cloud computing?
4. Describe the layer in which most people interact with Cloud Computing.
5. What has been called as the biggest issue with SaaS?

Appendices

Appendix 1 : References

Books Referred:

1. Human Resource Information Systems by Sage Publication.
2. Handbook of Human Resource Information Systems by McGraw-Hill.
3. Developing Human Resource Information System by Daya Publication House.

Websites:

1. phindia.com
2. www.hr.com
3. specht.com.au
4. www.shiftiq.com
5. www.successfactors.com
6. www.shrm.org

Appendix 2 : HR System to the Cloud

1. Core HRMS Transformation in the Cloud:

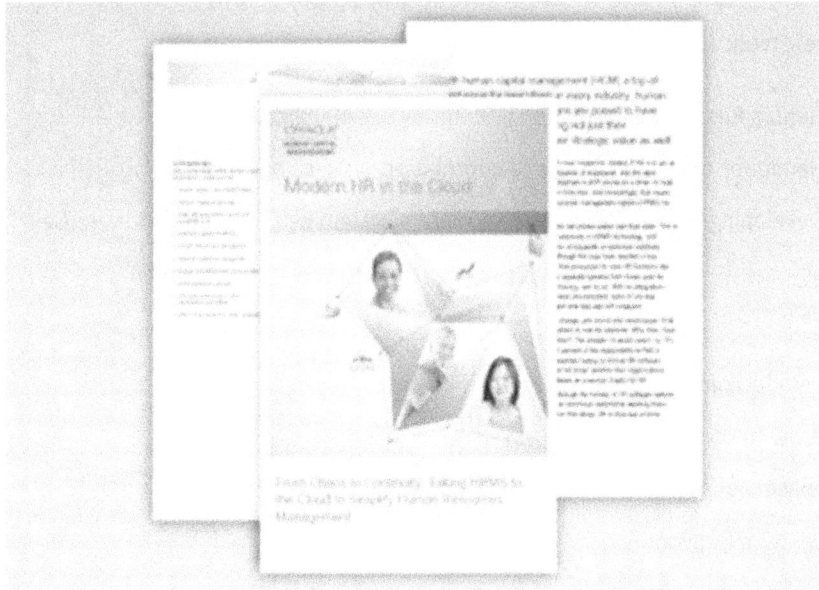

Taking your HR System to the Cloud:

Did you know that only 34% of HR organizations are prepared for the necessary transformative changes they need to make for the future? This disconcerting finding from the PwC's 17th Annual Global CEO Survey reveals the pressure put on business leaders to transform their HR organizations and drive business value. Making matters worse are cost constraints, demands to do more with fewer resources and, align HR with the business. Most HR leaders lack reliable and innovative HRMS tools to pursue transformative HR strategies that deliver value to their organization.

While many HR leaders have transformed their talent strategy by adopting talent management systems, only 16% of HR departments currently have their core HRMS application in the cloud. However, 45% of organizations will move their HRMS to the cloud within the next year, per PWC's 2013 HR technology survey.

To make good on the premise to align with the business, HR must modernize and transform. To be an agent of change, HR needs to choose the right human resource management system in the cloud to manage the entire employee lifecycle. Disparate, on-premise solutions where core HR functions like payroll and benefits are processed in separate systems are not integrated with those used for talent management, workforce optimization and training. This disconnect hinders ease of use, diminishes user experiences and makes data difficult to analyze for valuable insights.

Human Capital Management:

So what are the benefits of Oracle's cloud-based HRMS solution, Human Capital Management Cloud? Cedar Crestone sees lower annual costs per employee for a cloud-based HRMS, rather than for a licensed, on-premise solution. Its 2013-2014 HR Systems Survey (PDF) concludes that HR leaders are moving to a cloud-based HRMS because;

1. 69% see improved user experiences for employees, managers, and HR.
2. 58% see best practices functionality.
3. 55% experienced easier upgrades.

2. **The HRIS System Question: On-Premise or Cloud?**

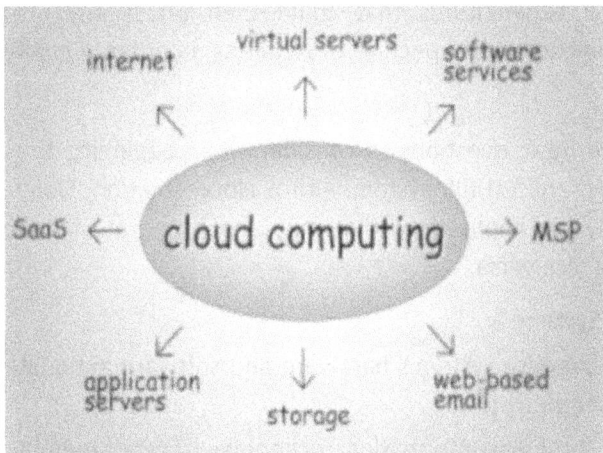

When you are faced with the question of choosing a Human Resource Information System (HRIS system) for your organization, one major factor to consider is whether it should reside on-premise or the cloud (also known as Software-as-a Service or SaaS).

The most efficient, reliable and cost-effective answer can be found by analyzing the pros and cons for each solution as it applies to your organization and its Information Technology (IT) structure.

With Human Resources (HR) needs rapidly changing, your HRIS system should not only be within budget, but also provide you with the functionality you require along with the highest level of data security and accessibility available. Some other top considerations include integration, control, tax implications, and mobile access.

Cloud Considerations:

The International Data Corporation (IDC), a group that provides insight and data for business and IT professionals, recently reported that expenditures for public IT cloud services are expected to rise to $107 billion by 2017, an increase from 2013 numbers of more than $60 billion. KPMG, LLP, the international audit, tax, and advisory firm, states in its survey report entitled The Cloud Takes Shape, that of its 674 respondents (287 business executives and 387 IT executives), currently 57 percent are using HR cloud solutions and, within the next 18 months, 30 percent expect to add an HR cloud component to their system.

On-Premise Considerations:

But, having your HRIS system on-premise is a viable option, at least until your IT organization is ready to make the transition to a cloud platform. According to the KPMG survey report, in the past it has been customary for IT groups to, many times, find software that met most of its needs, and then made adjustments as required by the organization. When purchasing an HRIS system cloud solution, however, it may be somewhat limited in the amount of customization that can be performed. That is, without additional expenditures that could then offset any attractive return on investment the company was expecting, or requiring, in order to justify the transition.

Sorting it Out:

Here are some basic questions to consider when beginning the analysis phase of comparing an on-premise HRIS system with a cloud solution. Don't forget about the importance of any tax implications that may apply, i.e., moving from fixed costs to operating costs, or vice versa.

On-Premise HRIS System:
1. Is your on-premise system's hardware and software antiquated, creating costly capital expenditures?
2. Is it taking too many Information Technology (IT) staff members to maintain the current system to be cost-effective?
3. Is your current system flexible enough to react to the complex HRIS system needs in today's competitive environment, or does a complex IT department bureaucracy exist?
4. Is the long-term strategy of your organization including keeping a robust IT department in place with adequate staff and equipment to maintain your HRIS system needs?

Cloud (or SaaS) HRIS System:
1. Can the system that resides in the cloud allow adequate cyber security for your employees' personal data?
2. Can the cloud provide you with the data storage space required? Can it be increased or decreased easily, depending on your needs?
3. Can the cloud ensure your system will be flexible but allow an adequate level of control over the content of your HRIS system?

4. Have you considered the geographic location of the servers hosting the cloud solution? Whether in the United States or elsewhere, be sure to research any privacy ramifications that may exist.

Charting it Out:

For a closer comparison of the top considerations discussed, as well as some other important considerations, review the following chart as you begin creating your own pros and cons analysis for your organization.

Consideration	On-Premise HRIS System	Cloud (SaaS) HRIS System
Size of Business	Considering number of employees, usually best for businesses with more than 100 employees.	Considering number of employees, usually best for businesses less than 100 employees.
Data Security/Privacy	Implementing security/privacy initiatives by IT department and possibly corporate security staff. May be very robust and more secure than transmitting via the Internet.	Providing assurance for security/privacy of data would be obtained from cloud provider. This agreement should be documented and tested for highest level of employee data security (especially if you are allowing a lot of employee self-service interaction via the company intranet and/or mobile apps). Security/Privacy should be scrutinized by your organization's IT security department as well.
Cost/Budget	Negotiating software and licensing fees and keeping up-to-date the hardware (servers, etc.), physical space, air conditioning, maintenance and upkeep of entire on-premise system.	Billing will most likely be on a monthly basis or possibly by user (total number).
Functionality/Flexibility/Upgrades(Application Maintenance, Support,	Depending on vendor, some customization may be provided, but IT department	Changing software configurations provided by cloud provider may be on a

and Customization)	will probably perform much of this work.	limited basis or additional charges may be incurred for it to conform to your needs.
Tax Implications	Depending on current status, either moving from fixed costs to operating costs, or vice versa.	Depending on current status, either moving from fixed costs to operating costs, or vice versa.
Implementation	Implementing the HRIS system may be controlled by your IT department. Authority for this would remain a part on your organization's IT strategy.	Implementing system parameters will be worked out with cloud provider.
Hardware	Dictating the equipment needs (hardware, servers, etc.) may be handled by you organization, which may or may not align with HRIS system current and/or future needs. However, it resides on company premises and the HRIS system is owned by the organization.	Updating/Upgrading hardware will not be a concern because HRIS system operates from cloud vendor site (hardware, servers, etc.).
Mobile Access	Accessing data would probably be via company intranet browsers on approved mobile devices.	Working with cloud provider will be necessary, but probably more limited access to programs running on approved company devices (laptops, desktops, mobile apps, etc.).
Integration	Integrating HRIS system with existing software is more likely achievable using an on-premise system.	Integrating the system may be limited. This would vary by cloud provider and should be researched thoroughly before purchase.

Control	Controlling your HRIS system will remain on-premise and your organization will have authority over program.	Controlling your HRIS system resides with cloud provider, which includes entrusting it with employees' personal data.
Data Center Location	Planning the location of your data centers is in the control of your organization.	Choosing the location of the data centers may be out of your control because this depends on the cloud provider. Remember to consider security/privacy laws in place at the various geographic locations of the cloud provider's centers.
IT Staff	Depending on IT staff configuration of your organization, it could be one or multiple locations. HR needs also would be placed in the hierarchy of corporate IT priorities and implementation schedule.	Servicing of your HRIS system is part of cloud provider services, so direct discussions between HR and cloud provider may be more collaborative. Also, system may implement faster because it's on HR's schedule, not a corporate IT department schedule.

Summary:

After a thorough study of solutions that offer the functionality you require within your security requirements and budget constraints, you will be well on your way to finding the right answer to the question of an on-premise or cloud solution for your HRIS system.

Appendix 3

Most Recommended Human Resources Systems:

BambooHR is an online HR software service for small and medium-sized businesses. As the price/performance leader, BambooHR makes it easy and affordable for small and growing companies to transition from spreadsheets to a Human Resource Information System (HRIS) that adapts to their changing needs. HR professionals can focus their time on meaningful work by using BambooHR's Applicant Tracking System (ATS) and HRIS to manage all aspects of the employee lifecycle.

Since 2008, BambooHR has helped thousands of organizations standardize and automate their HR processes. A winner of the 2013 Alfred P. Sloan Awards for Excellence in Workplace Effectiveness and Flexibility, BambooHR now serves tens of thousands of employees in 70 countries worldwide in English, Dutch, French Canadian, German, Portuguese, and Spanish—and in multiple currencies.

The information BambooHR provides gives HR a seat at the table by giving executives visibility into strategic indicators like employee turnover and retention. BambooHR is Software-as-a Service (SaaS) application, so businesses only need to pay a low monthly subscription based on the number of employees and a one-time implementation fee. There's no extra charge for customization, multiple administrators, enhanced features, support, or inactive employees.

Because it is so easy to use, the solution can be utilized by any member of the organization, from employee to executive, or limited to only those in the company that need it. Any facet of the organization buried under spreadsheets will definitely appreciate its streamlined, intuitive workflow.

Appendix 4 : Multiple Choice of Questions

Chapter 1: Different Types of Computer Based Information Systems

Q.1) HRIS gives firms several benefits and advantages, identify _____.
- (a) Understanding the needs of the organizing team
- **(b) Increasing competitiveness**
- (c) Diversified learning
- (d) and b of the above

Q.2) HRIS gives firms several benefits and advantages, identify _____.
- (a) Understanding the needs of the organizing team
- (b) Diversified learning
- **(c) Real-time HR-related reports**
- (d) and b of the above

Q.3) The Training and Development department at Intex Computers stresses the importance of managers experiencing things for themselves as the basis for their development.

There are various different ways to identify training needs select correct option from following.
- (a) Open learning
- (b) Meetings
- (c) Using HRIS
- **(d) All of the above**

Q.4) The Functions of HRIS firms looking for are _____.
- (a) Understanding the needs of the organizing team
- **(b) Increasing competitiveness**
- (c) Diversified learning
- (d) and b of the above

Q.5) HRIS does not produce real-time HR-related reports _____.
- (a) True
- **(b) False**

Q.6) Transaction Processing Systems is used for Order tracking _____.
- (a) True
- (b) False

Chapter 2: Management Information Systems

Q.1) You are HR manager of a software export company, involved in building company that could be divided based on their specialized knowledge and suggested HRIS software to buy.

What modules you will prefer?

(a) Organization charts
(b) Project format
(c) Employee self-service
(d) a and c of the above

Q.2) You are HR manager of a recruitment consultant, and suggested HRIS software to buy.

What modules you will prefer?

(a) Track training for employees
(b) Project format
(c) Work order reports
(d) a and c of the above

Q.3) The HRIS stakeholders in the organization need to consider the sum of the important components when overhauling or installing any system,

Identify from following _____.

(a) Identify the size range of solution
(b) Project format
(c) Work order reports
(d) a and c of the above

Q.4) The HRIS stakeholders in the organization need to consider the sum of the important components when overhauling or installing any system,

Identify from following _____.

(a) Project format
(b) Defining of business objectives
(c) Work order reports
(d) a and c of the above

Q.5) Adoptability, sequence of activities, controls to be exercised during the transition, in Merger of old and new systems while designing HRIS is to be considered _____.

(a) True
(b) False

Chapter 3 : Implementation of HRIS

Q.1) Designing an HRIS department essentially requires the following issues to be resolved_____.
  (a) **Level of Involvement of the people in the system**
  (b) Project Charter
  (c) Employee self-service
  (d) a and c of the above

Q.2) Designing an HRIS department essentially requires the following issues to be resolved_____.
  (a) Line Format
  (b) **Merger of old and new systems for running organization**
  (c) Employee self-service
  (d) a and c of the above

Q.3) Designing an HRIS department essentially requires the following issues to be resolved_____.
  (a) Line Format
  (b) **Financial Aspects**
  (c) Employee self-service
  (d) a and c of the above

Q.4) The key HRIS stakeholders need to be recognized at the inception of the implementation procedure of HRIS _____.
  (a) True
  (b) False

Q.5) Designing an HRIS department essentially requires the following issues to be Controlled
  Identify Correct option _____.
  (a) Line Format
  (b) Regulatory access
  (c) Security technology
  (d) **b and c of the above**

Chapter 4: HRIS Applications

Q.1) Internet selection has turned into one of the essential strategies utilized by Human Resource divisions to earn potential aspirants for accessible positions inside an association. Recruitment management frameworks normally include _____.

(a) Analyzing work force utilization inside a firm
(b) Potential candidate identification
(c) Security technology
(d) All of the above

Q.2) Recruitment application is very much alike the Customer Relationship Management frameworks, yet is composed particularly for recruitment following purposes.
Identify key features _____.
(a) Schedule feature for aspirants
(b) Project charter
(c) Feature of parsing to scan resumes and essential words
(d) a and c of the above

Q.3) Recruitment application is very much alike the Customer Relationship Management frameworks, yet is composed particularly for recruitment following purposes.
Identify key features _____.
(a) Configurable screening polls
(b) Candidate profile archive
(c) Hiring acceptances and exchanging representatives
(d) a and c of the above

Q.4) Employee referrals are considered as one of the most reliable systems to obtain quality candidates based on previous experience _____.
(a) True
(b) False

Q.5) What are key Components of Payroll (Compensation and Benefits) Management Module _____.
(a) Employee Profiling System
(b) Project Charter
(c) Hiring acceptances and exchanging representatives
(d) a and c of the above

Q.6) What are key Components of Payroll (Compensation and Benefits) Management Module _____.
(a) Time Management System
(b) Project Charter
(c) Hiring acceptances and exchanging representatives
(d) a and c of the above

Q.7) What are key Components of Payroll (Compensation and Benefits) Management Module _____.
(a) Income Tax Management (TDS)
(b) Project Charter
(c) Report Generation System
(d) a and c of the above

Q.8) Key features of Payroll Management Software are _____.
(a) Configure Payroll Components
(b) Create Payroll Templates
(c) Assign Payroll Templates
(d) All of the above

Q.9) The modules for Payroll Management Software also should define the sub-modules related to the requirements of the employees in the enterprise such as Transfer, Promotions and Increments.
(a) True
(b) False

Q.10) Key features of Leave Management Module are
(a) Configure Payroll Components
(b) Ability to define the types of leave
(c) Assign job Templates
(d) All of the above

Q.11) Key features of Leave Management Module are
(a) Configure new employees leave
(b) Tracking of Leave Balances
(c) Assign job Templates
(d) a and b of the above

Q.12) Key features of Leave Management Module are
(a) Cancel / revert any pending leave application functionality
(b) Linkage to Time Management System for identifying employees on Leave
(c) Linkage to Payroll System for the deduction of Unpaid Leave and Pay in Lieu
(d) All of the above

Q.13) Time sheets are used for Project tracking
(a) True
(b) False

Q.14) Key features of Key Features of Module on Performance Management are _____.
   (a) Key Performance Indicators
   (b) Linkage to Time Management System for identifying employees on Leave
   (c) Linkage to Payroll System for the deduction of Unpaid Leave and Pay in Lieu
   (d) All of the above

Q.15) Key features of Key Features of Module on Performance Management are
   (a) Performance Appraisal
   (b) Online Job/Role Descriptions
   (c) Linkage to Payroll System for the deduction of Unpaid Leave and Pay in Lieu
   (d) a and b of the above

Q.16) Examples of KPIs in HR _____.
   (a) Employee Retention
   (b) Customer care
   (c) Promotion mix completion
   (d) a and b of the above

Q.17) Examples of KPIs in sales _____.
   (a) Employee Retention
   (b) Customer care
   (c) Promotion mix completion
   (d) a and b of the above

Q.18) Examples of KPIs in marketing _____.
   (a) Employee Retention
   (b) Customer care
   (c) Promotion mix completion
   (d) a and b of the above

Q.19) Examples of KPIs in Procurement _____.
   (a) Cost of purchasing units
   (b) Customer care
   (c) Promotion mix completion
   (d) a and b of the above

Q.20) Examples of KPIs in Manufacturing
   (a) Planning order management
   (b) Customer care

(c) Promotion mix completion
(d) **a and b of the above**

Q.21) KPIs in Manufacturing are advertising, e-marketing
(a) True
(b) **False**

Q.22) What are the Pre-requisites of e-learning?
(a) **Involving Employees in an e-learning Environment**
(b) Customer care
(c) Promotion mix completion
(d) a and b of the above

Q.23) What are the Pre-requisites of e-learning?
(a) **Building an e-Learning Architecture**
(b) Customer care
(c) Promotion mix completion
(d) a and b of the above

Chapter 5: Other HRIS Applications (Ancillary Modules in the HRIS System)

Q.1) What are Key features of Policy and Procedures Model _____.
(a) Legislative requirements
(b) Codes of conduct
(c) Promotion mix completion
(d) **a and b of the above**

Q.2) What are Key features of Policy and Procedures Model _____.
(a) Employee entitlements
(b) Employee benefits
(c) Promotion mix completion
(d) **a and b of the above**

Q.3) Employee Self Service (ESS) is a combination of technology and organizational change that enables users to interact directly with their human resource data to inquire, review and act upon transactions in the workplace
(a) **True**
(b) False

Q.4) Identify Large Scale HRIS Vendors _____.
(a) SAP HR - SAP Human Resources
(b) JD Edwards Enterprise One

(c) Simple HR
(d) **a and b of the above**

Q.5) Identify Medium Scale HRIS Vendors _____.
(a) SAP HR - SAP Human Resources
(b) JD Edwards Enterprise One
(c) **Simple HR**
(d) a and b of the above

Q.6) SAP Human Resources (HR) Components or Sub-Components contain Time Management _____.
(a) **True**
(b) False

Chapter 6: Emerging Trends in HRIS

Q.1) Identify vendors providing Cloud Solutions
(a) **Cloud Business Solutions**
(b) JD Edwards Enterprise One
(c) Simple HR
(d) a and b of the above

Q.2) Talent management module contains
(a) Career development
(b) Performance management
(c) Retention planning
(d) **a and b of the above**

Q.3) Employee self-service provides a huge reduction in administrative work for your HR staff. With self-service, employees can get information and make changes to their HR information and benefit elections themselves, instead of calling an HR rep or completing a paper form.
(a) **True**
(b) False

Appendix 5: Question Bank

QUESTION BANK

Chapter 1 : Different Types of Computer Based Information Systems

1) Explain various Components of Computer System.
   (Ref 1.2.1)
2) State various types of computer.
   (Ref 1.2.1)
3) What is Computer Based Information System?
   (Ref 1.2.2)
4) Explain Evolution of Human Resource Management and Information System.
   (Ref 1.2.3)
5) Explain types of Information System and how Transaction Processing Systems (TPS) Forms basis of all.
   (Ref 1.3.1)
6) What is Management Information System?
   (Ref 1.3.1)
7) What is Expert System? Explain various components of Expert System.
   (Ref 1.3.1)
8) What is Expert System? Explain various components of Expert System.
   (Ref 1.3.4)
9) What is Decision Support System and how it is used in Human Resource Information Systems (HRIS).
   (Ref 1.3.5)
10) Explain Major Steps in Planning Human Resource Information Systems.
    (Ref 1.4.1.3)
11) Explain Functions and Attributes of Modern Human Resource Information System.
    (Ref 1.4.1.1)
12) What are Benefits of Human Resource Information System.
    (Ref 1.5)

Chapter 2 : Management Information Systems

1) What is need of Management Information Systems?
   (Ref 2.1.1)
2) What are Management Information Systems (MIS) Definitions?
   (Ref 2.1.1)
3) What are Functional Applications of HRIS?
   (Ref 2.2)
4) Explain HRIS Life Cycle
   (Ref 2.3)
5) Explain HRIS Expectation.
   (Ref 2.1.1)
6) Explain HRIS Cost Benefit Value Analysis.
   (Ref 2.7)
7) Write short note on: Getting Management Support and overcoming employee resistance to change.
   (Ref 2.8)
8) State Limitation of Computerization of HRIS.
   (Ref 2.9)

Chapter 3 : Implementation of HRIS

1) Explain factors that need to be considered during implementation of HRIS.
   (Ref 3.2.1)
2) Explain Tools in HRIS Development.
   (Ref 3.3)
3) Explain Issues needed to Control and Maintain Security of Data before Implementing a Computerized HRIS.
   (Ref 3.2.4)
4) Explain Major HRIS Solution Providers.
   (Ref 3.4)

Chapter 4: HRIS Application

1) Explain : Applicant and Employment Management.
   (Ref 4.2)

2) Explain Equal Employment Opportunity (EEC) and affirmative action.
    (Ref 4.3)
3) Define Compensation, State various factors affecting Compensation.
    (Ref 4.4)
4) State the meaning of benefits and services offered to employees.
    (Ref 4.5)
5) Explain the need of Employee and Industrial Relations.
    (Ref 4.6)
6) Explain Key features of Leave Management Module.
    (Ref 4.6.2)
7) Explain the need of Training and its importance in organization.
    (Ref 4.7)
8) What is Human Recourse Planning?
    (Ref 4.8)
9) State Key Features of Module on Performance Management.
    (Ref 4.8.2)
10) Write a note on OSHA.
    (Ref 4.9)

Chapter 5: Other HRIS Applications (Ancillary modules in the HRIS System)

1) Explain Key Components of Payroll Management Module.
    (Ref 5.2.2)

Chapter 6: Emerging Trends in HRIS

1) Explain Emerging Trends in HRIS.
    (Ref 6.2)
2) Explain different types of Network.
    (Ref 6.5)
3) What do you understand by Information Security and Privacy in Human Resource Information System.
    (Ref 6.6)

NOTES